Kidbits

Illustrated by
Bob Italiano

Text by
Jenny Tesar

Executive Editor
Bruce S. Glassman

BLACKBIRCH PRESS, INC.
WOODBRIDGE, CONNECTICUT

Special thanks to my wife Joan, without whom
this project would not have been possible.
–B.I.

Published by Blackbirch Press, Inc.
260 Amity Road
Woodbridge, CT 06525

©2001 by Blackbirch Press, Inc.
First Edition

e-mail: staff@blackbirch.com
Web site: www.blackbirch.com

Check out KidBits Online!
KidBits is now available as an online subscription
through EBSCO Publishing. In addition to all the
material contained in this book, KidBits Online
offers a wealth of additional research capability,
including access to thousands of related articles
from periodicals such as *Time*, *Newsweek*, and
Sports Illustrated. Check out KidBits Online at
www.web4school.com/reference.htm or call EBSCO
Publishing at 1-800-653-2726 for more information.

Photo Credits
Cover: Football, cellular phone, CD, film reel and PC ©PhotoDisc, kids ©Rubberball; all interior
photographs ©PhotoDisc.

Printed in Singapore

10 9 8 7 6 5 4 3 2 1

The Kidbits Staff
Executive Editor: Bruce S. Glassman
Production Designer: Calico Harington
Assistant Editor: Jenifer Morse

Library of Congress Cataloging-in-Publication Data
Kidbits: more than 1,500 eye-popping charts, graphs, maps, and visuals that instantly show you
everything you want to know about your world!/ by the editors of Blackbirch Press; illustrated by
Bob Italiano
    p.   cm.
    Includes bibliographical references and index.
    ISBN 1-56711-533-0
    1. Handbooks, vade-mecums, etc.—Juvenile literature.
I. Italiano, Bob, ill. II. Blackbirch Press
AG106.K54 2001
031.02—dc21   98-19623
                                                    CIP
                                                     AC

Table of Contents

Health — 102

Recreation — 124

Music — 134

Television — 156

Movies and Videos — 182

Pro Sports — 204

Who Are We?

By 2000, more than 275 million people lived in the United States. About 70 million were kids—that is, under age 18. Their ancestors came from every part of the world. They represented nearly every race and ethnic background. Most of them lived in cities and suburbs, and a growing number lived in the South and West.

Every ten years since 1790, the Census Bureau has made an official count of the U.S. population. It asks people about their place of birth, age, race, marital status, home, and other aspects of their lives. In 2000 the Census Bureau estimated that 82.1% of the population was white and 12.8% was black. The population also included Asians, Pacific Islanders, American Indians, Eskimos, and other people. According to the Census Bureau, Hispanics—people of Spanish or Spanish-American heritage—can be of any race; they made up 11.6% of the 2000 population.

The 2000 population included 26 million people who were born in other countries. About 27% had been born in Mexico and 17% in Asia. California had the largest foreign-born population, followed by New York, Florida, and Texas.

Kidbits Tidbits

● In 1999, there were 95.6 males for every 100 females in the U.S. Among young people, there are more males than females. But men die earlier than women, and among older people there are more women than men.

● In 1900, a newborn baby could expect to live to the age of 45. Today, a newborn can expect to live to age 76.

● About 3.95 million babies were born in the U.S. in 1999.

● Families are getting smaller. In 1970, the average size of a family was 3.58 people. By 1998, it was 3.18 people.

The population is expected to grow during the coming decades. By the year 2010, the Census Bureau predicts the U.S. will have 297.7 million people, including more than 72.5 million under age 18.

Each year, some 2.3 million marriages take place in the U.S. May through October are the most popular months for "getting hitched," with June ranking #1. In 1998, about 7% of the women and 3% of the men who got married were under age 20.

In 1999, 3.95 million babies were born in the U.S. They included 11,242 babies born to girls under age 15 and 385,802 born to girls ages 15 to 19. Those babies, like all babies born in America, could expect to live to an average age of 76. Most of them will grow up in middle- and upper-class families. But some will live in poverty. Today, about 20% of American children live in poverty. This means their families do not have enough income to buy adequate food and clothing.

There were 70.8 million families in the U.S. in 1998. About 50% of the families did not have any children. About 20% had one child, 19% had two children, and 11% had three or more children. Nearly one-third of all families with children were headed by a single parent.

Kidbits Tidbits

● 8.9 million kids (people under age 18) lived in California in 1998—more than in any other state. In comparison, Wyoming only had 130,000 residents under age 18.

● In Mississippi, over 36.4% of the population is black—more than in any other state.

● More than 29% of the population of California and Texas is Hispanic.

● Most U.S. Hispanics are of Mexican origin.

● In 1999, almost 16.9% of Americans under age 18 lived in poverty.

● In 1999, more than 20% of the people in New Mexico lived below the poverty level—more than in any other state.

● In 1790, about 5% of U.S. people lived in cities and 95% lived in rural areas. In 1998, some 79% lived in cities and 21% lived in rural areas.

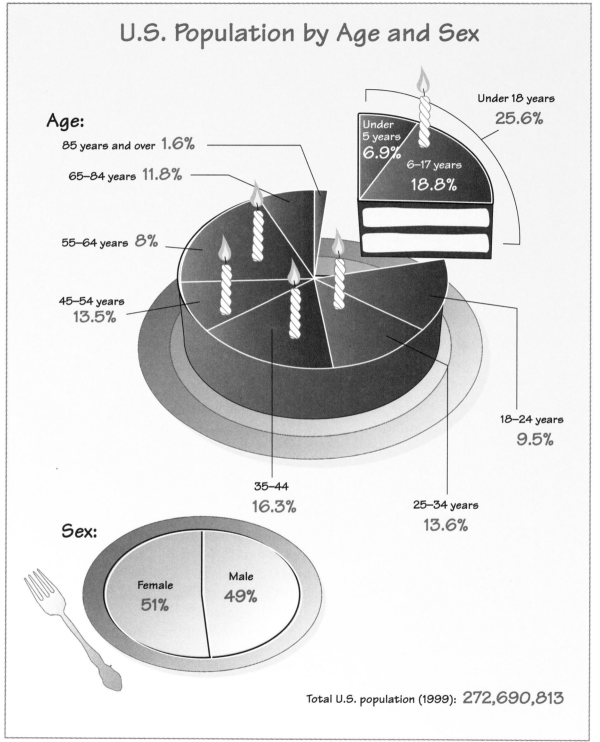

U.S. Population by Age and Sex

Age:

85 years and over 1.6%

65–84 years 11.8%

55–64 years 8%

45–54 years 13.5%

35–44 16.3%

25–34 years 13.6%

18–24 years 9.5%

Under 18 years 25.6%

Under 5 years 6.9%

6–17 years 18.8%

Sex:

Female 51%

Male 49%

Total U.S. population (1999): 272,690,813

SOURCE: Based on data from Bureau of the Census, U.S. Dept. of Commerce

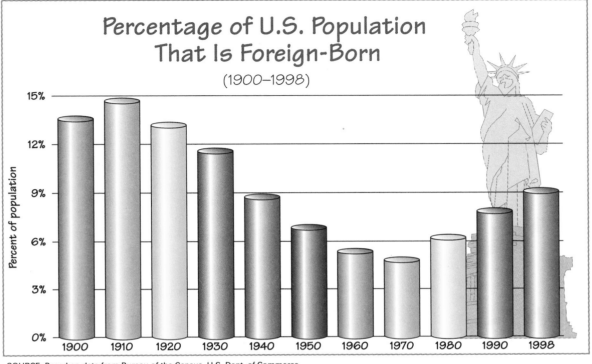

Percentage of U.S. Population That Is Foreign-Born

(1900–1998)

SOURCE: Based on data from Bureau of the Census, U.S. Dept. of Commerce

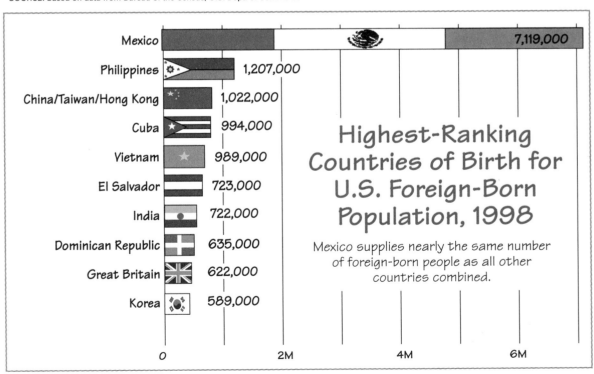

Country	Population
Mexico	7,119,000
Philippines	1,207,000
China/Taiwan/Hong Kong	1,022,000
Cuba	994,000
Vietnam	989,000
El Salvador	723,000
India	722,000
Dominican Republic	635,000
Great Britain	622,000
Korea	589,000

Highest-Ranking Countries of Birth for U.S. Foreign-Born Population, 1998

Mexico supplies nearly the same number of foreign-born people as all other countries combined.

SOURCE: Based on data from Bureau of the Census, U.S. Dept. of Commerce

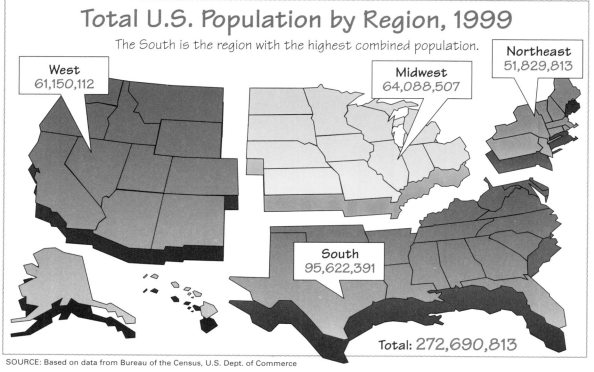

Total U.S. Population by Region, 1999

The South is the region with the highest combined population.

West 61,150,112

Midwest 64,088,507

Northeast 51,829,813

South 95,622,391

Total: 272,690,813

SOURCE: Based on data from Bureau of the Census, U.S. Dept. of Commerce

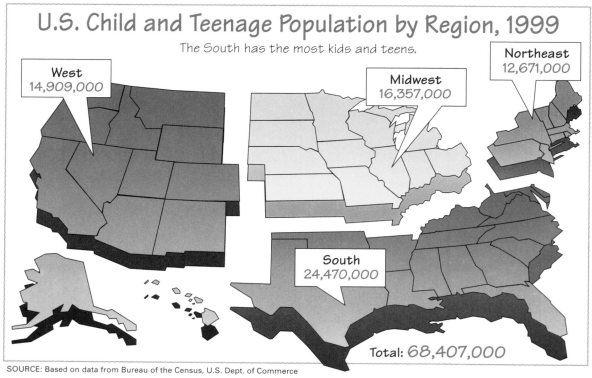

U.S. Child and Teenage Population by Region, 1999

The South has the most kids and teens.

West 14,909,000

Midwest 16,357,000

Northeast 12,671,000

South 24,470,000

Total: 68,407,000

SOURCE: Based on data from Bureau of the Census, U.S. Dept. of Commerce

U.S. Population by Region and Race, 1998

(In millions)

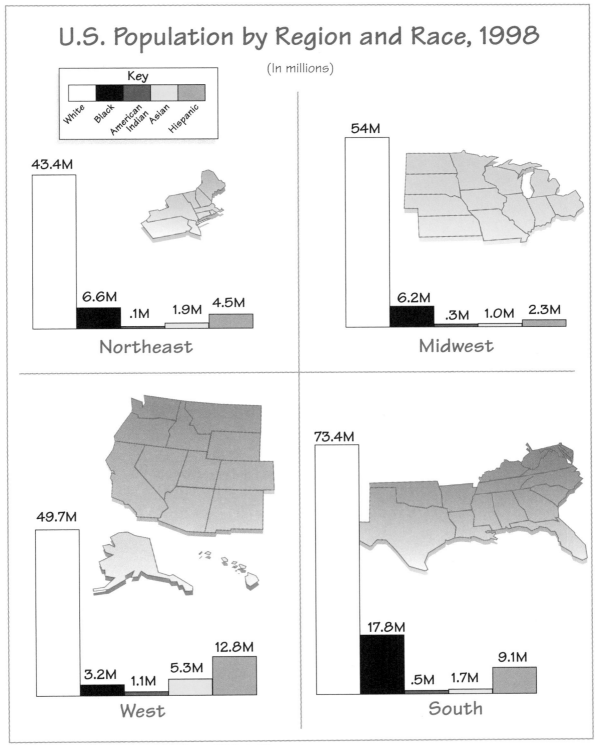

Key

White   Black   American Indian   Asian   Hispanic

Northeast
43.4M   6.6M   .1M   1.9M   4.5M

Midwest
54M   6.2M   .3M   1.0M   2.3M

West
49.7M   3.2M   1.1M   5.3M   12.8M

South
73.4M   17.8M   .5M   1.7M   9.1M

SOURCE: Based on data from Bureau of the Census, U.S. Dept. of Commerce

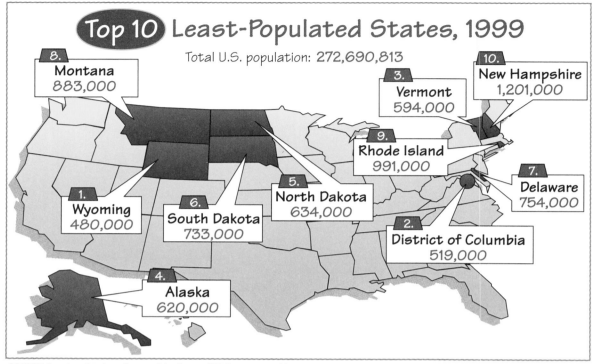

Top 10 Least-Populated States, 1999

Total U.S. population: 272,690,813

8. Montana 883,000

3. Vermont 594,000

10. New Hampshire 1,201,000

9. Rhode Island 991,000

7. Delaware 754,000

1. Wyoming 480,000

6. South Dakota 733,000

5. North Dakota 634,000

2. District of Columbia 519,000

4. Alaska 620,000

SOURCE: Based on data from Bureau of the Census, U.S. Department of Commerce

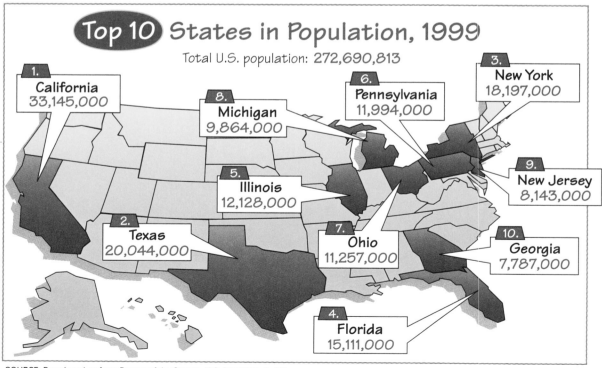

Top 10 States in Population, 1999

Total U.S. population: 272,690,813

1. California 33,145,000

6. Pennsylvania 11,994,000

3. New York 18,197,000

8. Michigan 9,864,000

9. New Jersey 8,143,000

5. Illinois 12,128,000

2. Texas 20,044,000

7. Ohio 11,257,000

10. Georgia 7,787,000

4. Florida 15,111,000

SOURCE: Based on data from Bureau of the Census, U.S. Department of Commerce

English and Non-English Speakers: Total Persons 5 to 17 Years Old

Most kids speak only English.

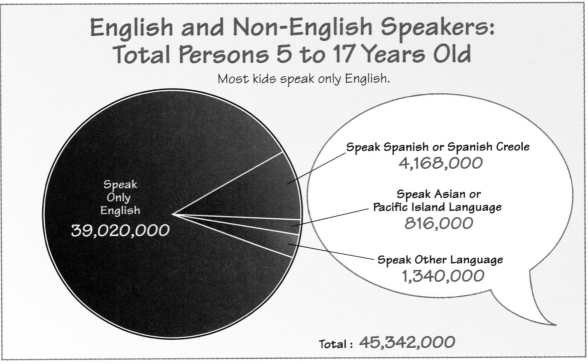

Speak Only English
39,020,000

Speak Spanish or Spanish Creole
4,168,000

Speak Asian or Pacific Island Language
816,000

Speak Other Language
1,340,000

Total : 45,342,000

SOURCE: Based on data from Bureau of the Census, U.S. Dept. of Commerce

Top 5 Non-English Languages Spoken at Home by Kids

(Persons 5 years old and over who speak language)

Chinese
1,249,000

Italian
1,309,000

German
1,547,000

French
1,702,000

Spanish
17,339,000

About 75% of all non-English speaking kids speak Spanish at home.

SOURCE: Based on data from Bureau of the Census, U.S. Dept. of Commerce

Who Are We?

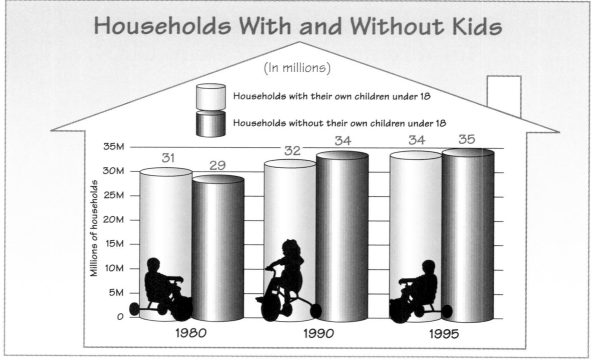

Households With and Without Kids

(In millions)

Households with their own children under 18

Households without their own children under 18

SOURCE: Based on data from Bureau of the Census, U.S. Dept. of Commerce

Children in One-Parent vs. Two-Parent Households

(Living arrangements of children under 18 years old, 1970 vs. 1998)

(In millions)

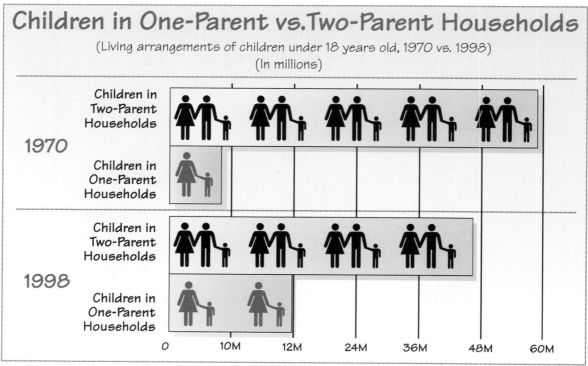

SOURCE: Based on data from Bureau of the Census, U.S. Dept. of Commerce

Size of U.S. Families, 1980 vs. 1998

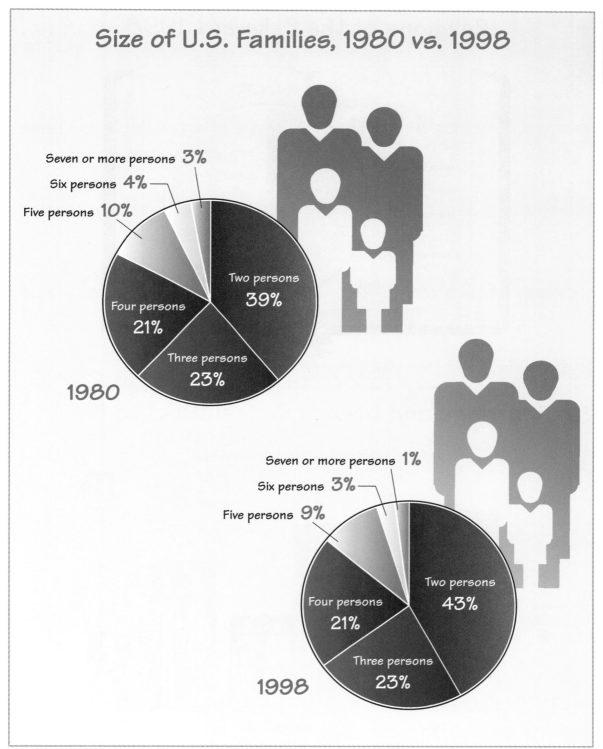

Seven or more persons **3%**
Six persons **4%**
Five persons **10%**
Four persons **21%**
Two persons **39%**
Three persons **23%**
1980

Seven or more persons **1%**
Six persons **3%**
Five persons **9%**
Four persons **21%**
Two persons **43%**
Three persons **23%**
1998

SOURCE: Based on data from Bureau of the Census, U.S. Dept. of Commerce

Religions of the Believers, 1998

(Percent of U.S. population affiliated with certain religions)

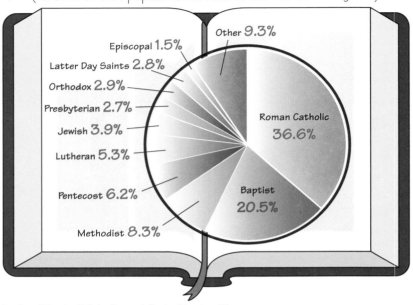

Other 9.3%

Episcopal 1.5%

Latter Day Saints 2.8%

Orthodox 2.9%

Presbyterian 2.7%

Jewish 3.9%

Lutheran 5.3%

Pentecost 6.2%

Methodist 8.3%

Roman Catholic 36.6%

Baptist 20.5%

SOURCE: Based on data from Princeton Religion Research Center, Princeton, NJ

Marriage and Divorce Rates: 1950 to 1998

Marriage and divorce have declined since 1980.
(Rate per 1,000 population)

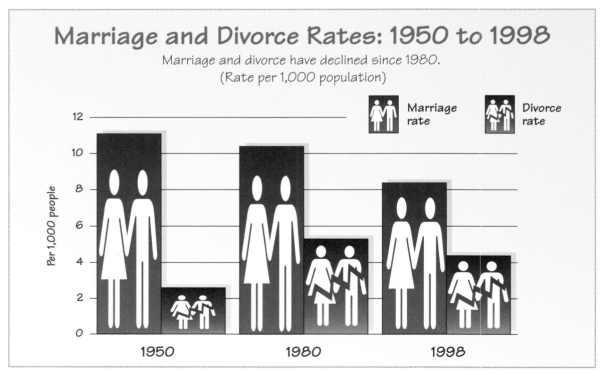

Marriage rate

Divorce rate

Per 1,000 people

1950   1980   1998

SOURCE: Based on data from U.S. National Center for Health Statistics

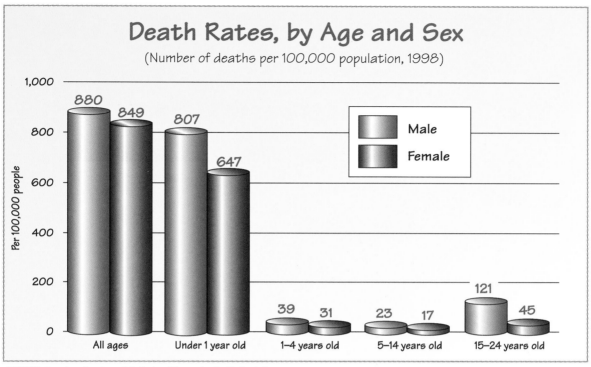

Death Rates, by Age and Sex

(Number of deaths per 100,000 population, 1998)

Per 100,000 people

Male
Female

880 / 849 — All ages
807 / 647 — Under 1 year old
39 / 31 — 1–4 years old
23 / 17 — 5–14 years old
121 / 45 — 15–24 years old

SOURCE: Based on data from U.S. National Center for Health Statistics

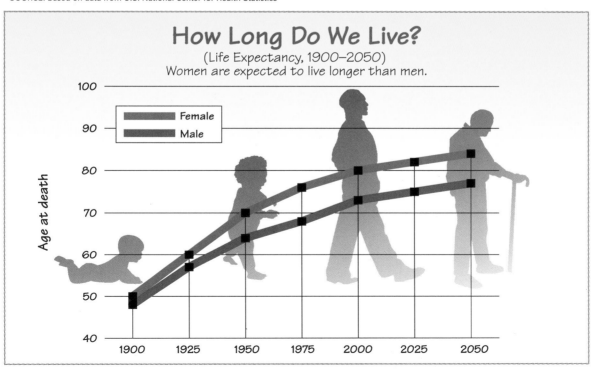

How Long Do We Live?

(Life Expectancy, 1900–2050)
Women are expected to live longer than men.

Age at death

Female
Male

1900   1925   1950   1975   2000   2025   2050

SOURCE: Based on data from Social Security Administration

Leading Causes of Death, Kids Ages 5 to 14

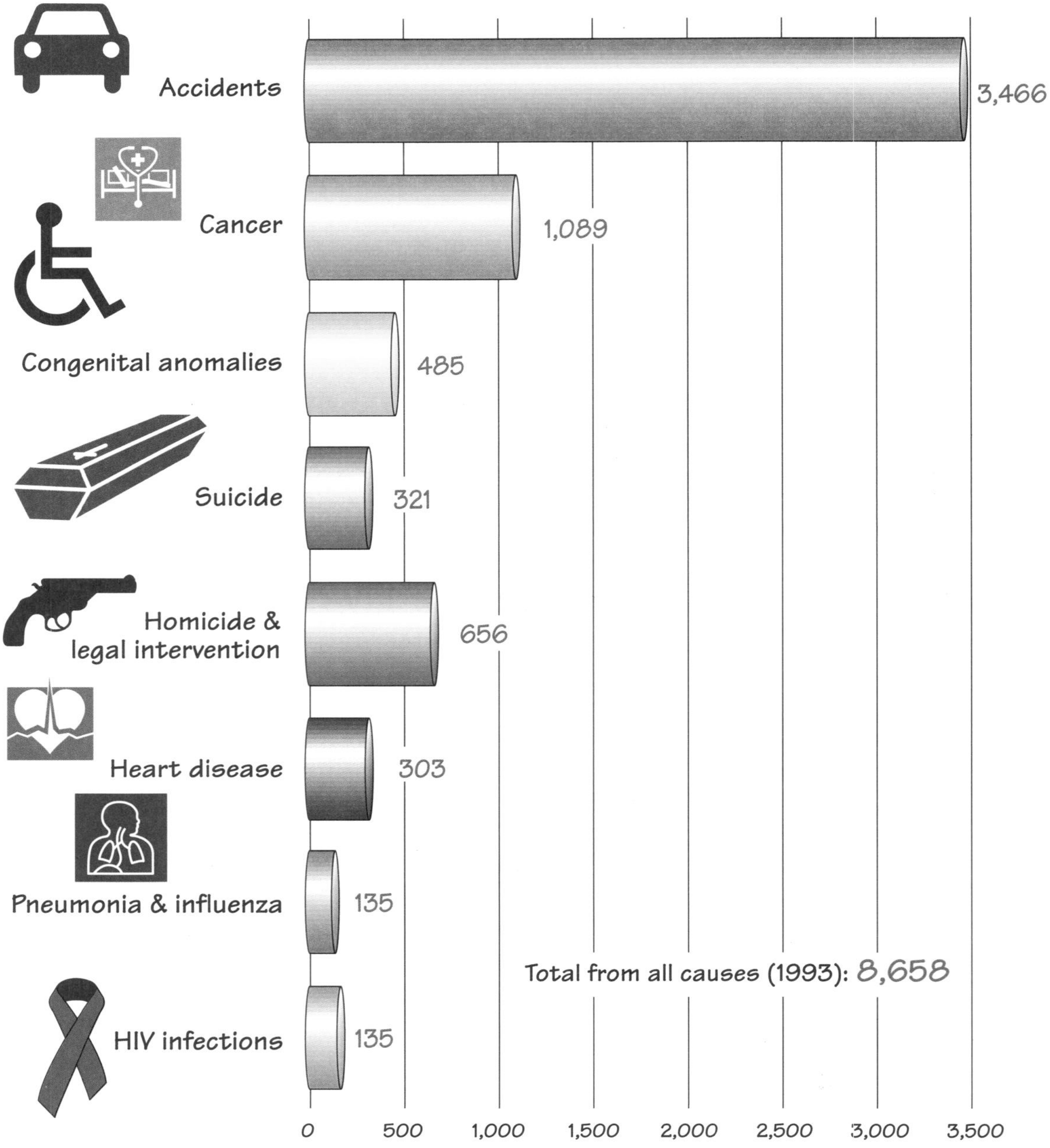

Accidents — 3,466

Cancer — 1,089

Congenital anomalies — 485

Suicide — 321

Homicide & legal intervention — 656

Heart disease — 303

Pneumonia & influenza — 135

Total from all causes (1993): 8,658

HIV infections — 135

0   500   1,000   1,500   2,000   2,500   3,000   3,500

SOURCE: Based on data from U.S. National Center for Health Statistics, Monthly Vital Statistics Report, 1996

Who Are We?

Leading Causes of Death for Americans
(As percentage of total deaths, 1995)

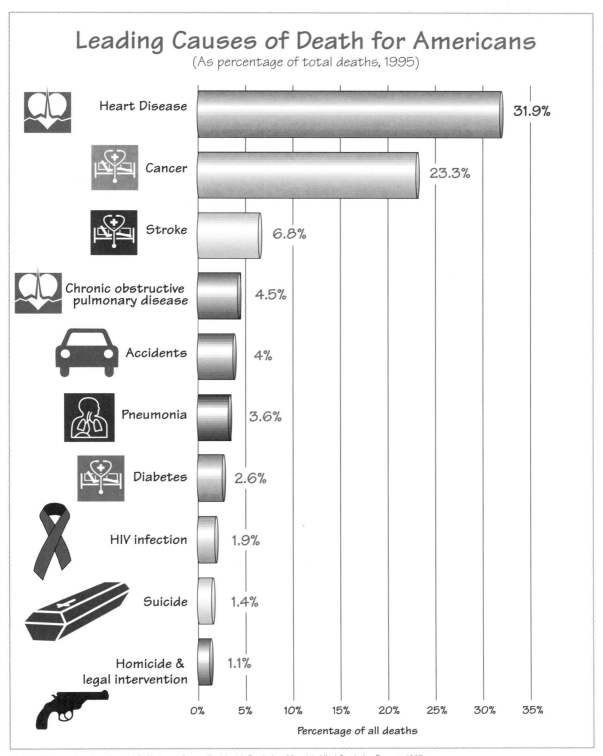

Heart Disease	31.9%
Cancer	23.3%
Stroke	6.8%
Chronic obstructive pulmonary disease	4.5%
Accidents	4%
Pneumonia	3.6%
Diabetes	2.6%
HIV infection	1.9%
Suicide	1.4%
Homicide & legal intervention	1.1%

0%   5%   10%   15%   20%   25%   30%   35%

Percentage of all deaths

SOURCE: Based on data from U.S. National Center for Health Statistics, Monthly Vital Statistics Report, 1997

Top 10 Countries with the Highest Male Life Expectancy

(U.S. = 72.0 years)
The U.S. is far behind the top 10 countries in male life expectancy.

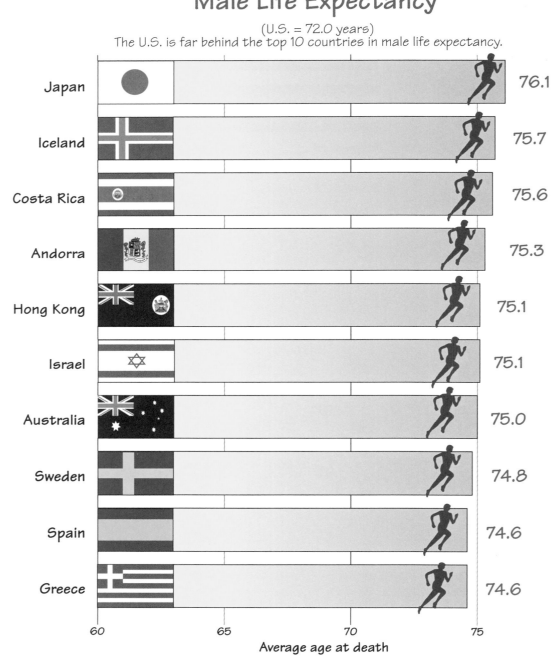

Country	Average age at death
Japan	76.1
Iceland	75.7
Costa Rica	75.6
Andorra	75.3
Hong Kong	75.1
Israel	75.1
Australia	75.0
Sweden	74.8
Spain	74.6
Greece	74.6

Average age at death

SOURCE: Based on information from the World Health Organization.

Top 10 Countries with the Highest Female Life Expectancy

(U.S. = 78.9 years)

The U.S. is far behind the top 10 countries in female life expectancy.

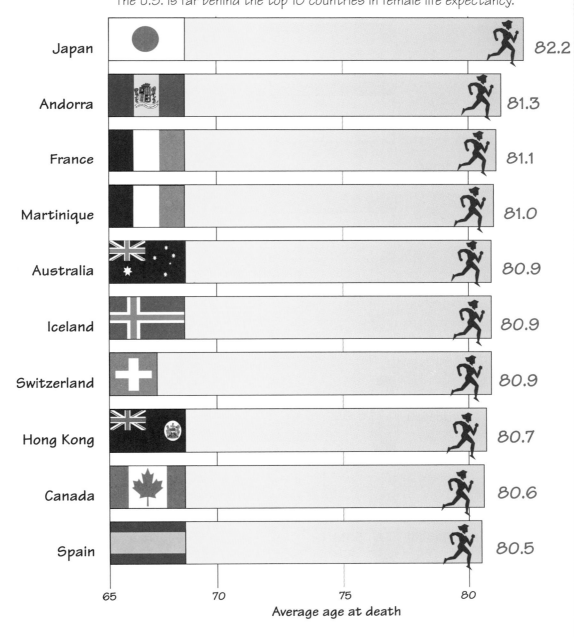

Country	Average age at death
Japan	82.2
Andorra	81.3
France	81.1
Martinique	81.0
Australia	80.9
Iceland	80.9
Switzerland	80.9
Hong Kong	80.7
Canada	80.6
Spain	80.5

Average age at death

SOURCE: Based on information from the World Health Organization.

Who Are We?

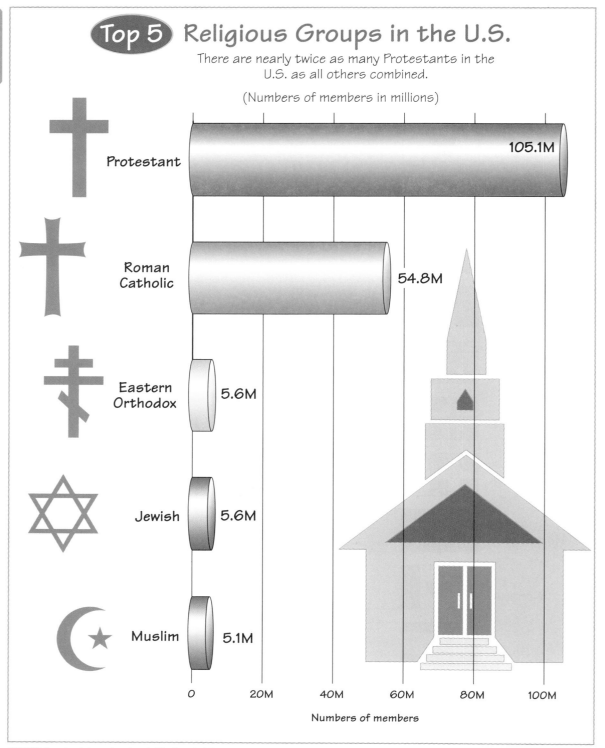

Top 5 Religious Groups in the U.S.

There are nearly twice as many Protestants in the U.S. as all others combined.

(Numbers of members in millions)

Protestant — 105.1M

Roman Catholic — 54.8M

Eastern Orthodox — 5.6M

Jewish — 5.6M

Muslim — 5.1M

0   20M   40M   60M   80M   100M

Numbers of members

SOURCE: Based on information given in *The Top 10 of Everything 1997,* Dorling Kindersley

U.S. Kids Are More Religious

The number of U.S. kids ages 7 - 12 who attend religious services is nearly four times more than the second highest country, the UK.

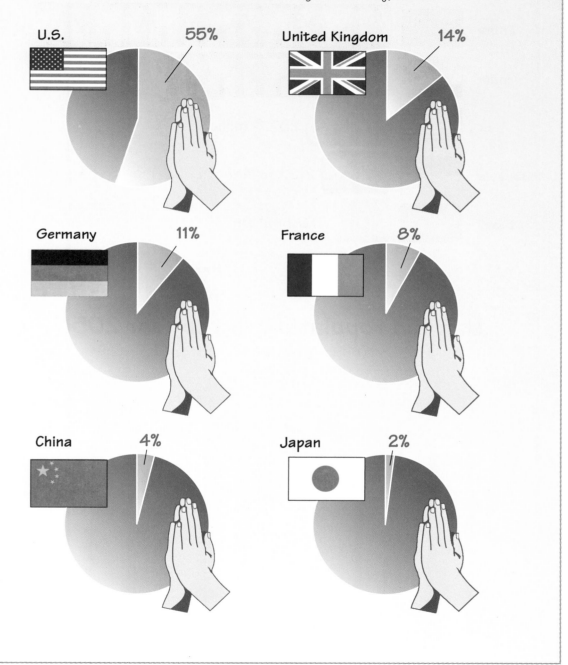

U.S. 55%

United Kingdom 14%

Germany 11%

France 8%

China 4%

Japan 2%

SOURCE: Based on data from Roper Starch Worldwide for A.B.C. Global Kids Study

Who Are We?

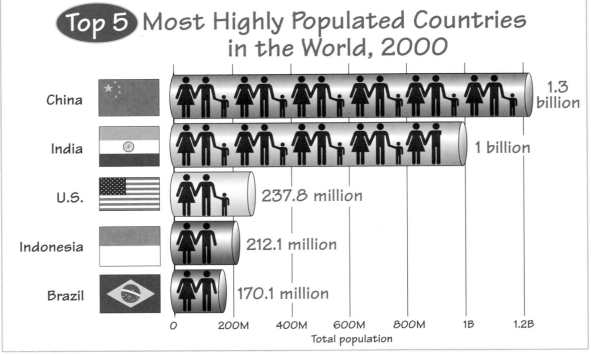

Top 5 Most Highly Populated Countries in the World, 2000

China		1.3 billion
India		1 billion
U.S.		237.8 million
Indonesia		212.1 million
Brazil		170.1 million

0   200M   400M   600M   800M   1B   1.2B

Total population

SOURCE: Based on data from United Nations Population Fund

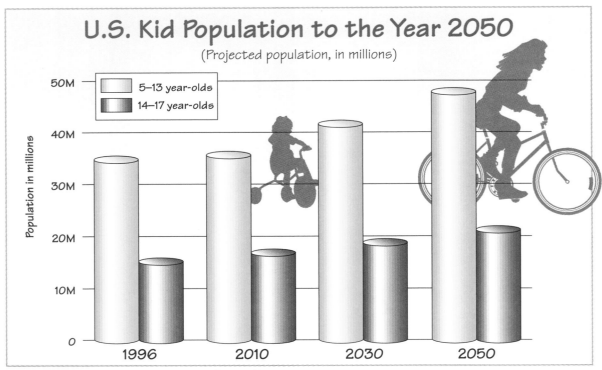

U.S. Kid Population to the Year 2050

(Projected population, in millions)

- 5–13 year-olds
- 14–17 year-olds

Population in millions

50M
40M
30M
20M
10M
0

1996   2010   2030   2050

SOURCE: Based on data from Bureau of the Census, U.S. Dept. of Commerce

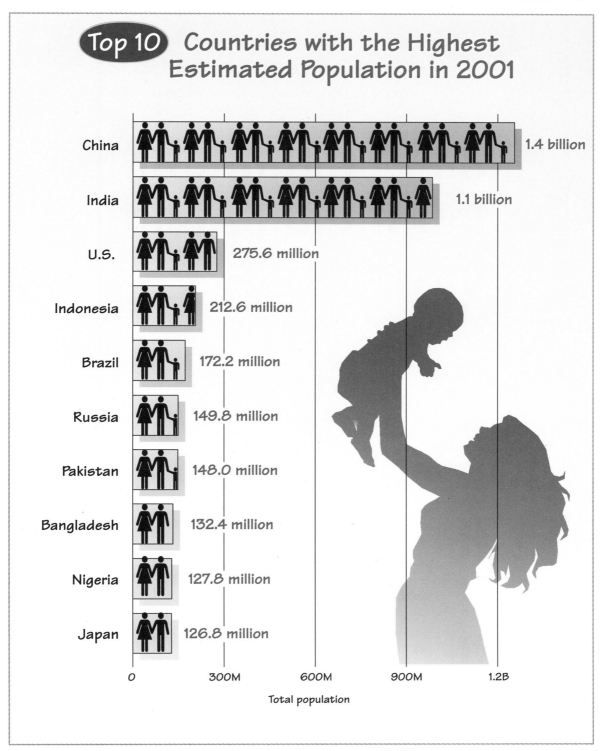

Top 10 Countries with the Highest Estimated Population in 2001

Country	Population
China	1.4 billion
India	1.1 billion
U.S.	275.6 million
Indonesia	212.6 million
Brazil	172.2 million
Russia	149.8 million
Pakistan	148.0 million
Bangladesh	132.4 million
Nigeria	127.8 million
Japan	126.8 million

0   300M   600M   900M   1.2B

Total population

SOURCE: Based on information from the United Nations Population Fund

Who Are We?

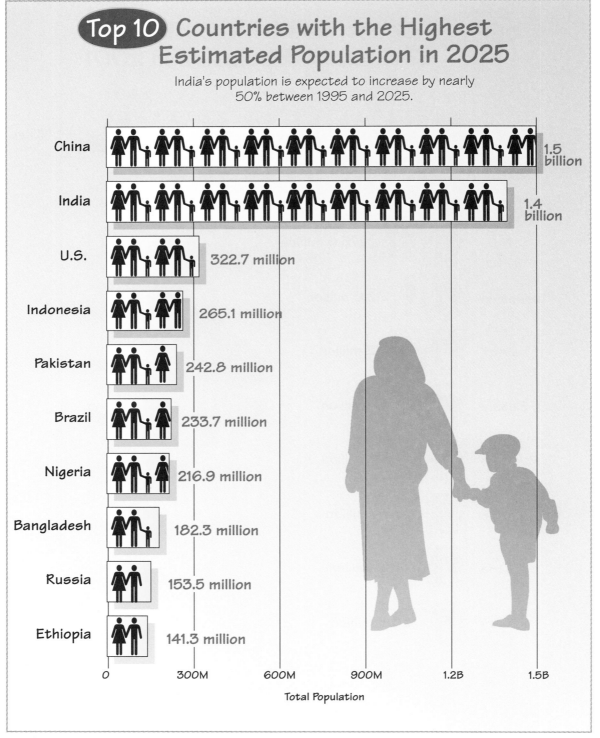

Top 10 Countries with the Highest Estimated Population in 2025

India's population is expected to increase by nearly 50% between 1995 and 2025.

Country	Population
China	1.5 billion
India	1.4 billion
U.S.	322.7 million
Indonesia	265.1 million
Pakistan	242.8 million
Brazil	233.7 million
Nigeria	216.9 million
Bangladesh	182.3 million
Russia	153.5 million
Ethiopia	141.3 million

Total Population

0   300M   600M   900M   1.2B   1.5B

SOURCE: Based on information from the United Nations Population Fund

Who Are We?

U.S. Doesn't Reach New Heights...
Top 5 Tallest Countries

(Average adult height)
(U.S. = 70.8 inches)

73.0 in.

72.6 in.

72.5 in.

72.2 in.

72.0 in.

71.9 in.

71.8 in.

71.6 in.

71.5 in.

71.0 in.

70.5 in.

70.0 in.

Netherlands   Denmark   Norway   Sweden   Germany

SOURCE: Based on data from Richard Steckel, Ohio State University

Money

Everyone can use money, which is one good reason why people work. Adults aren't the only workers. Many kids work, too. They earn money mowing lawns, babysitting, delivering newspapers, walking dogs, washing cars, and creating computer web sites. The older they are, the more likely they are to have a job. More than one-quarter of people ages 15 to 18 have part- or full-time jobs. Millions more pick up money doing odd jobs for family, neighbors, and other people.

When the U.S. first set a minimum wage, in 1938, it was 25 cents an hour. By 1999, it was $5.15 an hour! But while wages have increased, so has the cost of living. A comic book, a pair of jeans, a bicycle—they all cost a lot more today than they did when your parents and grandparents were your age.

Of course, jobs aren't the only source of money. Most kids also get money from their parents. Many receive allowances and gifts of money, especially on birthdays and at other special times of the year. Combine all those sources of income and kids have a lot of

Money

Kidbits Tidbits

- In 1998, some 8.2 million teenagers ages 16 to 19 worked. A total of 2.5 million worked full-time and 5.7 million worked part-time.
- In 1998, an *Amazing Fantasy* comic book that included the first appearance of Spider Man, sold for $2,000.
- American consumers owe more than $1.3 trillion dollars. In 1998, most of this—some $558 billion—was on credit card accounts. Another $447 billion was for automobiles.
- There are about 10,000 banks in the U.S.

spending power! American teenagers alone have more than $100 billion to spend each year!

The #1 item on kid shopping lists is candy. Kids spend their own money on candy more often than on anything else. Other foods are also popular. Surveys show that teenagers visit supermarkets more often than any other kind of store. Convenience stores, which stock tempting arrays of sodas and "junk food," aren't far behind.

Kids also spend lots of money on clothes, sporting goods, music, movies, toys, and books. They like to spend money on collecting stuff, too. Some 33-cent stamps, packs of stickers, or new comic books don't cost very much. But save them for a decade or two and they may be great investments as well as sources of pleasure. Over the years, they

can become very valuable. For instance, a Mickey Mantle rookie-year baseball card is now worth about $30,000!

The main way that kids invest money for the future is to save some of their income. On average, American kids save about 21 cents of every dollar they get. They save it for big purchases, such as a car or a computer. They also save money for college. And they see saving money as a first step toward becoming wealthy. Eighty percent of American kids dream about becoming rich one day!

If you're dreaming about getting rich, you should probably dream about the computer business and related businesses. In 2000, three of America's Top 10 richest people made their billions in the computer industry. Together, the three tycoons are worth an estimated $157 billion!

Kidbits Tidbits

- Almost all the geographical areas expected to have the fastest job growth in the coming decades are in the South. Heading the list are three Florida cities: Punta Gorda, Orlando, and Naples.
- The unemployment rate in 1999 fell to 4.3%—its lowest rate in 30 years.

Money

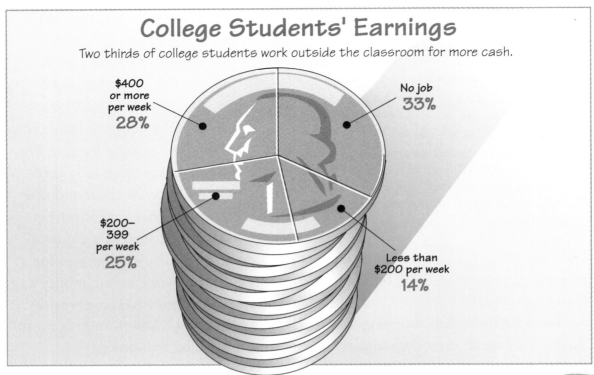

College Students' Earnings

Two thirds of college students work outside the classroom for more cash.

$400 or more per week **28%**

No job **33%**

$200–399 per week **25%**

Less than $200 per week **14%**

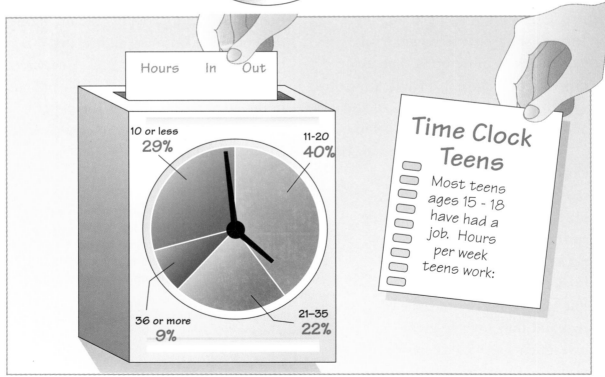

Hours   In   Out

10 or less **29%**

11-20 **40%**

36 or more **9%**

21–35 **22%**

Time Clock Teens

Most teens ages 15 - 18 have had a job. Hours per week teens work:

SOURCE: Based on data from Michaels Opinion Research for MassMutual

Money

Where Do Kids Dream Most About Being Rich?

In the world's leading industrial countries, more than half of kids
ages 7 - 12 daydream about being rich.

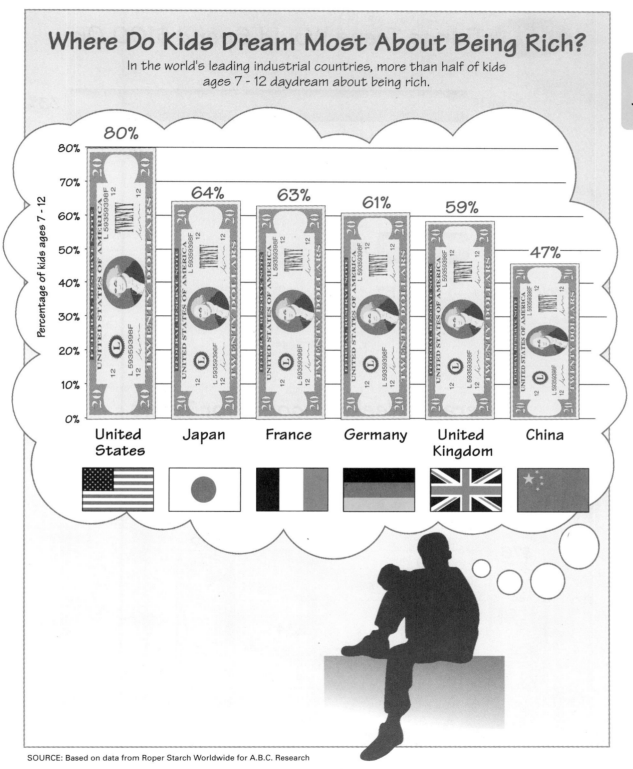

Percentage of kids ages 7 - 12

Country	Percentage
United States	80%
Japan	64%
France	63%
Germany	61%
United Kingdom	59%
China	47%

SOURCE: Based on data from Roper Starch Worldwide for A.B.C. Research

Money

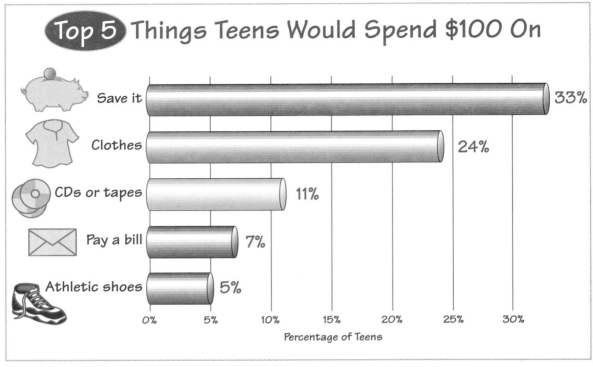

Top 5 Things Teens Would Spend $100 On

- Save it — 33%
- Clothes — 24%
- CDs or tapes — 11%
- Pay a bill — 7%
- Athletic shoes — 5%

Percentage of Teens

SOURCE: Based on data from Teenage Research Unlimited, Inc.

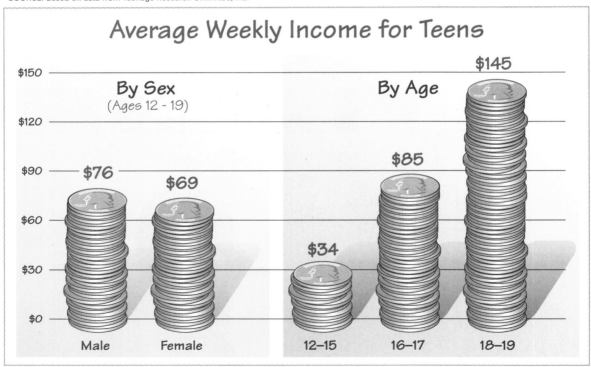

Average Weekly Income for Teens

By Sex (Ages 12 - 19)
- Male — $76
- Female — $69

By Age
- 12–15 — $34
- 16–17 — $85
- 18–19 — $145

SOURCE: Based on data from Teenage Research Unlimited, Inc.

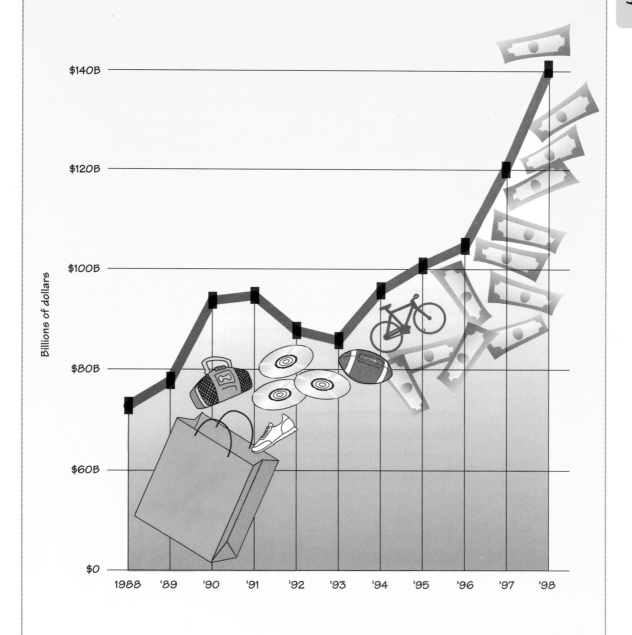

Teen Spending Power Grows, 1986–1998

In 1998, teens collectively spent more than $140 billion for the first time.
(In billions)

Billions of dollars

$140B

$120B

$100B

$80B

$60B

$0

1988 '89 '90 '91 '92 '93 '94 '95 '96 '97 '98

SOURCE: Based on data from Teenage Research Unlimited, Inc.

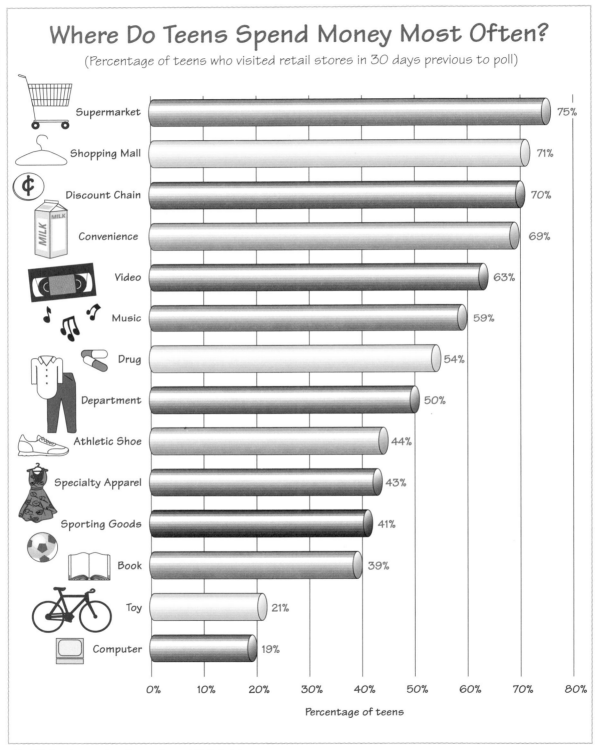

Where Do Teens Spend Money Most Often?

(Percentage of teens who visited retail stores in 30 days previous to poll)

Store	Percentage
Supermarket	75%
Shopping Mall	71%
Discount Chain	70%
Convenience	69%
Video	63%
Music	59%
Drug	54%
Department	50%
Athletic Shoe	44%
Specialty Apparel	43%
Sporting Goods	41%
Book	39%
Toy	21%
Computer	19%

Percentage of teens

SOURCE: Based on data from Teenage Research Unlimited, Inc.

Money

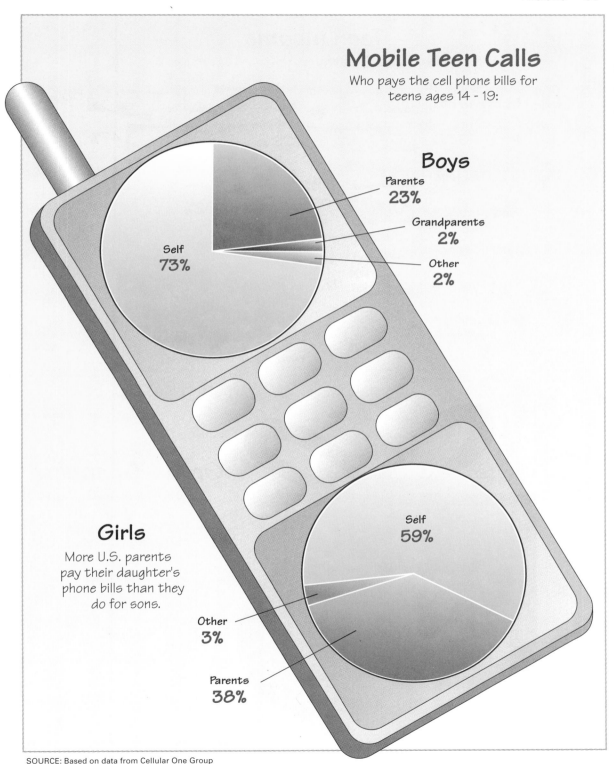

Mobile Teen Calls
Who pays the cell phone bills for teens ages 14 - 19:

Boys

Self
73%

Parents
23%

Grandparents
2%

Other
2%

Self
59%

Girls

More U.S. parents pay their daughter's phone bills than they do for sons.

Other
3%

Parents
38%

SOURCE: Based on data from Cellular One Group

Money

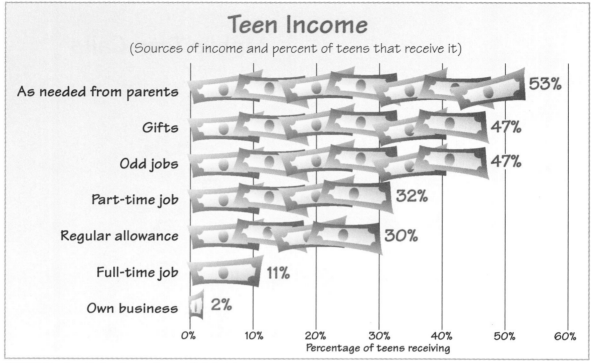

Teen Income
(Sources of income and percent of teens that receive it)

Source	Percentage
As needed from parents	53%
Gifts	47%
Odd jobs	47%
Part-time job	32%
Regular allowance	30%
Full-time job	11%
Own business	2%

Percentage of teens receiving

SOURCE: Based on data from Teenage Research Unlimited, Inc.

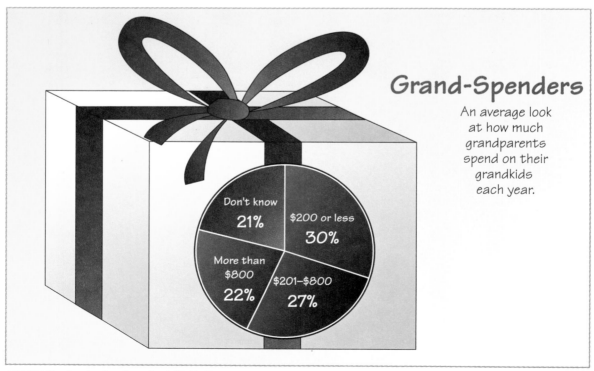

Grand-Spenders

An average look at how much grandparents spend on their grandkids each year.

Don't know 21%
$200 or less 30%
More than $800 22%
$201–$800 27%

SOURCE: Based on data from Roper Starch Worldwide, 1995

Kid Costs

Estimated yearly spending for a child born in 1995, for families in middle-income groups ($33,700 to $56,700).

| Age: | Under 1 | 1 | 2 | 3 | 4 | 5 | 6 | 7 | 8 | 9 | 10 | 11 | 12 | 13 | 14 | 15 | 16 | 17 |
| Year: | 1995 | '96 | '97 | '98 | '99 | '00 | '01 | '02 | '03 | '04 | '05 | '06 | '07 | '08 | '09 | '10 | '11 | '12 |

Cost per year

SOURCE: Based on data from Family Economics Research Group, U.S. Dept. of Agriculture

Which Kids Save the Most?

Studies show that Japanese kids save more of every dollar they earn or receive than do kids in the U.S. —about three times more. Here's how various countries stack up:

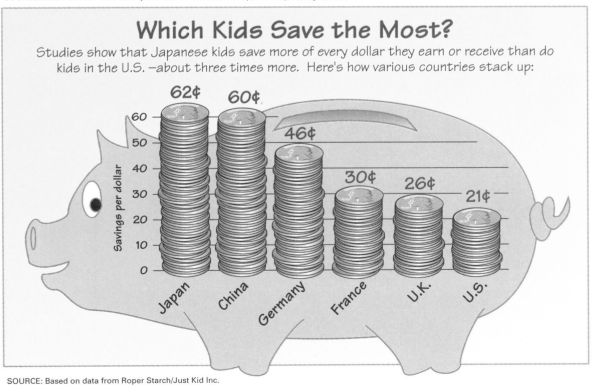

Savings per dollar

62¢ — Japan
60¢ — China
46¢ — Germany
30¢ — France
26¢ — U.K.
21¢ — U.S.

SOURCE: Based on data from Roper Starch/Just Kid Inc.

Money

America's Top 11 Richest People, 2000

Name	Source	Worth in billions of $
William Gates III	Computers	$63
Lawrence Ellison	Internet	$58
Paul Allen	Computers	$36
Warren Buffet	Investment	$28
Earle Moore	Internet	$26
Phillip Anschutz	Communications	$18
Alice Walton	Inheritance	$17
Helen Walton	Inheritance	$17
Jim Walton	Inheritance	$17
John Walton	Inheritance	$17
Steven Ballmer	Computers	$17

SOURCE: Based on data from *Forbes*

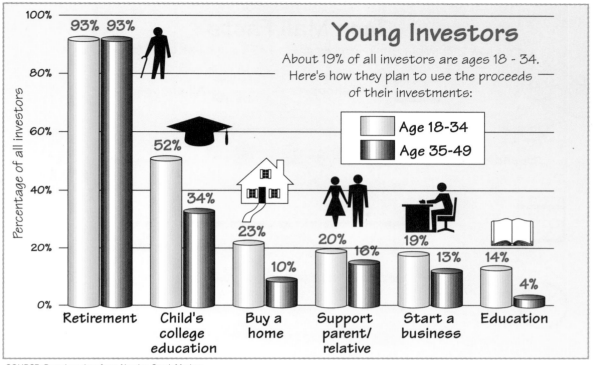

Young Investors

About 19% of all investors are ages 18 - 34.
Here's how they plan to use the proceeds
of their investments:

SOURCE: Based on data from Nasdaq Stock Market

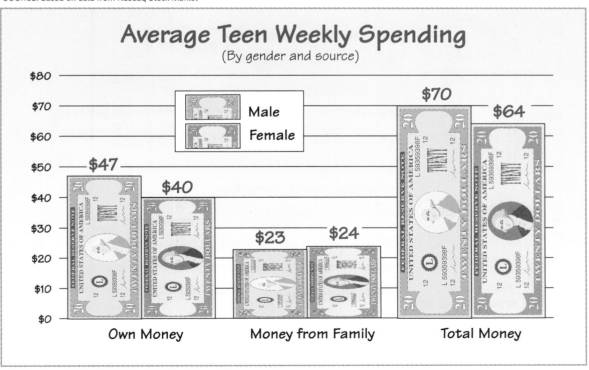

Average Teen Weekly Spending
(By gender and source)

SOURCE: Based on data from Teenage Research Unlimited, Inc.

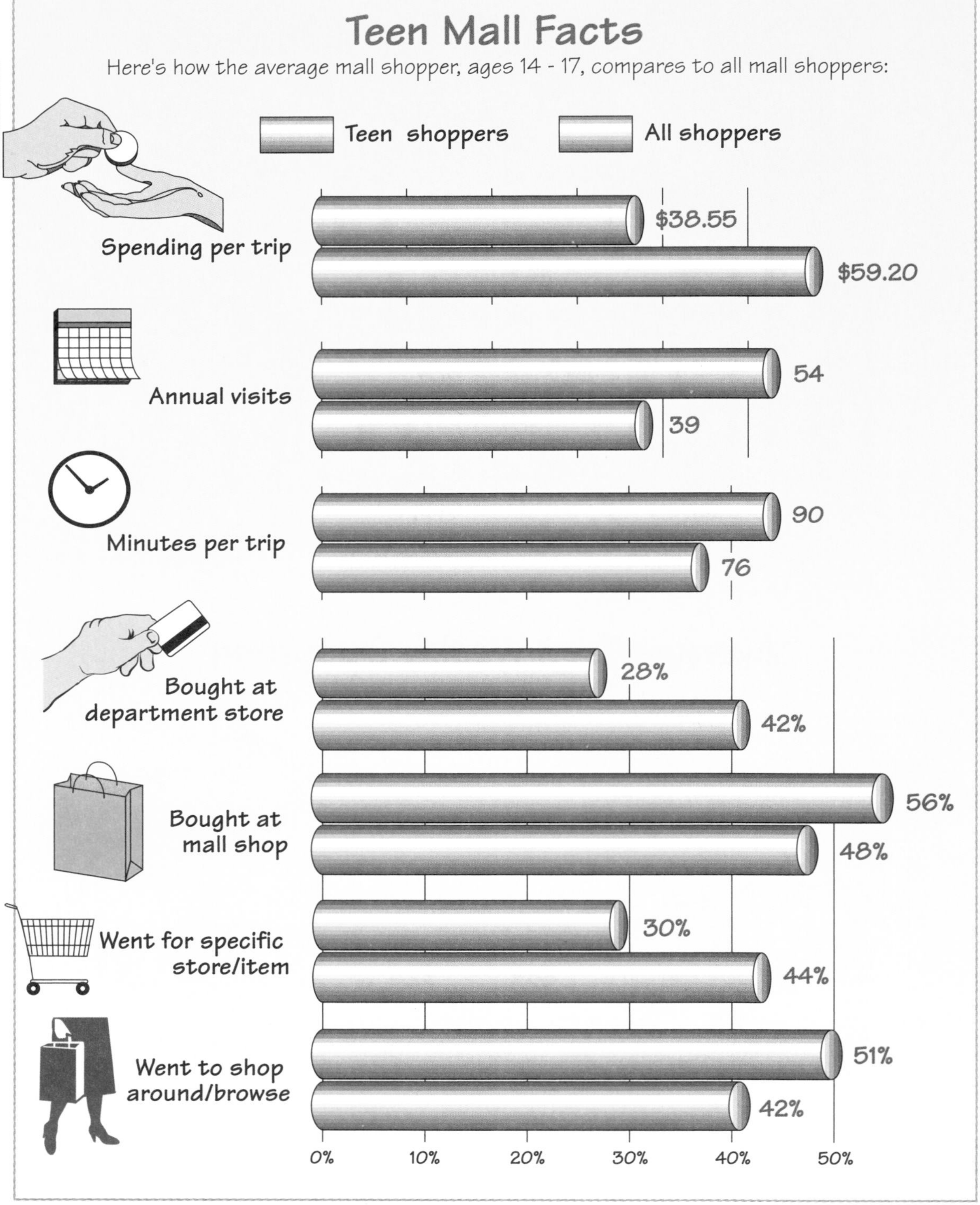

Money

Teen Mall Facts

Here's how the average mall shopper, ages 14 - 17, compares to all mall shoppers:

Teen shoppers　　**All shoppers**

Spending per trip
- Teen: $38.55
- All: $59.20

Annual visits
- Teen: 54
- All: 39

Minutes per trip
- Teen: 90
- All: 76

Bought at department store
- Teen: 28%
- All: 42%

Bought at mall shop
- Teen: 56%
- All: 48%

Went for specific store/item
- Teen: 30%
- All: 44%

Went to shop around/browse
- Teen: 51%
- All: 42%

0%　10%　20%　30%　40%　50%

SOURCE: Based on data from International Council of Shopping Centers

Money

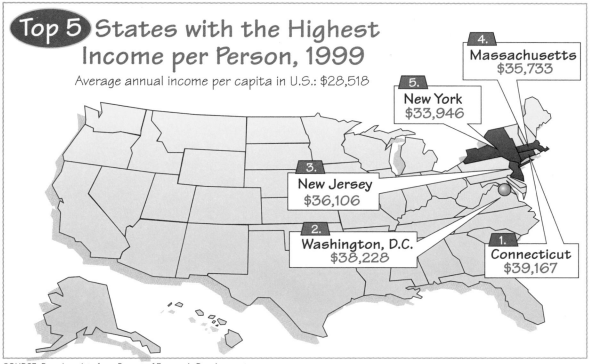

Top 5 States with the Highest Income per Person, 1999

Average annual income per capita in U.S.: $28,518

4. Massachusetts $35,733

5. New York $33,946

3. New Jersey $36,106

2. Washington, D.C. $38,228

1. Connecticut $39,167

SOURCE: Based on data from Bureau of Economic Development

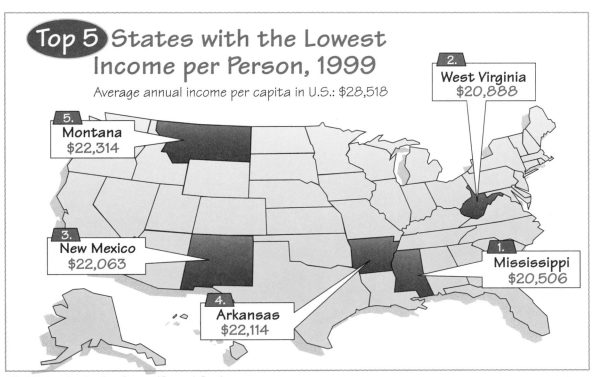

Top 5 States with the Lowest Income per Person, 1999

Average annual income per capita in U.S.: $28,518

2. West Virginia $20,888

5. Montana $22,314

3. New Mexico $22,063

4. Arkansas $22,114

1. Mississippi $20,506

SOURCE: Based on data from Bureau of Economic Development

Sports for Fun

Kids are sports crazy! They kick soccer balls, take jump shots, swing bats, tumble, run, swim, and skate. While some prefer team sports such as soccer and basketball, others are into one-on-one sports such as tennis and golf. Activities that can be pursued by oneself, such as running and bicycling, also are popular. And so are new twists on old sports, such as snowboarding, ultimate frisbee, and glow bowling (also called "cosmic bowling" or "xtreme bowling").

As years pass, some sports become more popular among kids while others attract fewer participants. Soccer in America is one sport that has grown in popularity. (It's about time—soccer is by far the most popular sport throughout the rest of the world!) Track and field has declined, in part because many kids prefer to play soccer.

Some kids commit a lot of time to their sports, training to become eligible for national teams and even for professional competitions. Michelle Kwan was only 15 in 1996 when she won

Kidbits Tidbits

- Basketball is the top high school sport for women in the U.S. In the '99-00 school year, a total of 451,6000 girls played. Football tops boys sports with just more than 1 million players.
- Girls participation in U.S. high school sports has risen dramatically from 294,015 in 1971 to 2.67 million in 2000.
- Americans spent $3.6 billion on exercise equipment, a 12% increase from 1998.

both the U.S. and world women's figure-skating championships. Tiger Woods won his first world golfing title at age 8—and, in 1997, at age 21, he became the youngest person ever to win the Masters. Also in 1997, 16-year-old Martina Hingis became the youngest woman to earn the #1 ranking in tennis. These and other young athletes have become top role models for America's aspiring athletes. They have also greatly increased interest and participation in their sports.

Whether on or off the playing fields, kids like to wear sports attire. For example, people under age 18 account for 57% of all gym shoe and sneaker purchases, and 25% of all jogging and running shoe purchases. They also use 71% of all team sports equipment that is bought each year.

Kids play sports because it's fun. But they also want to be physically fit. Sports help kids build muscle strength, improve posture and balance, and develop agility and endurance. When playing sports, it's important to try to avoid injuries and accidents. Each year, more than 550,000 Americans are injured riding their bikes; almost 170,000 are injured playing soccer; and more than 600,000 are injured playing basketball. (In fact, basketball is one of the top causes of injury in America.) So wear a helmet on your bike, strap on a life jacket when in a boat, and be sure to use the right equipment when playing sports!

Kidbits Tidbits

- Americans of all ages list walking as their #1 sports activity. Swimming is #2 and bike riding is #3.
- Americans spent over $61 billion on sporting goods in 1999. This included approximately $13 billion on clothing, $11.8 billion on footwear, $19.6 billion on equipment, and $29 billion on transport (boats, bicycles, snowmobiles, etc.).
- It's definitely "cool" to play on the ice and snow. In 1999, a total of 7.4 million Americans reported that they downhill ski. About 7.7 million said they ice or figure skate, and 2.2 million reported cross-country skiing. A total of 1.9 million people play ice hockey, and 3.3 million snowboarded two or more times during the year.

Sports for Fun

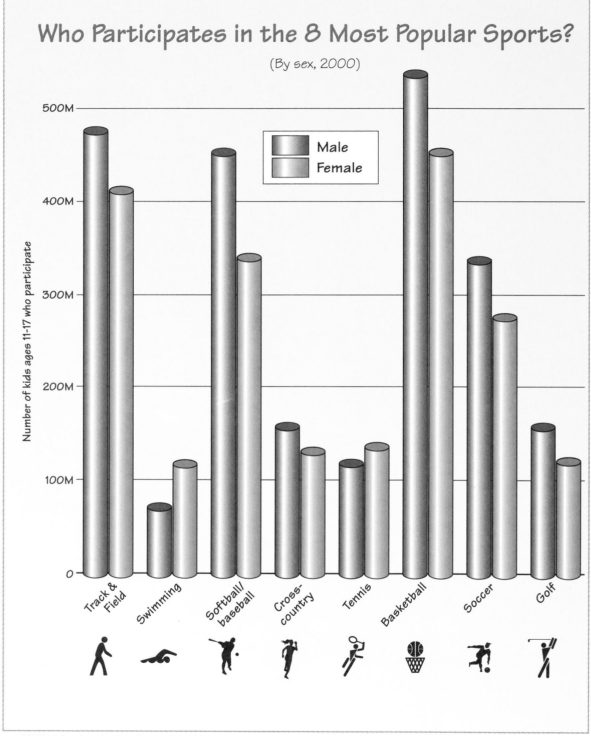

Who Participates in the 8 Most Popular Sports?
(By sex, 2000)

Male
Female

Number of kids ages 11-17 who participate

500M
400M
300M
200M
100M
0

Track & Field · Swimming · Softball/baseball · Cross-country · Tennis · Basketball · Soccer · Golf

SOURCE: Based on data from Bureau of the Census, U.S. Dept. of Commerce

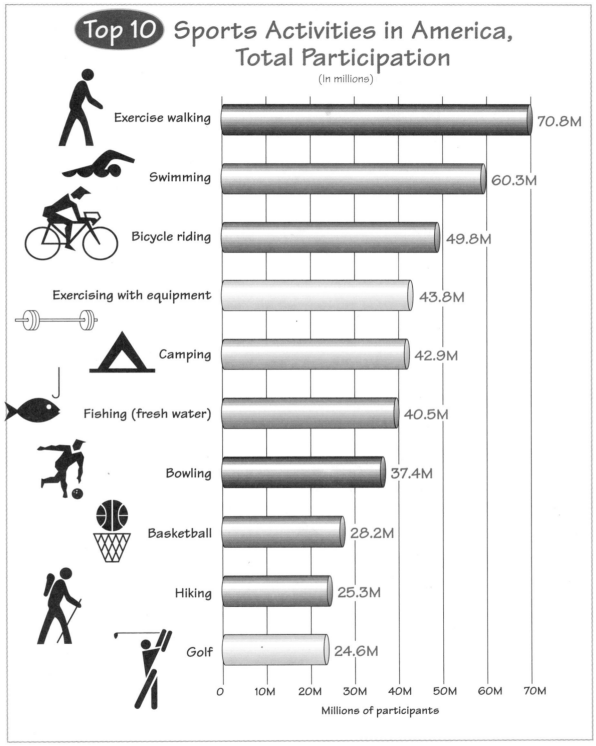

Top 10 Sports Activities in America, Total Participation

(In millions)

Sports for Fun

Activity	Participants
Exercise walking	70.8M
Swimming	60.3M
Bicycle riding	49.8M
Exercising with equipment	43.8M
Camping	42.9M
Fishing (fresh water)	40.5M
Bowling	37.4M
Basketball	28.2M
Hiking	25.3M
Golf	24.6M

0 10M 20M 30M 40M 50M 60M 70M

Millions of participants

SOURCE: Based on data from National Sporting Goods Association, Mt. Prospect, IL

Sports for Fun

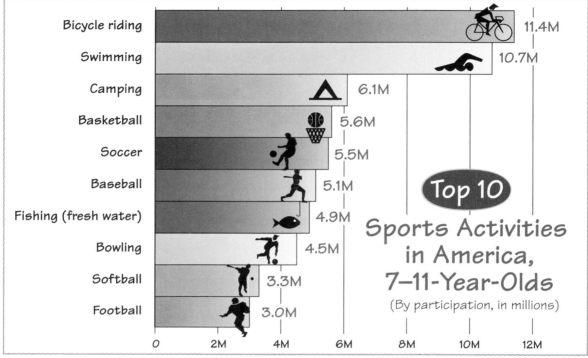

Bicycle riding	11.4M
Swimming	10.7M
Camping	6.1M
Basketball	5.6M
Soccer	5.5M
Baseball	5.1M
Fishing (fresh water)	4.9M
Bowling	4.5M
Softball	3.3M
Football	3.0M

Top 10

Sports Activities in America, 7–11-Year-Olds

(By participation, in millions)

SOURCE: Based on data from National Sporting Goods Association, Mt. Prospect, IL

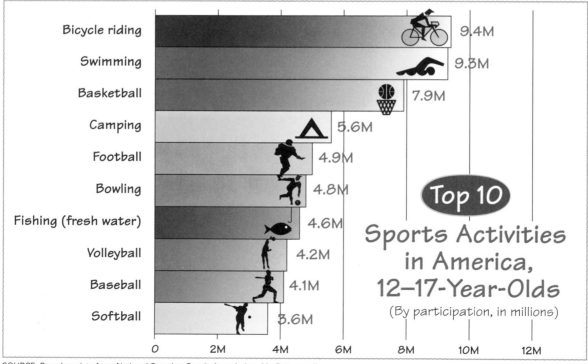

Bicycle riding	9.4M
Swimming	9.3M
Basketball	7.9M
Camping	5.6M
Football	4.9M
Bowling	4.8M
Fishing (fresh water)	4.6M
Volleyball	4.2M
Baseball	4.1M
Softball	3.6M

Top 10

Sports Activities in America, 12–17-Year-Olds

(By participation, in millions)

SOURCE: Based on data from National Sporting Goods Association, Mt. Prospect, IL

Participation in Sports and Activities by Percentage of Total Population, Ages 12–19

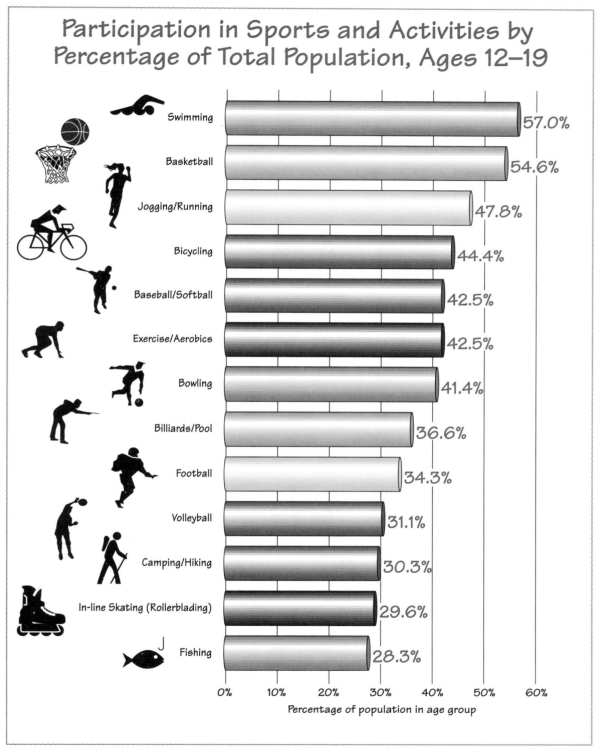

Activity	Percentage
Swimming	57.0%
Basketball	54.6%
Jogging/Running	47.8%
Bicycling	44.4%
Baseball/Softball	42.5%
Exercise/Aerobics	42.5%
Bowling	41.4%
Billiards/Pool	36.6%
Football	34.3%
Volleyball	31.1%
Camping/Hiking	30.3%
In-line Skating (Rollerblading)	29.6%
Fishing	28.3%

Percentage of population in age group

SOURCE: Based on data from Teenage Research Unlimited Inc.

Sports for Fun

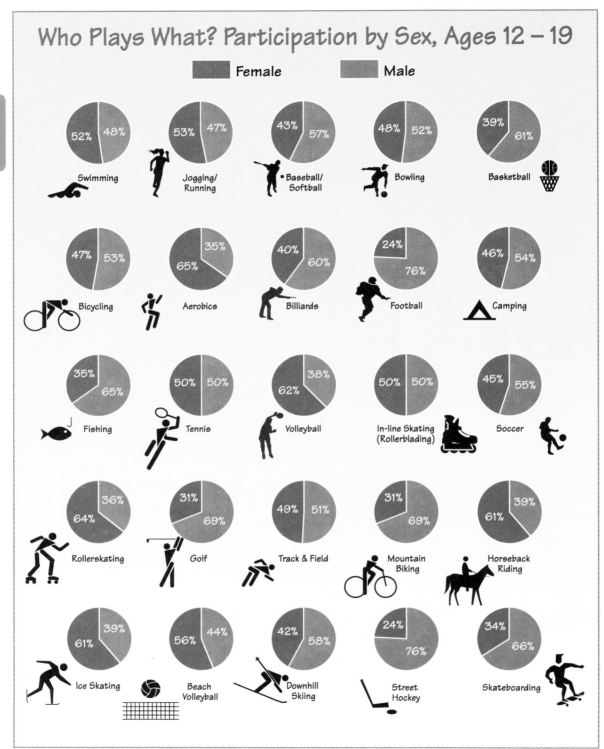

Who Plays What? Participation by Sex, Ages 12 – 19

Female   Male

	Female	Male
Swimming	52%	48%
Jogging/Running	53%	47%
Baseball/Softball	43%	57%
Bowling	48%	52%
Basketball	39%	61%
Bicycling	47%	53%
Aerobics	65%	35%
Billiards	40%	60%
Football	24%	76%
Camping	46%	54%
Fishing	35%	65%
Tennis	50%	50%
Volleyball	62%	38%
In-line Skating (Rollerblading)	50%	50%
Soccer	45%	55%
Rollerskating	64%	36%
Golf	31%	69%
Track & Field	49%	51%
Mountain Biking	31%	69%
Horseback Riding	61%	39%
Ice Skating	61%	39%
Beach Volleyball	56%	44%
Downhill Skiing	42%	58%
Street Hockey	24%	76%
Skateboarding	34%	66%

SOURCE: Based on data from Teenage Research Unlimited Inc.

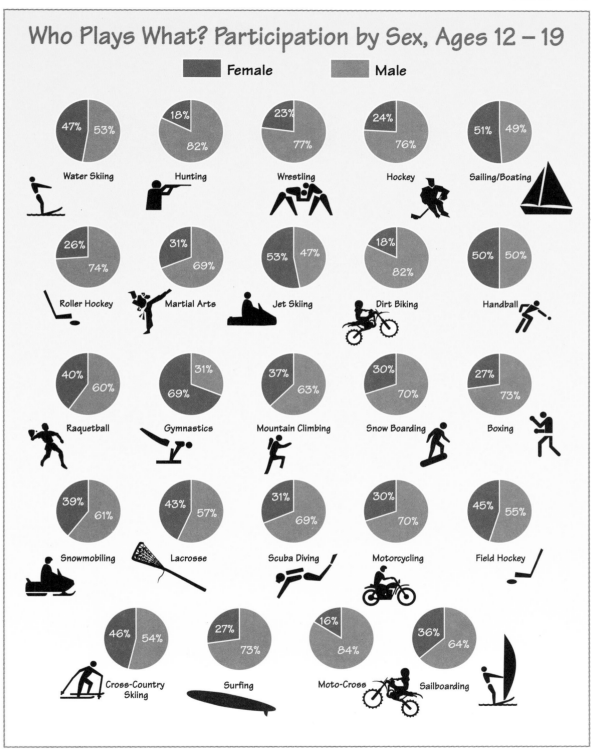

Who Plays What? Participation by Sex, Ages 12 – 19

Female   Male

Water Skiing — 47% / 53%
Hunting — 18% / 82%
Wrestling — 23% / 77%
Hockey — 24% / 76%
Sailing/Boating — 51% / 49%

Roller Hockey — 26% / 74%
Martial Arts — 31% / 69%
Jet Skiing — 53% / 47%
Dirt Biking — 18% / 82%
Handball — 50% / 50%

Raquetball — 40% / 60%
Gymnastics — 69% / 31%
Mountain Climbing — 37% / 63%
Snow Boarding — 30% / 70%
Boxing — 27% / 73%

Snowmobiling — 39% / 61%
Lacrosse — 43% / 57%
Scuba Diving — 31% / 69%
Motorcycling — 30% / 70%
Field Hockey — 45% / 55%

Cross-Country Skiing — 46% / 54%
Surfing — 27% / 73%
Moto-Cross — 16% / 84%
Sailboarding — 36% / 64%

SOURCE: Based on data from Teenage Research Unlimited Inc.

Sports for Fun

The Rules "Rule"

Boys and girls claim to understand the most about the rules of basketball.
Percentages of kids, ages 9 - 13, who say they know the rules of the following sports:

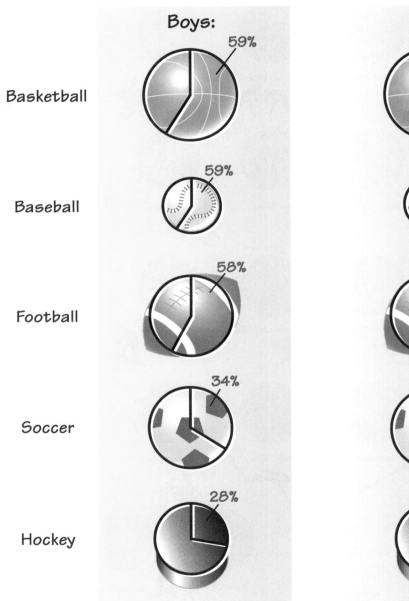
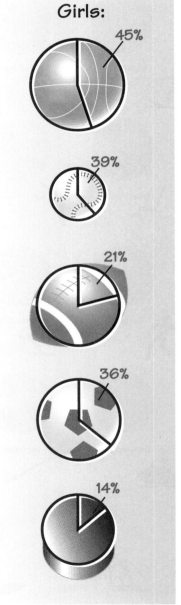

Boys: **Girls:**

Basketball   59%   45%

Baseball   59%   39%

Football   58%   21%

Soccer   34%   36%

Hockey   28%   14%

SOURCE: Based on data from *Sports Illustrated for Kids Omnibus*

Sports for Fun

Sneaker Specs
Who bought athletic shoes in 1999.

Gender

Men
47.1%

Women
52.9%

Age

65+
7.5%

18–24
5.3%

14–17
9.9%

25–34
12%

35–44
15.4%

Under 14
30%

45–64
19.9%

SOURCE: Based on data from National Sporting Goods Association

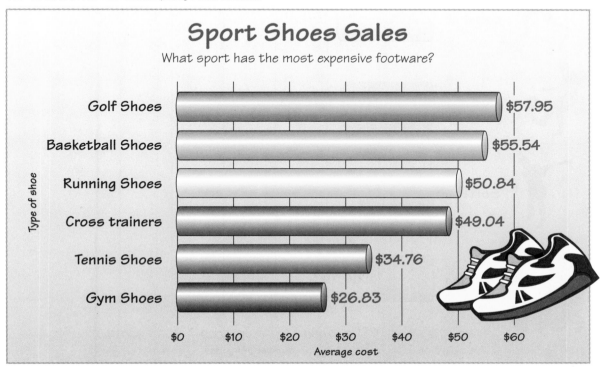

Sport Shoes Sales
What sport has the most expensive footware?

Type of shoe

Type of shoe	Average cost
Golf Shoes	$57.95
Basketball Shoes	$55.54
Running Shoes	$50.84
Cross trainers	$49.04
Tennis Shoes	$34.76
Gym Shoes	$26.83

$0 $10 $20 $30 $40 $50 $60

Average cost

Sports for Fun

No Pain, No Gain

In 1998 hospital emergency rooms treated thousands of sports injuries.
Here's a run-down of the top sports by number of E.R. visits:

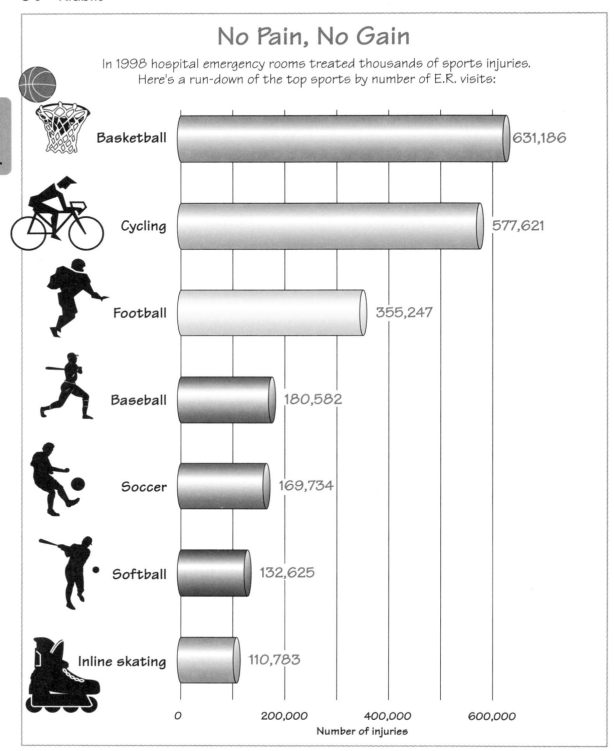

Basketball — 631,186
Cycling — 577,621
Football — 355,247
Baseball — 180,582
Soccer — 169,734
Softball — 132,625
Inline skating — 110,783

0   200,000   400,000   600,000

Number of injuries

SOURCE: Based on data from Consumer Product Safety Commission

Sports for Fun

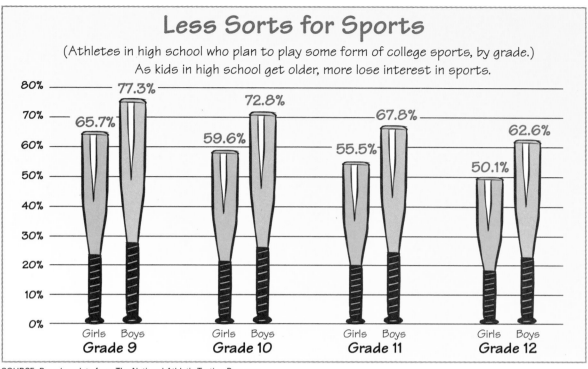

Less Sorts for Sports

(Athletes in high school who plan to play some form of college sports, by grade.)
As kids in high school get older, more lose interest in sports.

- Grade 9: Girls 65.7%, Boys 77.3%
- Grade 10: Girls 59.6%, Boys 72.8%
- Grade 11: Girls 55.5%, Boys 67.8%
- Grade 12: Girls 50.1%, Boys 62.6%

SOURCE: Based on data from The National Athletic Testing Program

Golf Course Cash

Total revenue collected for the four major men's golf championships in 1997. (In millions)

- U.S. Open: $35M
- PGA Championship: $30.5M
- The Masters: $22M
- British Open: $20M

SOURCE: Based on data from *Golf Digest*

Sports for Fun

Goal-Oriented Girls

Number of girls, by age group, playing soccer (1996)

Number of girls playing soccer

50,000

45,181 46,758

40,000

39,939

30,000

26,157

23,805

20,000

11,518

10,000

4,430

0

| 5–6 | 7–8 | 9–10 | 11–12 | 13–14 | 15–16 | 17–18 |

Age group

SOURCE: Based on data from American Youth Soccer Organization

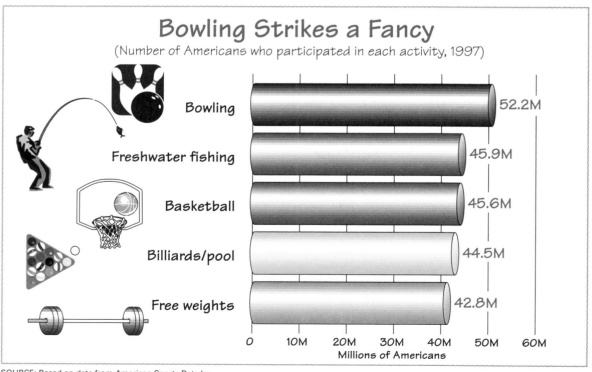

Bowling Strikes a Fancy

(Number of Americans who participated in each activity, 1997)

Bowling — 52.2M

Freshwater fishing — 45.9M

Basketball — 45.6M

Billiards/pool — 44.5M

Free weights — 42.8M

0   10M   20M   30M   40M   50M   60M

Millions of Americans

SOURCE: Based on data from American Sports Data Inc.

Sports for Fun

Not Board in the Snow

A total of 3.3 million Americans went snowboarding more than once in 1999. Here's a profile of the snowboarding population:

Age:
18-34
43%

Sex:
Male
74%

Average cost of a snowboard: $309

SOURCE: Based on data from SnowSports Industries America, National Sporting Goods Association

Spending Dough in the Snow

The top-selling kinds of sports equipment for snow sports in 1997-98:
(In millions of dollars)

Shaped Alpine skis — $84M

Snowboards — $71.2M

Straight Alpine skis — $20.4M

Cross-country skis — $9.7M

$0 $20M $40M $60M $80M $100M

SOURCE: Based on data from SnowSports Industries America

Clothes

Mission: wearing stuff that's fashionable, "cool," practical, exactly like everyone else's clothing—except for the fact that it is a part of your unique identity. When it comes to clothing, kids are the ultimate consumers. They know what they like, and they'll spend time and money to get it. They haunt the malls, sneaker superstores, vintage clothing shops, even tag sales and thrift shops. And if they can't find what they want, some kids will buy fabric and sew up their own clothes.

Casual wear, such as T-shirts, sweaters, jeans, and sports shoes form the basis of most kids' wardrobes. But not just any T-shirt or sweater will do. Brand names are very important among kids—even for the most ordinary attire. And a brand that's "in" one year may be "out" the next. Kids say that quality is the most important criterion when choosing brand-name clothing. But their parents may question the value of that brand-name label, particularly if it's the parents who are forking over $50 for jeans or $100 for sneakers that are likely to be outgrown in a few months.

Kidbits
Tidbits

● In 1996 there were more than 42,000 shopping centers in the U.S., with a total of 5.10 billion square feet of retail area.

● More than 14 million people worked in the retail industry in 1998.

● The Mall of America in Bloomington, Minnesota, is the nation's largest mall, with some 500 stores.

● In 1998, the U.S. had 11,314 department stores, 24,527 sporting goods and bicycle shops, 29,459 jewelry stores, and 125,093 apparel and accessory stores.

It's not just what you wear, it's how you wear it. Kids notice who's wearing caps backwards, jeans artfully ripped, or tees too tight. They get inspiration for new trends from their peers, from models in teen magazines, and from their favorite TV, movie, music, and sports personalities.

Some adults feel that kids place too much importance on clothing. They suspect that kids are more interested in what's being worn at school than in what's being taught there. Parochial and private schools have long used school uniforms to provide a more serious approach to learning. They feel this also removes some of the distractions and other problems connected with clothing fashions and fads. Requiring uniforms in public schools is a matter of much debate, though the trend gained momentum during the 1990s. And there was some evidence that wearing uniforms improved students' lives. For example, beginning in 1994, Long Beach, California, required uniforms for its 70,000 students in kindergarten through grade 8. In the first year of the program there was a 43% reduction in suspensions, 54% fewer fights, and more than 20% fewer cases of weapons possession and robbery. Is there a connection? You be the judge.

Kidbits
Tidbits

● People spent $21.5 billion in shoe stores in 1999.

● Clothing is the third most popular item purchased at yard sales.

● Nike's "Swoosh" logo represents the wing of the Greek goddess Nike.

● Each year, Nike recycles over 2 million athletic shoes into basketball courts and other sports courts.

● Gap spent $206.9 million in advertising in 1998; Nike spent $198 million.

● December is the busiest shopping month. Americans spent $184 billion on shopping during the 1999 holiday season. About $4 billion was spent shopping on-line.

● In a typical month, 185 million adults shop at shopping centers.

Clothes

Frequency of Teen Clothing Care Activities

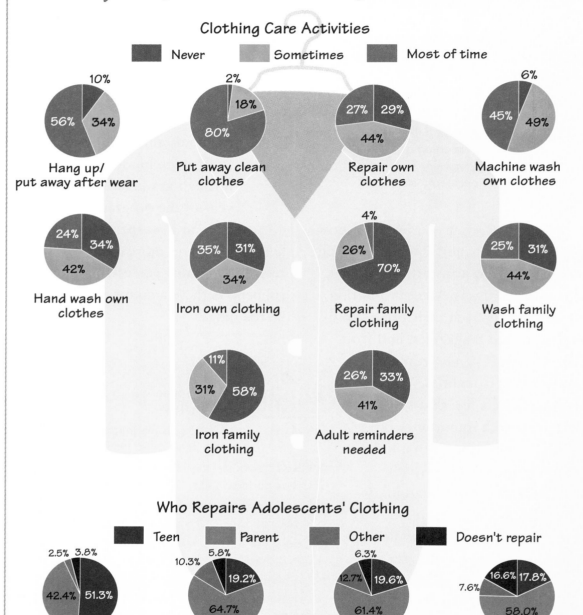

Clothing Care Activities

■ Never   ■ Sometimes   ■ Most of time

Hang up/ put away after wear
10%, 34%, 56%

Put away clean clothes
2%, 18%, 80%

Repair own clothes
27%, 29%, 44%

Machine wash own clothes
6%, 49%, 45%

Hand wash own clothes
24%, 34%, 42%

Iron own clothing
35%, 31%, 34%

Repair family clothing
4%, 26%, 70%

Wash family clothing
25%, 31%, 44%

Iron family clothing
11%, 31%, 58%

Adult reminders needed
26%, 33%, 41%

Who Repairs Adolescents' Clothing

■ Teen   ■ Parent   ■ Other   ■ Doesn't repair

Replace buttons
2.5%, 3.8%, 42.4%, 51.3%

Repair hems
5.8%, 10.3%, 19.2%, 64.7%

Repair seams
6.3%, 12.7%, 19.6%, 61.4%

Patch holes
16.6%, 17.8%, 7.6%, 58.0%

SOURCE: Based on data from *Journal of Extension*

Clothes

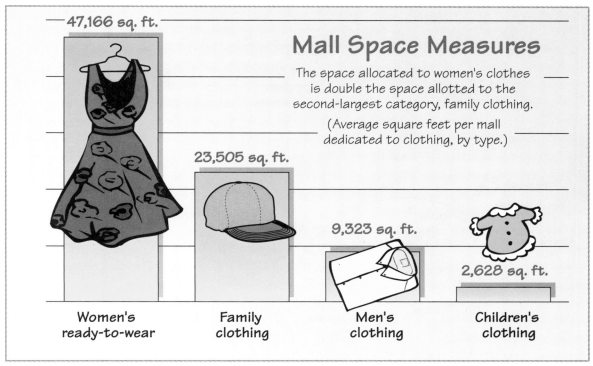

Mall Space Measures

The space allocated to women's clothes is double the space allotted to the second-largest category, family clothing.

(Average square feet per mall dedicated to clothing, by type.)

47,166 sq. ft.

23,505 sq. ft.

9,323 sq. ft.

2,628 sq. ft.

| Women's ready-to-wear | Family clothing | Men's clothing | Children's clothing |

SOURCE: Based on data from Gallup poll for Intl. Council of Shopping Centers

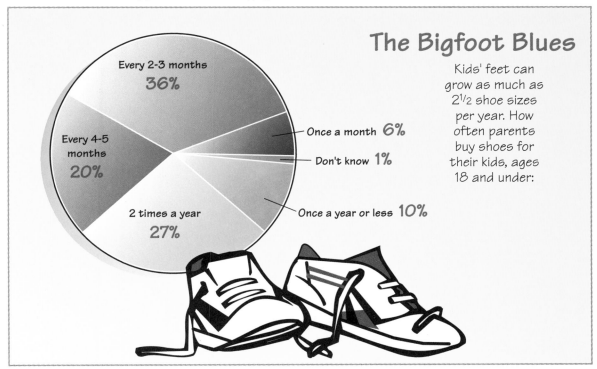

The Bigfoot Blues

Kids' feet can grow as much as $2\frac{1}{2}$ shoe sizes per year. How often parents buy shoes for their kids, ages 18 and under:

Every 2-3 months
36%

Every 4-5 months
20%

2 times a year
27%

Once a month 6%

Don't know 1%

Once a year or less 10%

SOURCE: Based on data from Opinion Research for Payless ShoeSource

Clothes

Sport-Shoe Sales, by Type

Sport shoes account for about $14 billion in sales each year. About 13% of all purchases are made by kids ages 12 and younger.

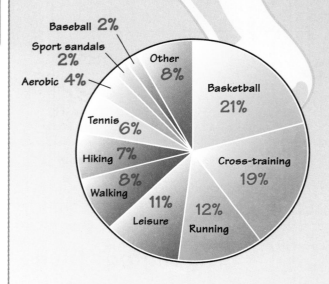

Baseball **2%**
Sport sandals **2%**
Aerobic **4%**
Other **8%**
Basketball **21%**
Tennis **6%**
Hiking **7%**
Cross-training **19%**
Walking **8%**
Leisure **11%**
Running **12%**

Who Buys Sport-Shoes? By Sex
(Percentage of gender population)

Males   **Females**

42%   45%

SOURCE: Based on data from NPD Group

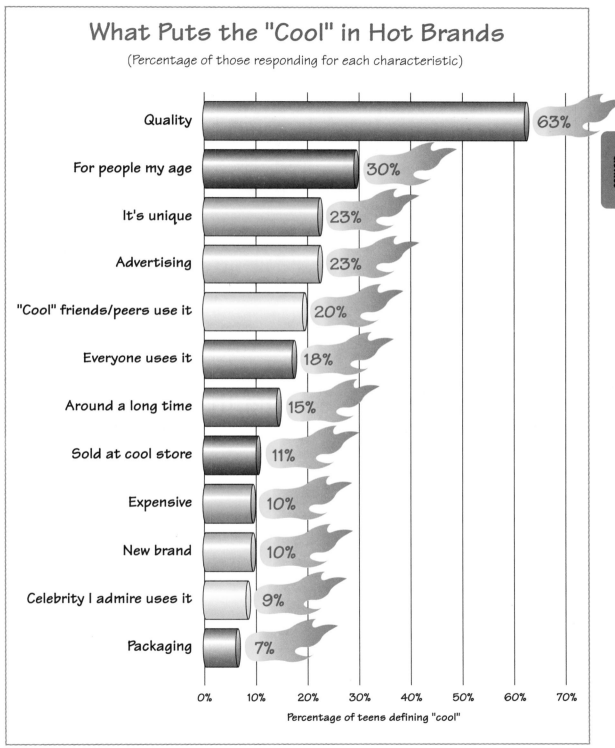

What Puts the "Cool" in Hot Brands

(Percentage of those responding for each characteristic)

Clothes

Quality	63%
For people my age	30%
It's unique	23%
Advertising	23%
"Cool" friends/peers use it	20%
Everyone uses it	18%
Around a long time	15%
Sold at cool store	11%
Expensive	10%
New brand	10%
Celebrity I admire uses it	9%
Packaging	7%

0%　10%　20%　30%　40%　50%　60%　70%

Percentage of teens defining "cool"

SOURCE: Based on data from Teenage Research Unlimited, Inc.

Clothes

Who Rules Cool?

Top 5 "coolest" brand names, by sex
(Percentage of each gender group that voted it "the coolest")

	1. Nike	2. Levi's	3. Calvin Klein	4. Sony	5. Pepsi
Females	38%	13%	20%	8%	8%
Males	49%	14%	5%	16%	10%

SOURCE: Based on data from Teenage Research Unlimited, Inc.

Online Shopping Trends

The average online shopper is white (74%), male (62%), and rich ($74K+).
It is estimated that by 2002, U.S. online customers will spend
one third of their shopping income via the Internet.

Percent of all shoppers

1995

- Men: 81%
- Women: 19%

1999

- Men: 62%
- Women: 38%

Average number of purchases per household

- 1996: 9
- 1999: 120

SOURCE: Based on data from *Canada One Magazine*

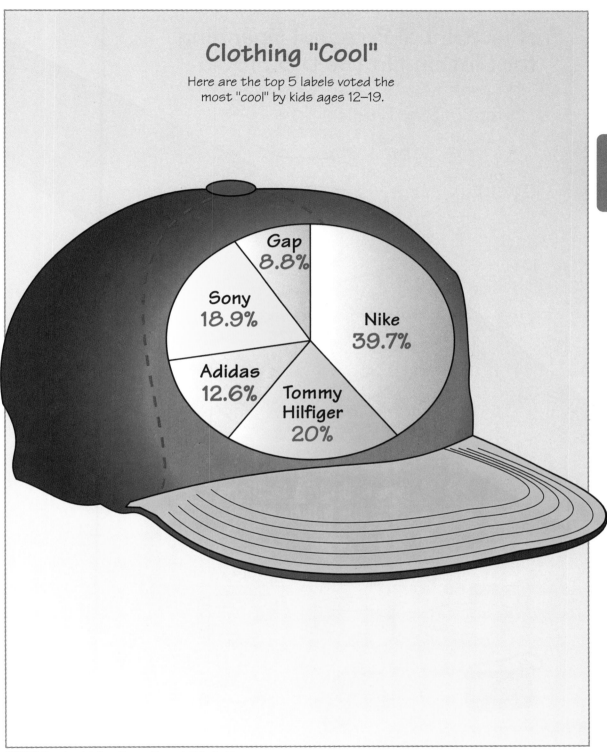

Clothing "Cool"

Here are the top 5 labels voted the most "cool" by kids ages 12–19.

Gap
8.8%

Sony
18.9%

Nike
39.7%

Adidas
12.6%

Tommy Hilfiger
20%

Clothes

SOURCE: Based on data from Teenage Research Unlimited, Inc.

Clothes

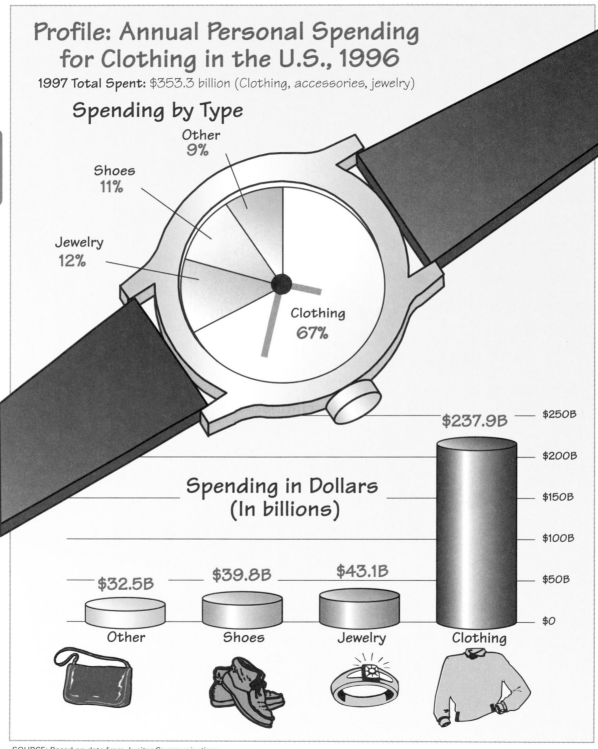

Profile: Annual Personal Spending for Clothing in the U.S., 1996

1997 Total Spent: $353.3 billion (Clothing, accessories, jewelry)

Spending by Type

Other
9%

Shoes
11%

Jewelry
12%

Clothing
67%

Spending in Dollars
(In billions)

$237.9B — $250B

$200B

$150B

$100B

$32.5B — $39.8B — $43.1B — $50B

$0

Other   Shoes   Jewelry   Clothing

SOURCE: Based on data from Jupiter Communications

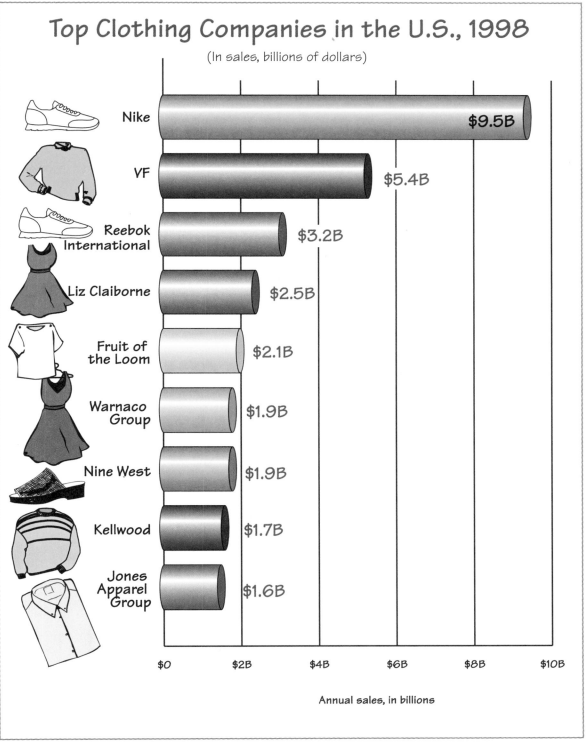

Top Clothing Companies in the U.S., 1998

(In sales, billions of dollars)

Company	Sales
Nike	$9.5B
VF	$5.4B
Reebok International	$3.2B
Liz Claiborne	$2.5B
Fruit of the Loom	$2.1B
Warnaco Group	$1.9B
Nine West	$1.9B
Kellwood	$1.7B
Jones Apparel Group	$1.6B

$0 $2B $4B $6B $8B $10B

Annual sales, in billions

Clothes

SOURCE: Based on data from *FORTUNE* Magazine

Entertainment

Screaming on scary rides at the amusement park, checking out the latest models at an auto show, putting together a jigsaw puzzle, attacking aliens in an arcade game, curling up with a good book, visiting a sports hall of fame—the list of ways to be entertained goes on and on!

Video games are especially popular with many young people. They let you fly an airplane, visit spooky caves, battle fierce robots, and maneuver a hang glider through the canyons of a crowded city. Lots of other types of toys and games are popular, too. Some are silly and easy to learn. Others require lots of practice if you want to be really, really good at them. Etienne Bacrot of France started playing the game of chess when he was only four years old. He practiced every day. Determined to be among the world's best players, he got a professional chess coach. In 1997, Etienne became the youngest chess grandmaster ever—he was only 14!

Some kinds of entertainment are fads that are quickly replaced by new pleasures. Others remain popular for many, many years.

Kidbits Tidbits

- The longest-running musical in history is *Cats* (7,485 performances).
- About 1,500 daily newspapers and 7,500 weekly newspapers are published in the U.S.
- The very first newspaper comic strip, "Hogan's Alley," appeared in 1895.
- The world's best-selling fiction author is British mystery writer Agatha Christie, who died in 1976. More than two billion copies of her books have been sold so far.

A metal coil called the Slinky was first sold in 1945. By the time it celebrated its 50th birthday in 1995, some 250 million of these bouncy gizmos had been sold. A big hit in 1999 was the Furby—a funny-looking, hairy creature that says "Feed me!" and "Pet me!" Do you think Furbies will be around as long as Slinky?

Maybe cyberpets will become collectibles, like Barbie and G.I. Joe dolls. Some collectibles become very valuable—if they are rare and if there is a big demand for them. The hottest toys of 1997 were Beanie Babies, bean-bag animals such as Snort the Bull and Nuts the Squirrel. The first Beanie Babies were introduced in 1994, but they were soon "retired." That is, the company stopped making those designs. By 1997, many collectors were willing to pay thousands of dollars for retired Beanie Babies, which originally only sold for about $5!

Despite all the new toy and game fads that come and go, a few forms of entertainment remain consistent favorites. Reading, watching television, and listening to music are still the most popular means by which kids and adults entertain themselves. In fact, nearly every home in America has at least one color television and one radio, and 88% of all U.S. households now have a VCR. But, even with all those electronics, the majority of people in America still rank reading as their favorite leisure and entertainment activity.

Kidbits Tidbits

- R. L. Stine's *Goosebumps* books have sold more copies than any other kids' books.
- In 1999 Americans purchased 2.46 billion books. The majority were adult fiction and mass market paperbacks.
- State parks and recreational areas had more than 780 million visitors in 1998. National parks had 64.4 million visitors.
- About 300 million people visited amusement parks in the U.S. in 1997. The parks took in $11.2 billion.
- *Teen Magazine* is read by 2.1 million people every month; 1.3 million people read *Boy's Life*.

Entertainment

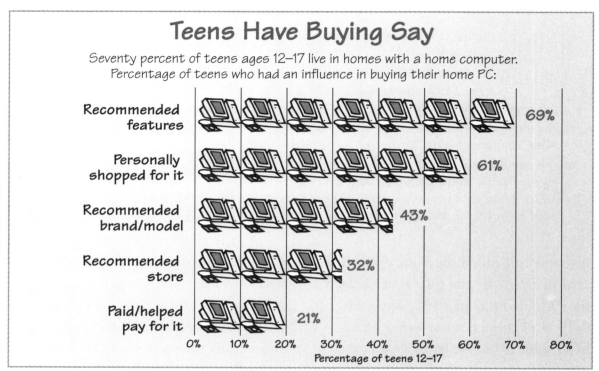

Teens Have Buying Say

Seventy percent of teens ages 12–17 live in homes with a home computer. Percentage of teens who had an influence in buying their home PC:

Recommended features — 69%
Personally shopped for it — 61%
Recommended brand/model — 43%
Recommended store — 32%
Paid/helped pay for it — 21%

0% 10% 20% 30% 40% 50% 60% 70% 80%
Percentage of teens 12–17

SOURCE: Based on data from Millward Brown for Channel One

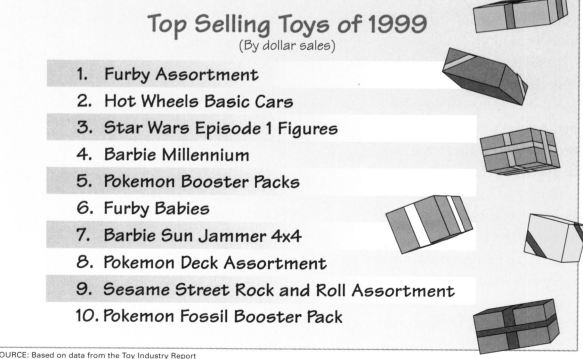

Top Selling Toys of 1999
(By dollar sales)

1. Furby Assortment
2. Hot Wheels Basic Cars
3. Star Wars Episode 1 Figures
4. Barbie Millennium
5. Pokemon Booster Packs
6. Furby Babies
7. Barbie Sun Jammer 4x4
8. Pokemon Deck Assortment
9. Sesame Street Rock and Roll Assortment
10. Pokemon Fossil Booster Pack

SOURCE: Based on data from the Toy Industry Report

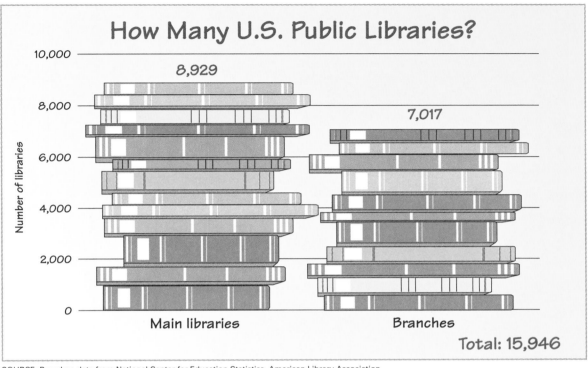

How Many U.S. Public Libraries?

Number of libraries

Main libraries: 8,929

Branches: 7,017

Total: 15,946

SOURCE: Based on data from National Center for Education Statistics, American Library Association

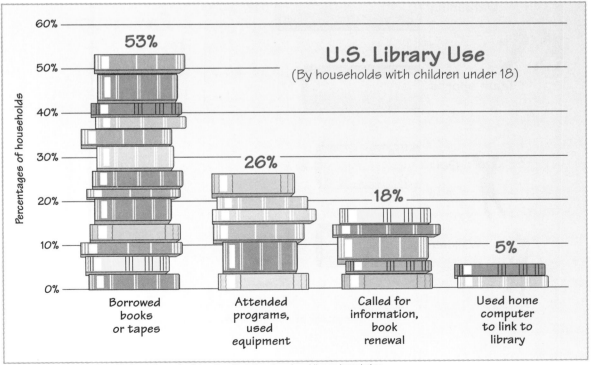

U.S. Library Use
(By households with children under 18)

Percentages of households

- Borrowed books or tapes: 53%
- Attended programs, used equipment: 26%
- Called for information, book renewal: 18%
- Used home computer to link to library: 5%

SOURCE: Based on data from National Center for Education Statistics, American Library Association

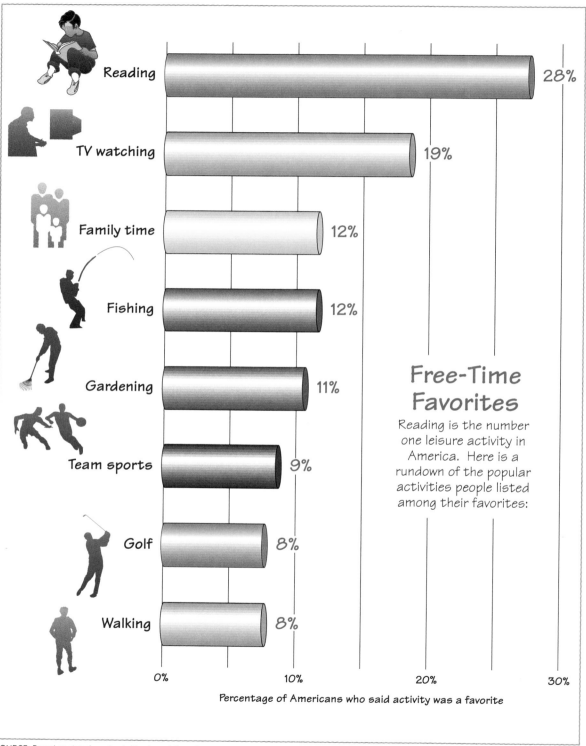

Entertainment

Reading — 28%

TV watching — 19%

Family time — 12%

Fishing — 12%

Gardening — 11%

Team sports — 9%

Golf — 8%

Walking — 8%

Free-Time Favorites

Reading is the number one leisure activity in America. Here is a rundown of the popular activities people listed among their favorites:

0%   10%   20%   30%

Percentage of Americans who said activity was a favorite

SOURCE: Based on data from Louis Harris and Associates

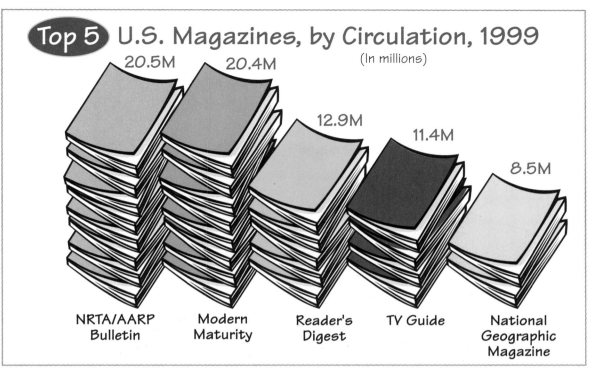

Top 5 U.S. Magazines, by Circulation, 1999

(In millions)

- NRTA/AARP Bulletin — 20.5M
- Modern Maturity — 20.4M
- Reader's Digest — 12.9M
- TV Guide — 11.4M
- National Geographic Magazine — 8.5M

SOURCE: Based on data from Audit Bureau of Circulations, Schaumberg, IL

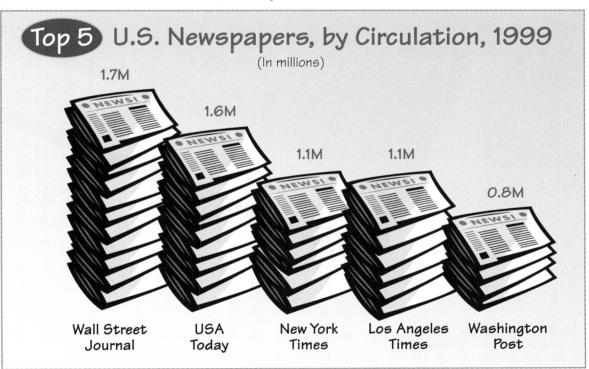

Top 5 U.S. Newspapers, by Circulation, 1999

(In millions)

- Wall Street Journal — 1.7M
- USA Today — 1.6M
- New York Times — 1.1M
- Los Angeles Times — 1.1M
- Washington Post — 0.8M

SOURCE: Based on data from *Editor & Publisher International Yearbook, 1999*

Entertainment

Entertainment

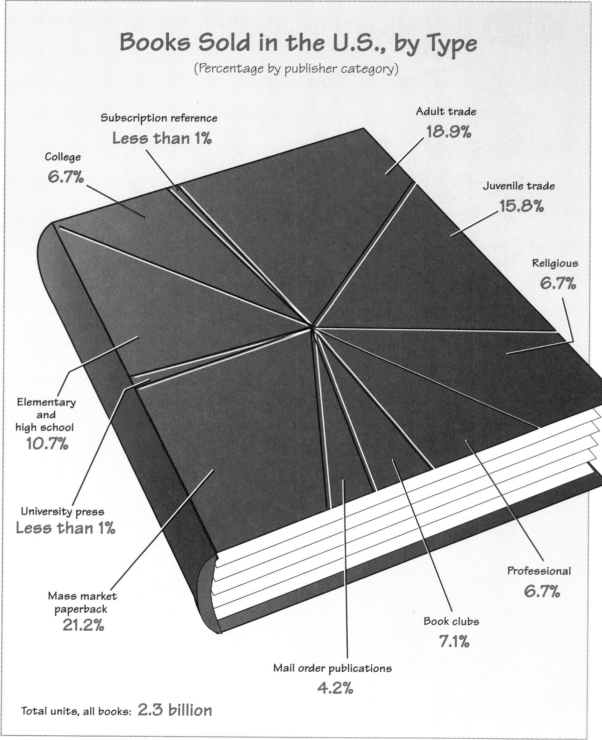

Books Sold in the U.S., by Type

(Percentage by publisher category)

Subscription reference
Less than 1%

Adult trade
18.9%

College
6.7%

Juvenile trade
15.8%

Religious
6.7%

Elementary
and
high school
10.7%

University press
Less than 1%

Professional
6.7%

Mass market
paperback
21.2%

Book clubs
7.1%

Mail order publications
4.2%

Total units, all books: **2.3 billion**

SOURCE: Based on data from Book Industry Study Group, Inc.

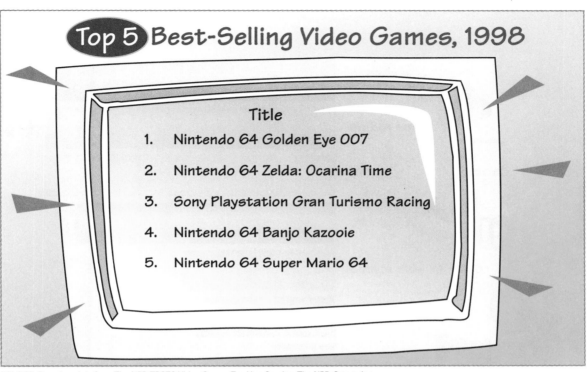

Top 5 Best-Selling Video Games, 1998

Title

1. Nintendo 64 Golden Eye 007
2. Nintendo 64 Zelda: Ocarina Time
3. Sony Playstation Gran Turismo Racing
4. Nintendo 64 Banjo Kazooie
5. Nintendo 64 Super Mario 64

SOURCE: Based on data from The NPD TRSTS Video Games Tracking Service, The NPD Group, Inc.

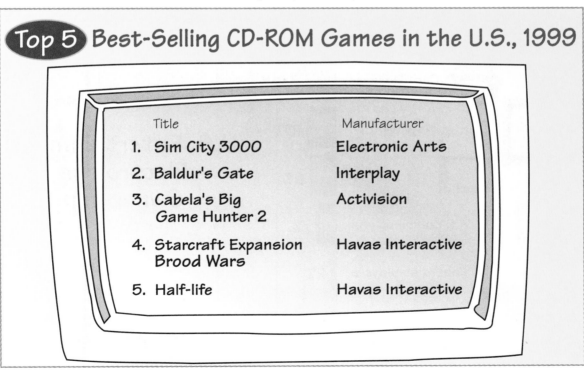

Top 5 Best-Selling CD-ROM Games in the U.S., 1999

Title	Manufacturer
1. Sim City 3000	Electronic Arts
2. Baldur's Gate	Interplay
3. Cabela's Big Game Hunter 2	Activision
4. Starcraft Expansion Brood Wars	Havas Interactive
5. Half-life	Havas Interactive

SOURCE: Based on information from PC Data

Entertainment

Entertainment

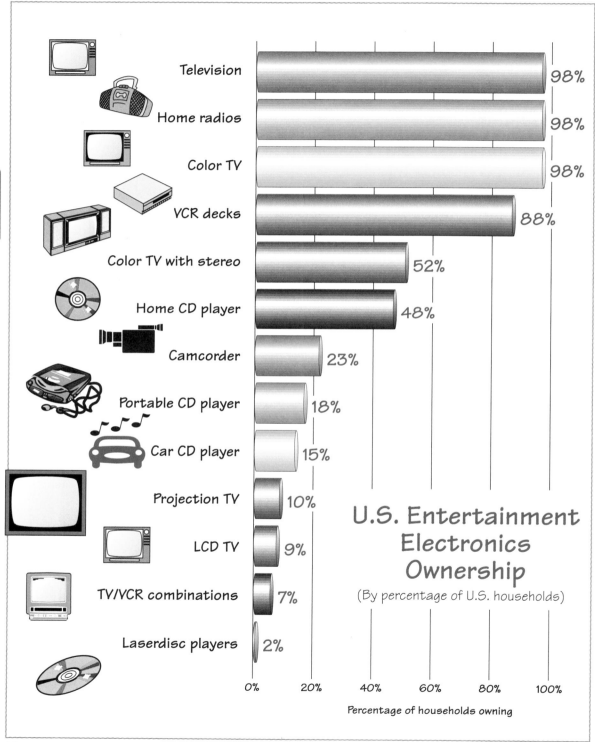

U.S. Entertainment
Electronics
Ownership

(By percentage of U.S. households)

Device	Percentage
Television	98%
Home radios	98%
Color TV	98%
VCR decks	88%
Color TV with stereo	52%
Home CD player	48%
Camcorder	23%
Portable CD player	18%
Car CD player	15%
Projection TV	10%
LCD TV	9%
TV/VCR combinations	7%
Laserdisc players	2%

0%   20%   40%   60%   80%   100%

Percentage of households owning

SOURCE: Based on data from Electronic Industries Association, Market Research Department

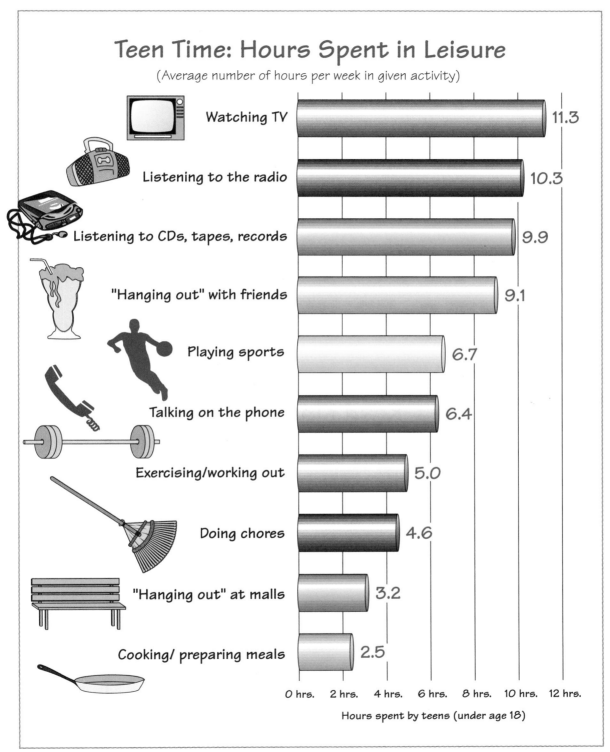

Teen Time: Hours Spent in Leisure

(Average number of hours per week in given activity)

Activity	Hours
Watching TV	11.3
Listening to the radio	10.3
Listening to CDs, tapes, records	9.9
"Hanging out" with friends	9.1
Playing sports	6.7
Talking on the phone	6.4
Exercising/working out	5.0
Doing chores	4.6
"Hanging out" at malls	3.2
Cooking/ preparing meals	2.5

0 hrs. 2 hrs. 4 hrs. 6 hrs. 8 hrs. 10 hrs. 12 hrs.

Hours spent by teens (under age 18)

Entertainment

SOURCE: Based on data from Teenage Research Unlimited, Inc.

Entertainment

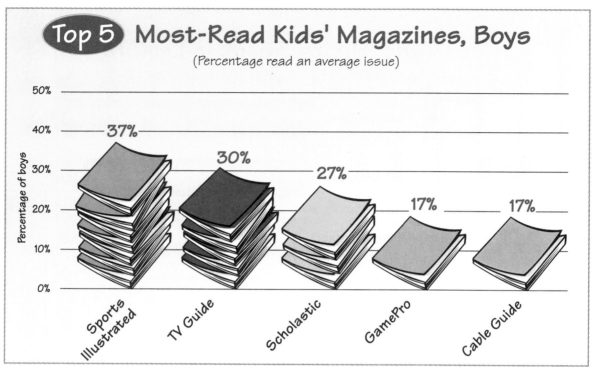

Top 5 Most-Read Kids' Magazines, Boys

(Percentage read an average issue)

Percentage of boys

- Sports Illustrated — 37%
- TV Guide — 30%
- Scholastic — 27%
- GamePro — 17%
- Cable Guide — 17%

SOURCE: Based on data from Teenage Research Unlimited, Inc.

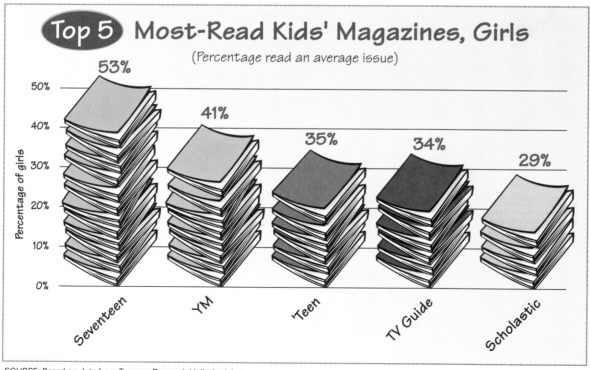

Top 5 Most-Read Kids' Magazines, Girls

(Percentage read an average issue)

Percentage of girls

- Seventeen — 53%
- YM — 41%
- 'Teen — 35%
- TV Guide — 34%
- Scholastic — 29%

SOURCE: Based on data from Teenage Research Unlimited, Inc.

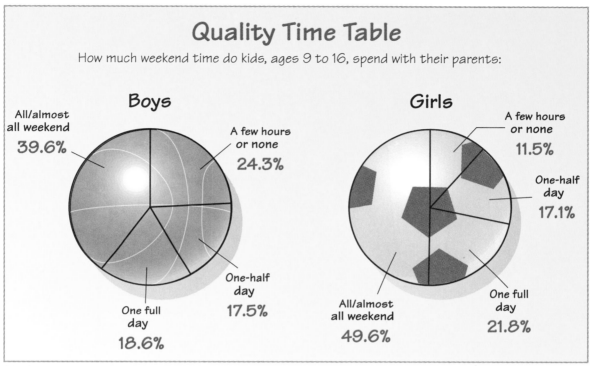

Quality Time Table

How much weekend time do kids, ages 9 to 16, spend with their parents:

Boys

All/almost all weekend
39.6%

A few hours or none
24.3%

One full day
18.6%

One-half day
17.5%

Girls

A few hours or none
11.5%

One-half day
17.1%

All/almost all weekend
49.6%

One full day
21.8%

SOURCE: Based on data from *KidSpeak* survey

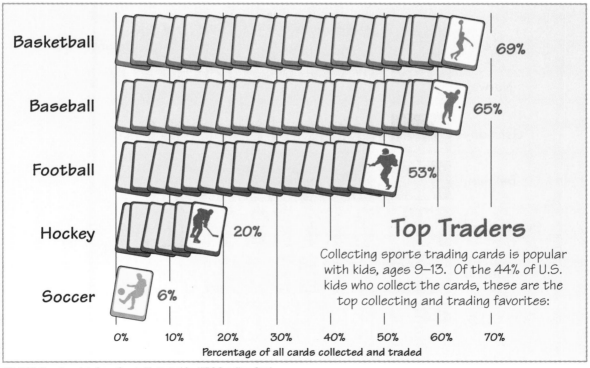

Basketball — 69%

Baseball — 65%

Football — 53%

Hockey — 20%

Soccer — 6%

0% 10% 20% 30% 40% 50% 60% 70%

Percentage of all cards collected and traded

Top Traders

Collecting sports trading cards is popular with kids, ages 9–13. Of the 44% of U.S. kids who collect the cards, these are the top collecting and trading favorites:

SOURCE: Based on data from *Sports Illustrated for KIDS* Omnibus Study

Entertainment

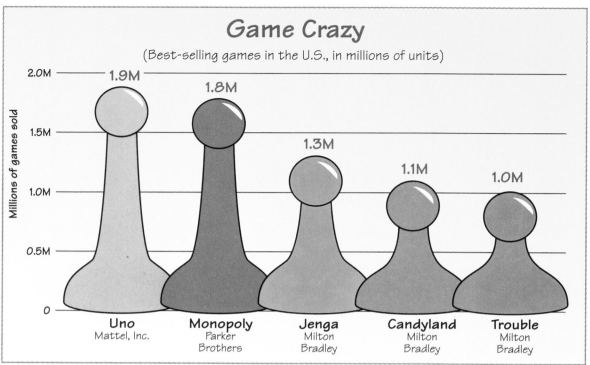

Game Crazy

(Best-selling games in the U.S., in millions of units)

Millions of games sold

Uno	1.9M
Monopoly	1.8M
Jenga	1.3M
Candyland	1.1M
Trouble	1.0M

Uno
Mattel, Inc.

Monopoly
Parker
Brothers

Jenga
Milton
Bradley

Candyland
Milton
Bradley

Trouble
Milton
Bradley

SOURCE: Based on data from *Trsts,* NPD Group

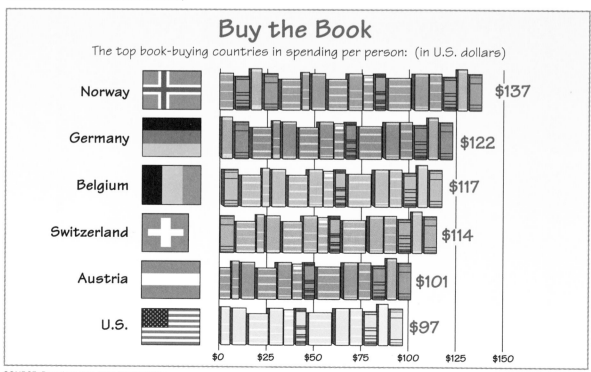

Buy the Book

The top book-buying countries in spending per person: (in U.S. dollars)

Country	Spending
Norway	$137
Germany	$122
Belgium	$117
Switzerland	$114
Austria	$101
U.S.	$97

$0 $25 $50 $75 $100 $125 $150

SOURCE: Based on data from Euromonitor

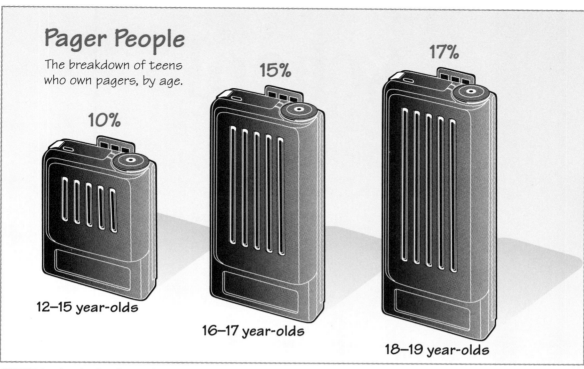

Pager People

The breakdown of teens who own pagers, by age.

10%
12–15 year-olds

15%
16–17 year-olds

17%
18–19 year-olds

SOURCE: Based on data from Teenage Research Unlimited, Inc.

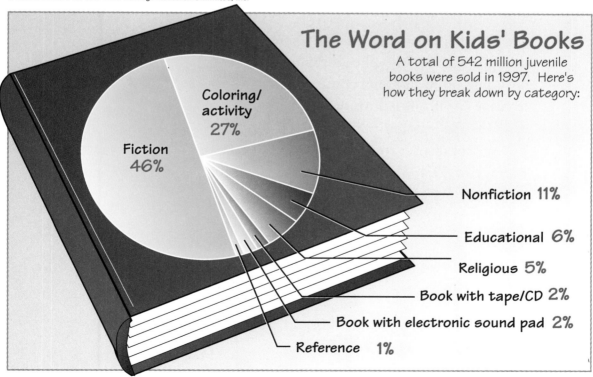

The Word on Kids' Books

A total of 542 million juvenile books were sold in 1997. Here's how they break down by category:

Fiction 46%

Coloring/activity 27%

Nonfiction 11%

Educational 6%

Religious 5%

Book with tape/CD 2%

Book with electronic sound pad 2%

Reference 1%

SOURCE: Based on data from *1997 Consumer Research Study on Book Purchasing*

Entertainment

School

More than 52.8 million kids attend school—38.1 million in grades K through 8, and 14.7 million in grades 9 through 12. Most of them—46.8 million—attend public schools. About 6.0 million students attend private schools, the majority of which are affiliated with a religion. In 1998, each teacher had an average of 16.7 students per class. In general, elementary school classes were larger than high school classes, and classes in public schools were larger than classes in private schools.

The U.S. has about 76,350 elementary schools, 22,800 high schools, and 10,700 schools that cover grades K through 12. Total spending on K-12 education is more than $300 billion a year! The average spent on each student in the 1997-98 school year was $6,943. The amount varied greatly from state to state, and from one school district to another. New Jersey spent the most—an average of $9,455 per student. Utah spent the least—an average of $3,837 per student.

Kidbits Tidbits

- About 9% of public schools have fewer than 100 students; 9.2% have 1,000 or more students.
- Most private schools are affiliated with a religion.
- In 1998, the average elementary school classroom had 18.8 students. The average high school classroom had 14.5 students.
- 600,000 children eat lunch in school, and 140,000 eat breakfast there.

Most kids graduate from high school, though about 5% of 16- and 17-year-olds are dropouts. Getting a high school degree and doing well in school can pay off in many ways. For example, it makes it easier to get a good job or go to college. It can mean money, too! When Rebecca Sealfon won the National Spelling Bee she received a new computer and $5,000 in prize money. Seyi Fayanju got a $25,000 scholarship when he won the National Geography Bee.

Today, a record number of high school graduates continue their education at the college level. More than 14.5 million people are currently enrolled in college, the great majority of them in public institutions. More women than men are enrolled in college. Attending college can be very expensive.

The average yearly cost of tuition and fees at 4-year colleges in 1999 was $3,356 at public colleges and $15,380 at private colleges. But there's a financial payoff: The greater the amount of education people have, the better their chances of getting jobs—and earning good salaries. In 1998, only 72.1% of people with less than a high school degree had jobs, but 91.1% of college graduates had jobs. The average earnings of people age 18 and older who did not have high school degrees was $20,650. Earnings of people with a bachelor's degree were $45,700; with a master's degree it was $55,227.

Kidbits Tidbits

- College graduates can expect to earn about $600,000 more during their lifetimes than high school graduates can expect to earn.
- 43% of children from low-income families enter college after high school, compared with 83% of children from higher-income families.
- In 1999, the cost of tuition and fees for an average year at a private college was nearly 4.5 times more than a public college.
- In 1998, the average salary of public school teachers was $35,924—up from only $15,913 in 1980.
- A study of 12th graders in 23 countries found that U.S. students scored close to the international average in math, but below average in advanced math and physics.

School

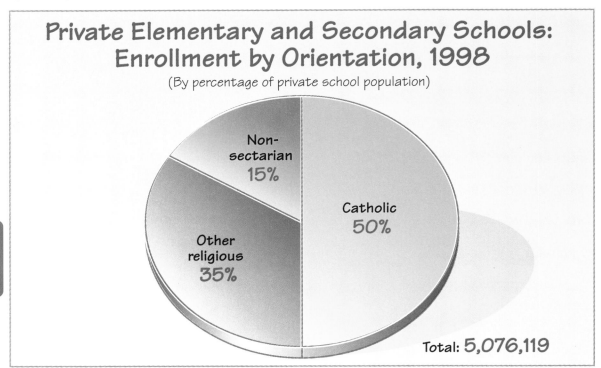

Private Elementary and Secondary Schools: Enrollment by Orientation, 1998

(By percentage of private school population)

Non-sectarian 15%

Catholic 50%

Other religious 35%

Total: 5,076,119

SOURCE: Based on data from U.S. National Center for Education Statistics, *Digest of Educational Statistics*

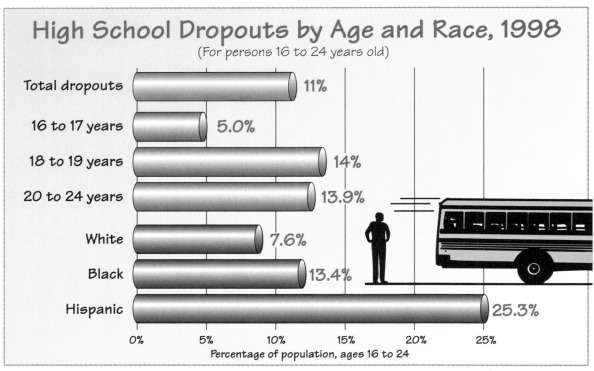

High School Dropouts by Age and Race, 1998

(For persons 16 to 24 years old)

Total dropouts	11%
16 to 17 years	5.0%
18 to 19 years	14%
20 to 24 years	13.9%
White	7.6%
Black	13.4%
Hispanic	25.3%

0%   5%   10%   15%   20%   25%

Percentage of population, ages 16 to 24

SOURCE: Based on data from U.S. Bureau of the Census, *Current Population Reports*

Average Monthly Income, by Highest Educational Degree Earned

(For persons 18 and over)

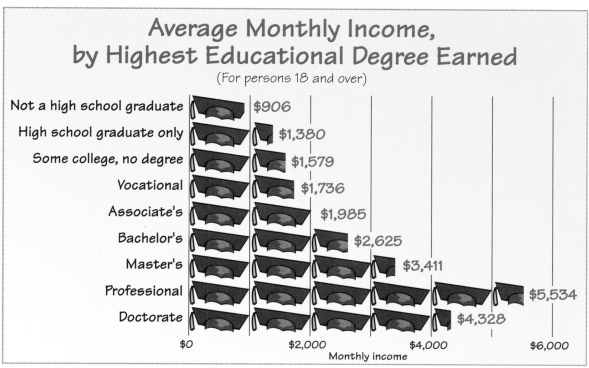

Not a high school graduate	$906
High school graduate only	$1,380
Some college, no degree	$1,579
Vocational	$1,736
Associate's	$1,985
Bachelor's	$2,625
Master's	$3,411
Professional	$5,534
Doctorate	$4,328

Monthly income

$0 $2,000 $4,000 $6,000

School

SOURCE: Based on data from U.S. Bureau of the Census, *Current Population Reports*

U.S. Public Elementary and Secondary School Enrollment, 1980 to 1999

(In millions)

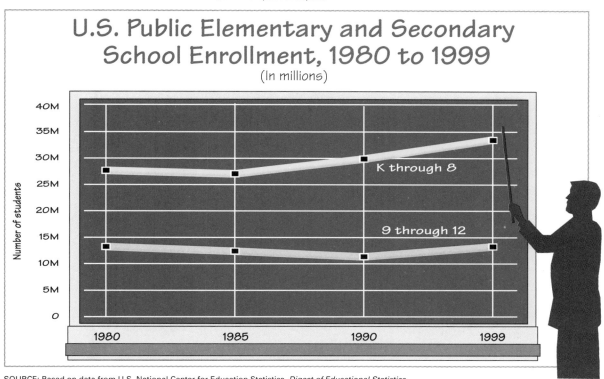

Number of students

K through 8

9 through 12

1980   1985   1990   1999

SOURCE: Based on data from U.S. National Center for Education Statistics, *Digest of Educational Statistics*

School

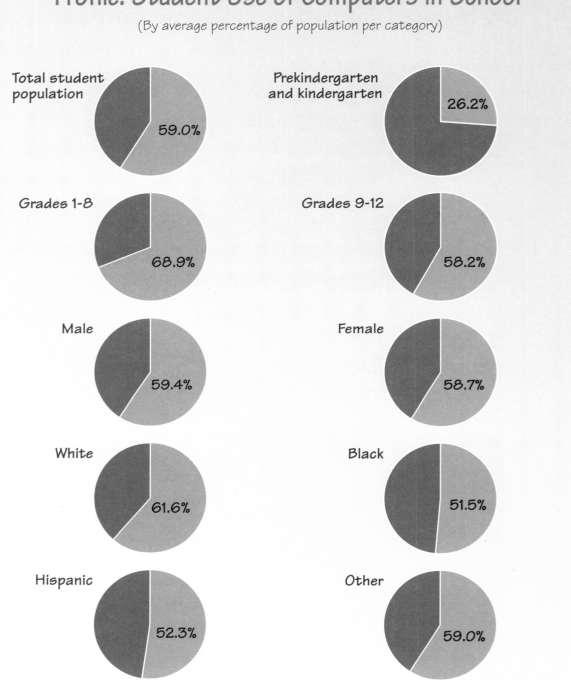

Profile: Student Use of Computers in School

(By average percentage of population per category)

Total student population — 59.0%

Prekindergarten and kindergarten — 26.2%

Grades 1-8 — 68.9%

Grades 9-12 — 58.2%

Male — 59.4%

Female — 58.7%

White — 61.6%

Black — 51.5%

Hispanic — 52.3%

Other — 59.0%

SOURCE: Based on data from U.S. National Center for Education Statistics, *Digest of Educational Statistics*

Profile: Student Use of Computers at Home for School Work

(By average percentage of population per category)

Total student population

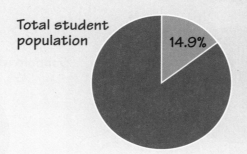

14.9%

Male

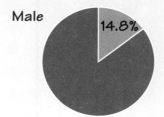

14.8%

Female

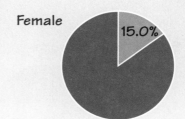

15.0%

White

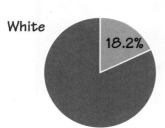

18.2%

Black

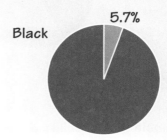

5.7%

Hispanic

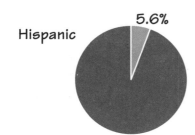

5.6%

Other

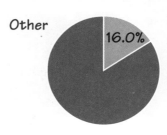

16.0%

School

SOURCE: Based on data from U.S. National Center for Education Statistics, *Digest of Educational Statistics*

School

Profile: Technology in U.S. Public Schools, 1999

(By percentage of total)

Schools with computers

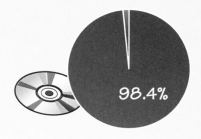

98.4%

Schools with internet access

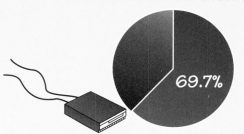

69.7%

Schools with networks

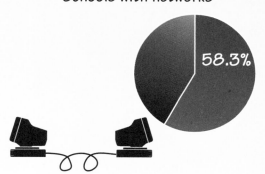

58.3%

Schools with CD-ROMs

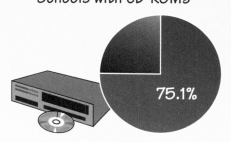

75.1%

Schools with satellite dishes

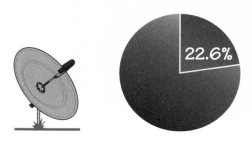

22.6%

Schools with cable

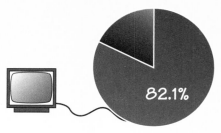

82.1%

SOURCE: Based on data from Quality Education Data, Inc., Denver, CO., *Technology in Public Schools*

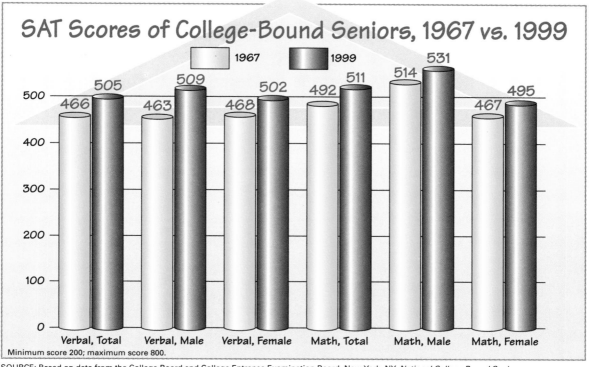

SAT Scores of College-Bound Seniors, 1967 vs. 1999

1967
1999

| | 466 | 505 | 463 | 509 | 468 | 502 | 492 | 511 | 514 | 531 | 467 | 495 |

Verbal, Total · Verbal, Male · Verbal, Female · Math, Total · Math, Male · Math, Female

Minimum score 200; maximum score 800.

SOURCE: Based on data from the College Board and College Entrance Examination Board, New York, NY, *National College Bound Senior*

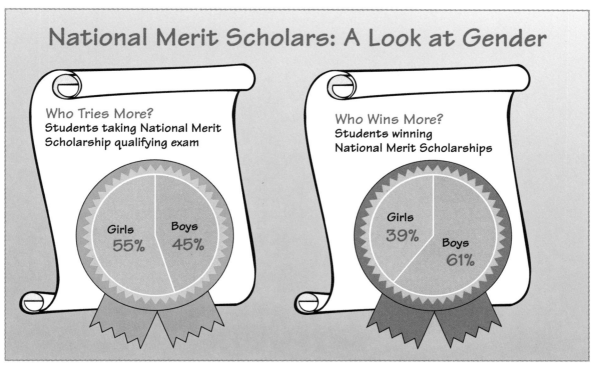

National Merit Scholars: A Look at Gender

Who Tries More?
Students taking National Merit Scholarship qualifying exam

Girls 55%
Boys 45%

Who Wins More?
Students winning National Merit Scholarships

Girls 39%
Boys 61%

SOURCE: Based on data from National Center for Fair & Open Testing

School

School

A Profile of U.S. College Freshmen

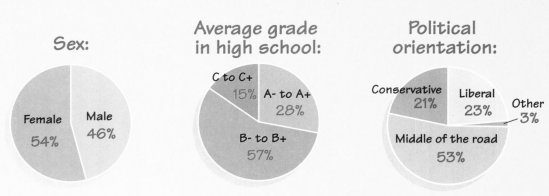

Sex:
- Female 54%
- Male 46%

Average grade in high school:
- C to C+ 15%
- A- to A+ 28%
- B- to B+ 57%

Political orientation:
- Conservative 21%
- Liberal 23%
- Other 3%
- Middle of the road 53%

Probable field of study:

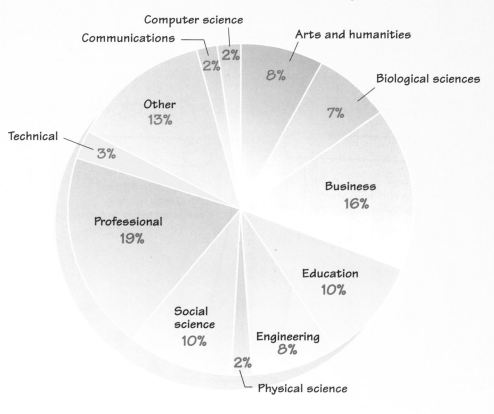

- Computer science 2%
- Communications 2%
- Arts and humanities 8%
- Biological sciences 7%
- Other 13%
- Technical 3%
- Business 16%
- Professional 19%
- Education 10%
- Social science 10%
- Engineering 8%
- Physical science 2%

SOURCE: Based on data from The Higher Education Research Institute, University of California, Los Angeles, CA.
The American Freshman: National Norms

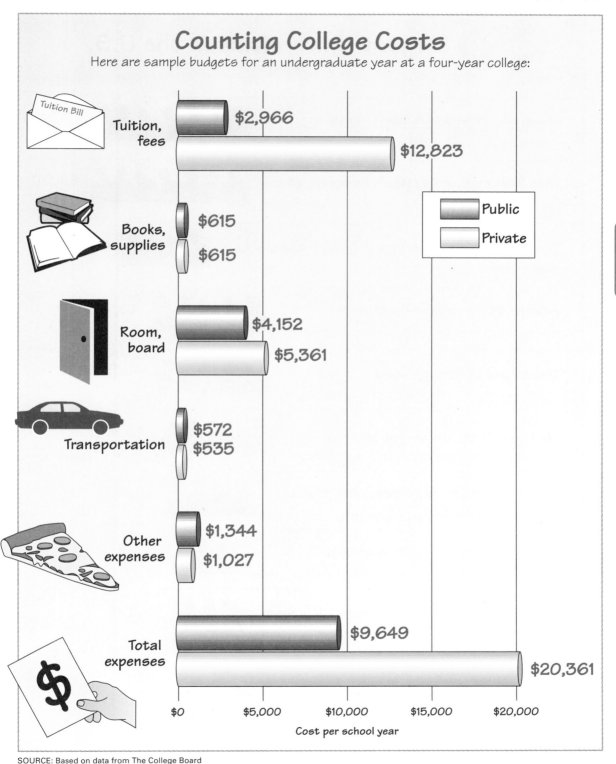

Counting College Costs

Here are sample budgets for an undergraduate year at a four-year college:

Tuition, fees
$2,966
$12,823

Books, supplies
$615
$615

Room, board
$4,152
$5,361

Transportation
$572
$535

Other expenses
$1,344
$1,027

Total expenses
$9,649
$20,361

Public
Private

$0 $5,000 $10,000 $15,000 $20,000

Cost per school year

School

SOURCE: Based on data from The College Board

School

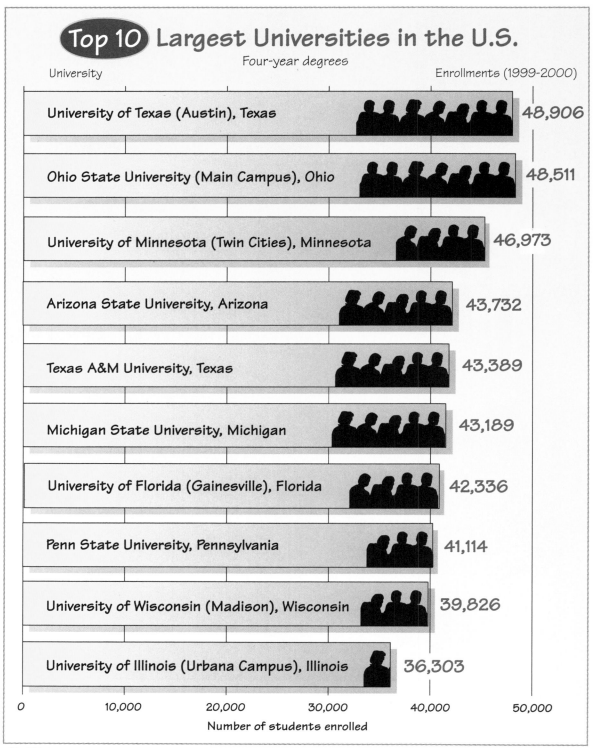

Top 10 Largest Universities in the U.S.

Four-year degrees

University

Enrollments (1999-2000)

University	Number of students enrolled
University of Texas (Austin), Texas	48,906
Ohio State University (Main Campus), Ohio	48,511
University of Minnesota (Twin Cities), Minnesota	46,973
Arizona State University, Arizona	43,732
Texas A&M University, Texas	43,389
Michigan State University, Michigan	43,189
University of Florida (Gainesville), Florida	42,336
Penn State University, Pennsylvania	41,114
University of Wisconsin (Madison), Wisconsin	39,826
University of Illinois (Urbana Campus), Illinois	36,303

0   10,000   20,000   30,000   40,000   50,000

Number of students enrolled

SOURCE: Based on data from National Center for Educational Statistics, U.S. Department of Education

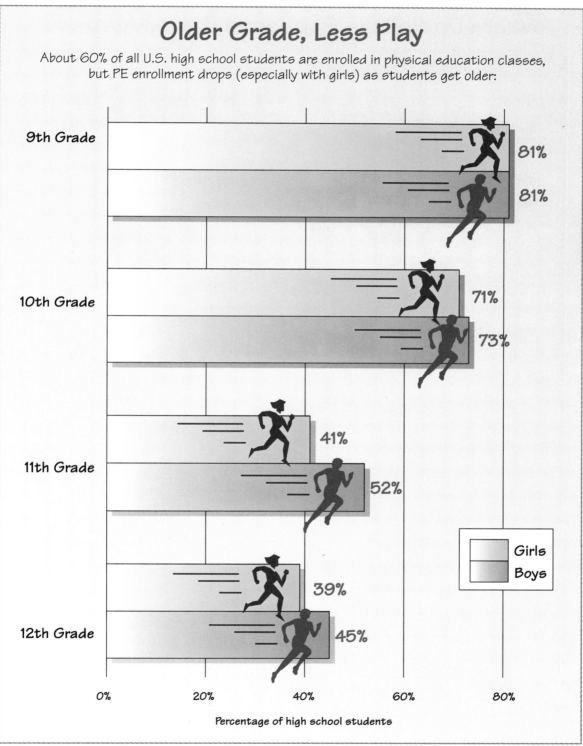

Older Grade, Less Play

About 60% of all U.S. high school students are enrolled in physical education classes, but PE enrollment drops (especially with girls) as students get older:

9th Grade — 81% / 81%

10th Grade — 71% / 73%

11th Grade — 41% / 52%

12th Grade — 39% / 45%

0%   20%   40%   60%   80%

Percentage of high school students

Girls
Boys

School

SOURCE: Based on data from Department of Health and Human Services for "Girl Power!"

School

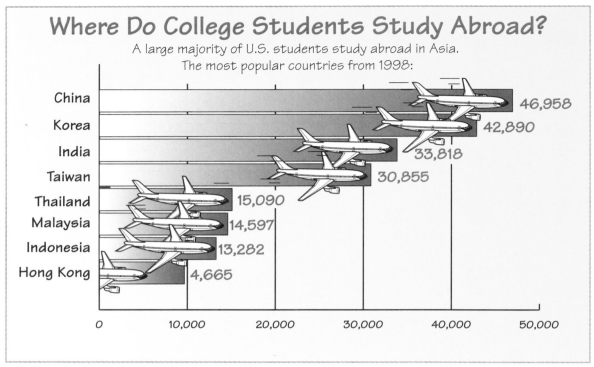

Where Do College Students Study Abroad?

A large majority of U.S. students study abroad in Asia.
The most popular countries from 1998:

Country	Students
China	46,958
Korea	42,890
India	33,818
Taiwan	30,855
Thailand	15,090
Malaysia	14,597
Indonesia	13,282
Hong Kong	4,665

SOURCE: Based on data from Asia Week

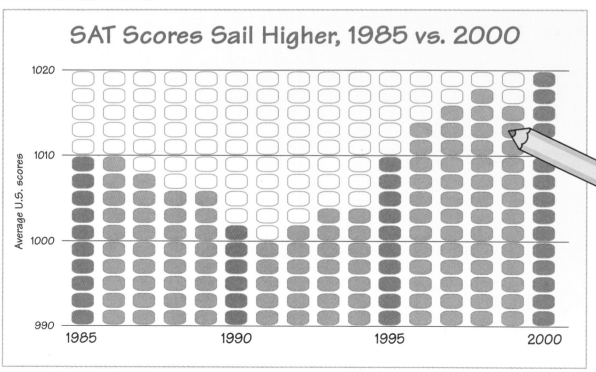

SAT Scores Sail Higher, 1985 vs. 2000

Average U.S. scores

1020
1010
1000
990

1985   1990   1995   2000

SOURCE: Based on data from The College Board

Comparing Countries: How Do We Stack Up in Math?

Here's a look at how U.S. 13-year-olds compare to their peers in nine other countries for math skills. (By test score averages)

Mathematics proficiency scores for 13-year-olds

Taiwan	285
Korea	283
Russia	279
Switzerland	279
France	273
Israel	272
Canada	270
Slovenia	266
Spain	263
USA	262

School

SOURCE: Based on data from National Science Foundation, "Learning Curve" report

School

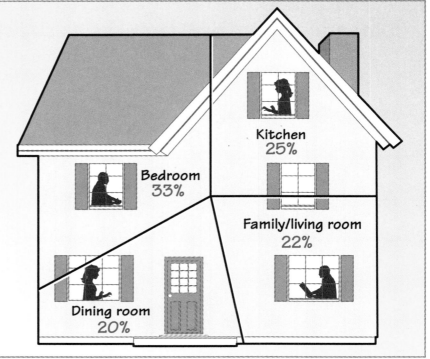

House for Homework

Most parents say homework is the first thing kids do when they get home from school. Here's a look at where kids say they do their homework:

Kitchen
25%

Bedroom
33%

Family/living room
22%

Dining room
20%

SOURCE: Based on data from Federal National Mortgage Association

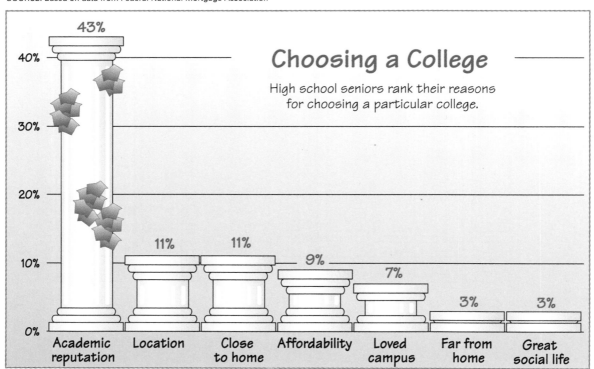

Choosing a College

High school seniors rank their reasons for choosing a particular college.

43%	Academic reputation
11%	Location
11%	Close to home
9%	Affordability
7%	Loved campus
3%	Far from home
3%	Great social life

SOURCE: Based on data from Kaplan Educational Centers

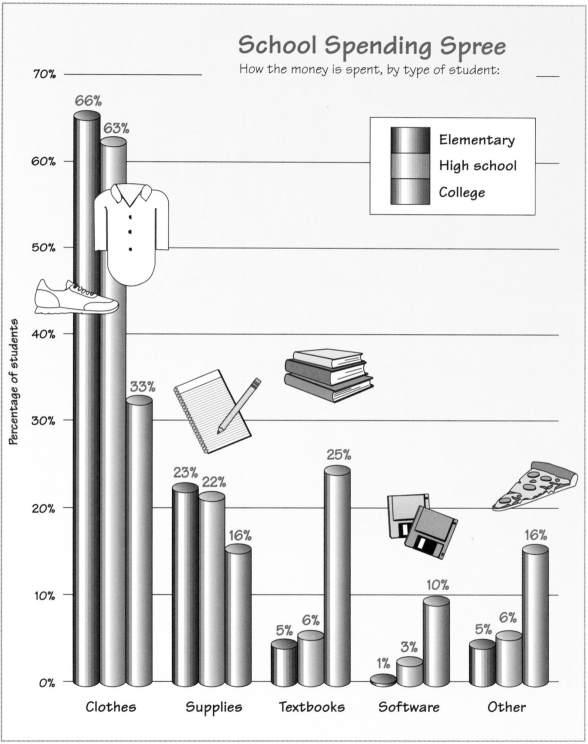

School Spending Spree

How the money is spent, by type of student:

Percentage of students

Legend:
- Elementary
- High school
- College

Category	Elementary	High school	College
Clothes	66%	63%	33%
Supplies	23%	22%	16%
Textbooks	5%	6%	25%
Software	1%	3%	10%
Other	5%	6%	16%

School

SOURCE: Based on data from American Express Retail Index

School

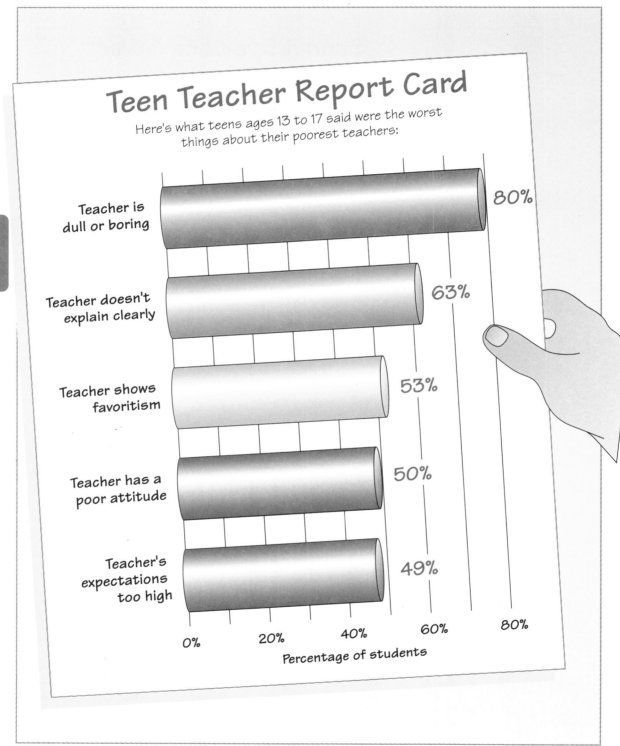

Teen Teacher Report Card

Here's what teens ages 13 to 17 said were the worst things about their poorest teachers:

- Teacher is dull or boring — 80%
- Teacher doesn't explain clearly — 63%
- Teacher shows favoritism — 53%
- Teacher has a poor attitude — 50%
- Teacher's expectations too high — 49%

0%   20%   40%   60%   80%

Percentage of students

SOURCE: Based on data from 1996 *Mood of American Youth* by NFO Research for Horatio Alger Association, National Association of Secondary School Principals

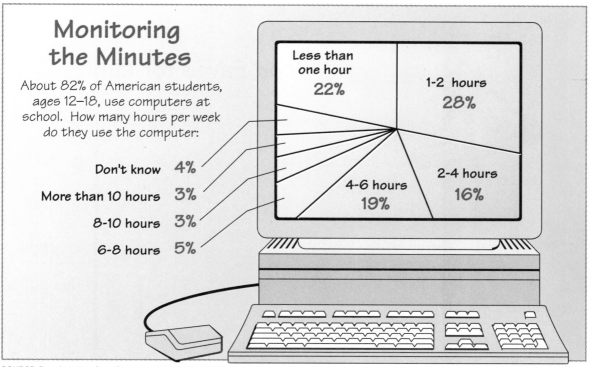

Monitoring the Minutes

About 82% of American students, ages 12–18, use computers at school. How many hours per week do they use the computer:

Don't know	4%
More than 10 hours	3%
8-10 hours	3%
6-8 hours	5%

Less than one hour
22%

1-2 hours
28%

2-4 hours
16%

4-6 hours
19%

SOURCE: Based on data from Consumer Electronics Manufacturers Association survey

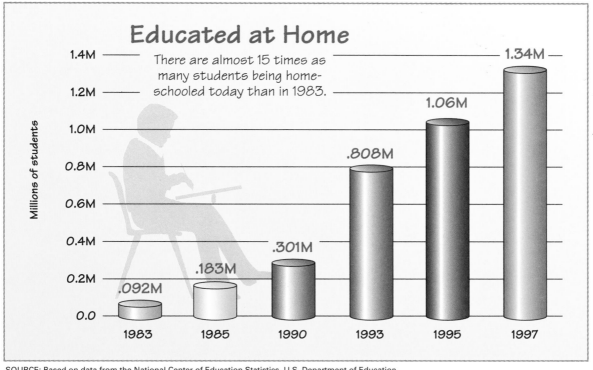

Educated at Home

There are almost 15 times as many students being home-schooled today than in 1983.

Millions of students

1.4M
1.2M
1.0M
0.8M
0.6M
0.4M
0.2M
0.0

.092M — 1983
.183M — 1985
.301M — 1990
.808M — 1993
1.06M — 1995
1.34M — 1997

SOURCE: Based on data from the National Center of Education Statistics, U.S. Department of Education

School

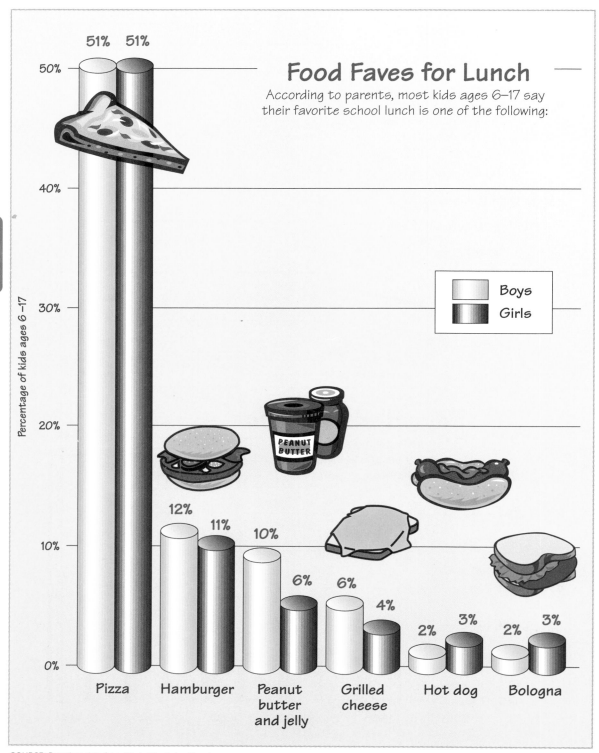

Food Faves for Lunch

According to parents, most kids ages 6–17 say their favorite school lunch is one of the following:

Percentage of kids ages 6 –17

Boys
Girls

Pizza	Hamburger	Peanut butter and jelly	Grilled cheese	Hot dog	Bologna
51% 51%	12% 11%	10% 6%	6% 4%	2% 3%	2% 3%

SOURCE: Based on data from Market Facts for Shout

Daily Diet in School

The average public school student spends 1,000 hours in the school cafeteria, from first grade to high school graduation. Here's an example of what's served every day in the lunchrooms:

**Fresh fruit
4.9 million
pounds**

**Milk
1.9 million
gallons**

**Slices of bread
65 million**

**Vegetables
375,000
pounds**

SOURCE: Based on data from American School Food Service Association

Health

To be healthy and physically fit, you need good health habits. These habits include eating properly, exercising regularly, getting enough sleep, and taking precautions to avoid accidents. For example, using safety belts reduces the risk of fatal injury to people riding in the front seat of a car by 45%. Receiving recommended childhood vaccines reduces the risk of contracting polio, hepatitis, and other diseases. Exercising reduces the risk of heart disease, cancer, and diabetes. Following good habits does more than lower your risk of getting sick or injured. It's also the key to living to a healthy old age.

One of the saddest but most serious U.S. health problems is the use of alcohol, tobacco, and illegal drugs. These substances are bad news—they ruin health and often cause death. Teachers, parents, and others try to make sure that kids know about the dangers of using drugs. But many of these substances are easily available, and kids continue to use them. For example, each day about 3,000 kids start smoking cigarettes.

Kidbits Tidbits

- Of the 33 largest cities in the U.S., New Orleans has the highest percentage of fat people. More than 37% of its residents are considered obese.
- At conception, you consisted of one cell. By the time you're an adult, your body will consist of 100 trillion cells.
- The largest organ in your body is your skin. An adult has about 20 square feet of skin.

Another serious problem is weight control. People of all ages are more likely to be overweight than they were 20 years ago. A full one-third of Americans are obese, or seriously over-weight. About 300,000 people die each year because their excess weight led to diabetes, heart disease, and other deadly illnesses. Many people try to fight the "battle of the bulge" by dieting. Billions of dollars are spent annually on special foods, diet clubs, and medicines—all in unsuccessful efforts to lose weight. Americans also spend billions of dollars yearly on vitamins and minerals, to try to make up for not eating enough of the proper foods.

Heart disease and cancer are the major causes of death in the United States. Accidents are the fifth-leading cause. Every 10 minutes, 2 people are killed in accidents. Deadly infectious diseases also claim many lives each year. These are illnesses caused by viruses and other germs—they include AIDS, pneumonia, and the flu.

In comparison to many other countries, Americans are very healthy. Excellent medical care, safe food and water, and good sanitation means that Americans can expect to live an average of 76 years. In some countries, the average life expectancy is less than 50 years. In the U.S., 7.6 infants one year old or less die per 1,000 live births. In more than a dozen countries where most people are very poor, over 100 infants die per 1,000 live births.

Kidbits Tidbits

- The U.S. spends more than $1 trillion a year on health care.
- In 1998, heart disease accounted for 31% of the total deaths in America.
- Unintentional injuries are the main cause of death for Americans between the ages of 1 and 24.
- Each year, more than 3,000 Americans under age 15 die in motor-vehicle accidents. Almost 11,000 people between the ages of 15 and 24 die in auto accidents.
- Americans consumed 435 billion cigarettes in 1999. That's almost 2,146 for each person in the country.

Who Exercises the Least?

Studies show that people between the ages of 35–44 excercise the least as a group. Percentage of age group that excercises regularly:

Percentage of age group

- 18–24: 21%
- 25–34: 23%
- 35–44: 20%
- 45–54: 27%
- 55 and up: 28%

Age

SOURCE: Based on data from American Sports Data for SGMA, Active and Ageless

Health

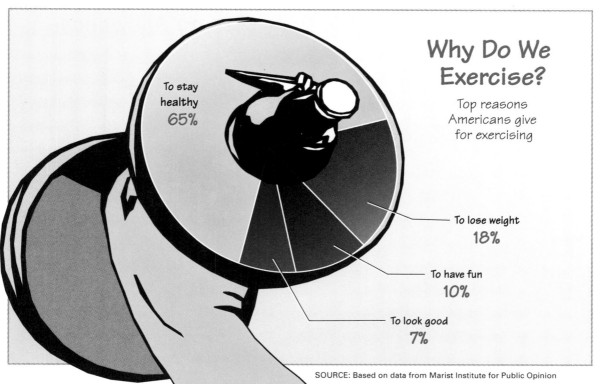

Why Do We Exercise?

Top reasons
Americans give
for exercising

To stay
healthy
65%

To lose weight
18%

To have fun
10%

To look good
7%

SOURCE: Based on data from Marist Institute for Public Opinion

Health

Who Uses Mouthwash the Most?

(By age)

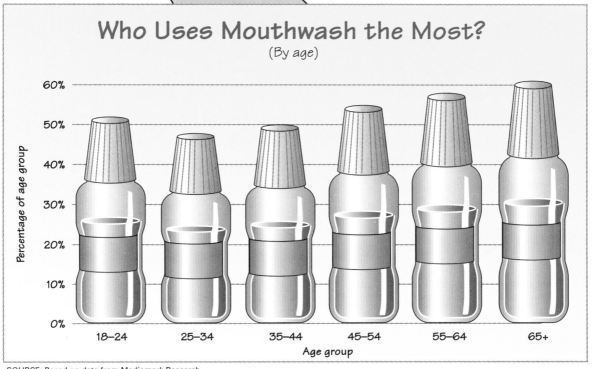

Percentage of age group

60%
50%
40%
30%
20%
10%
0%

18–24   25–34   35–44   45–54   55–64   65+

Age group

SOURCE: Based on data from Mediamark Research

Health

Recommended Daily Dietary Allowances

	Weight (lbs.)	Protein (grams)	Vitamin A	Vitamin D	Vitamin E	Vitamin K (mcg.)	Vitamin C (mg.)	Thiamine (mg.)	Riboflavin (mg.)	Niacin (mg.)	Vitamin B 6 (mg.)	Folate (mcg.)	Vitamin B 12 (mcg.)	Calcium (mg.)	Phosphorus (mg.)	Magnesium (mg.)	Iron (mg.)	Zinc (mg.)	Iodine (mcg.)
			Fat soluble vitamins				Water soluble vitamins							Minerals					
Children																			
1–3	29	16	400	10	6	15	40	0.7	0.8	9	1.0	50	0.7	800	800	80	10	10	70
4–6	44	24	500	10	7	20	45	0.9	1.1	12	1.1	75	1.0	800	800	120	10	10	90
7–10	62	28	700	10	7	30	45	1.0	1.2	13	1.4	100	1.4	800	800	170	10	10	120
Males																			
11–14	99	45	1000	10	10	45	50	1.3	1.5	17	1.7	150	2.0	1200	1200	270	12	15	150
15–18	145	59	1000	10	10	65	60	1.5	1.8	20	2.0	200	2.0	1200	1200	400	12	15	150
Females																			
11–14	101	46	800	10	8	45	50	1.1	1.3	15	1.4	150	2.0	1200	1200	280	15	12	150
15–18	120	44	800	10	8	55	60	1.1	1.3	15	1.5	180	2.0	1200	1200	300	15	12	150

SOURCE: Based on data from the Food and Nutrition Board, National Academy of Sciences–National Research Council; 1989

How Many Calories Do I Need Per Day?

Recommended Daily Dietary Allowances (RDA's)

	Age	Weight (in pounds)	Height (in inches)	Calories needed	Grams of protein needed
Males	11–14	97	63	2,800	44
	15–18	134	69	3,000	54
	19–22	147	69	3,000	54
Females	11–14	97	62	2,400	44
	15–18	119	65	2,100	48
	19–22	128	65	2,100	46

SOURCE: Based on data from *The New York Public Library Desk Reference*

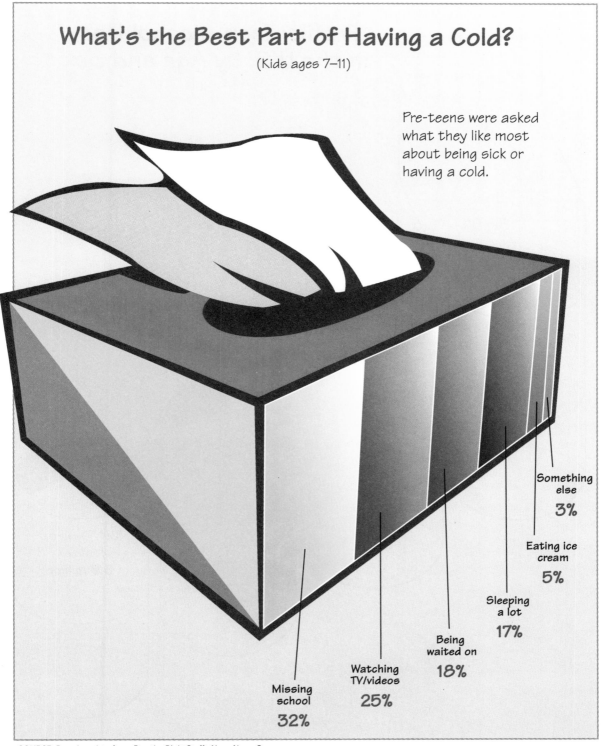

What's the Best Part of Having a Cold?

(Kids ages 7–11)

Pre-teens were asked what they like most about being sick or having a cold.

Health

Something else
3%

Eating ice cream
5%

Sleeping a lot
17%

Being waited on
18%

Watching TV/videos
25%

Missing school
32%

SOURCE: Based on data from *Breathe Right* Stuffy Nose News Survey

Health

Profile: Teen Alcohol Use in the U.S. by Age and Sex

(Teens ages 12–17)

66.9%

Total users in U.S. population
140 million

35.5%

12–17 year olds
7.8 million

34.1%

12–17-year-old males
3.8 million

36.1%

12–17-year-old females
3.9 million

SOURCE: Based on data from U.S. Dept. of Health and Human Services

How Long Does It Take My Body to Absorb Alcohol?

Drinking and driving is a very dangerous combination. Many states have very strict laws for people who drive while intoxicated. The following chart is intended as a general guideline of how long to wait after drinking before driving a motor vehicle. The time varies, however, from person to person. The best rule is "Never drink and drive." In the following chart, one drink equals 1 1/2 ounces of liquor (86 proof) or 4 ounces of wine or champagne or 12 ounces of beer.

Body weight (in pounds)	1 drink	2 drinks	3 drinks	4 drinks	5 drinks	6 drinks
100–119	30–45 min.	3 hours	6 hours	10 hours	13 hours	16 hours
120–139	30–45 min.	2 hours	5 hours	8 hours	10 hours	12 hours
140–159	30–45 min.	2 hours	4 hours	6 hours	8 hours	10 hours
160–179	30–45 min.	1 hour	3 hours	5 hours	7 hours	9 hours
180–199	30–45 min.	30–45 min	2 hours	4 hours	6 hours	7 hours
200–219	30–45 min.	30–45 min	2 hours	3 hours	5 hours	6 hours
Over 220	30–45 min.	30–45 min	1 hour	3 hours	4 hours	6 hours

SOURCE: Based on data from *The New York Public Library Desk Reference*

Health

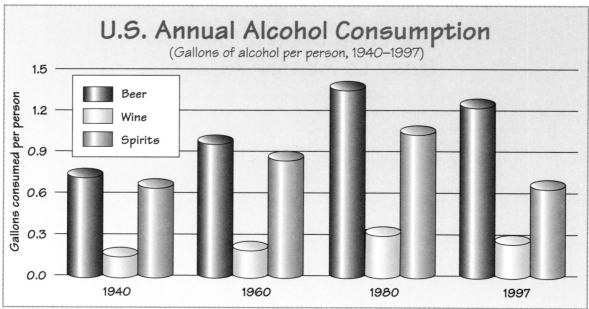

U.S. Annual Alcohol Consumption
(Gallons of alcohol per person, 1940–1997)

Legend:
- Beer
- Wine
- Spirits

Y-axis: Gallons consumed per person (1.5, 1.2, 0.9, 0.6, 0.3, 0.0)

X-axis: 1940, 1960, 1980, 1997

SOURCE: Based on data from U.S. Dept. of Health and Human Services

What Are the Most Commonly Abused Drugs?

Drug	Primary Effect	Popular Names
Alcohol	Depressant	Drink, booze
Amphetamines	Stimulant	Pep pills, uppers; *methamphetamines:* speed, crystal, crank, ice
Amyl or butyl nitrites	Stimulant	Poppers, snappers, rush, locker room
Barbituates	Depressant	Sleeping pills, dolls
Cocaine	Stimulant	Coke, snow, lady; *smokable form:* crack
Ephedra	Stimulant	Ma huang; *brand names:* Herbal Ecstacy, Euphoria, Buzz Tablets, Brain Wash
Heroin	Depressant	Snow, smack; *synthetic form:* China white, Persian heroin, gasoline dope; *combined heroin & cocaine:* speedball
D-lysergic acid diethylamide	Hallucinogen	LSD, acid
Marijuana	Hallucinogen/ depressant	Pot, grass, joint, cannabis, dope, reefer, weed, herb, skunk
MDMA (combination of synthetic mescaline and an amphetamine)	Stimulant/ hallucinogen	Ecstacy, love potion
Mescaline	Hallucinogen	Peyote, cactus
Morphine	Depressant	
PCP (phencyclidine)	Hallucinogen	Angel dust
Tranquilizers	Depressants	Downers, *brand names:* Valium, Librium, Darvon

SOURCE: Based on data from U.S. Dept. of Health and Human Services

Profile: Drug Use by U.S. High School Seniors, 1998

(By percentage of students who used within a month of the survey)

Alcohol
52.0%

LSD
3.2%

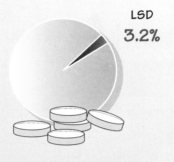

Cigarettes
35.1%

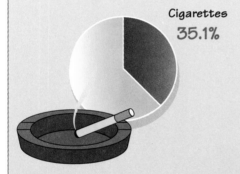

Cocaine
2.4%

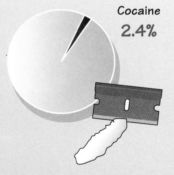

Marijuana
22.8%

Heroin
.05%

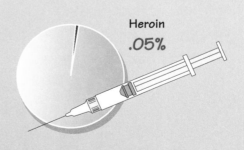

SOURCE: Based on data from Department of Health

Health

Smoking: What Does Starting Age Have to Do With Quitting Age?

Adults who start smoking in their early teens are more likely to still be smoking at age 30. Of those who've quit by age 30, the percentage of smokers who:

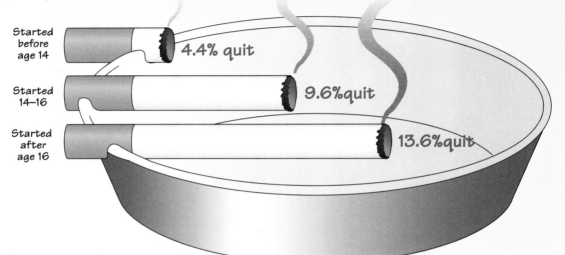

Started before age 14   4.4% quit

Started 14–16   9.6% quit

Started after age 16   13.6% quit

SOURCE: Based on data from *American Journal of Public Health*

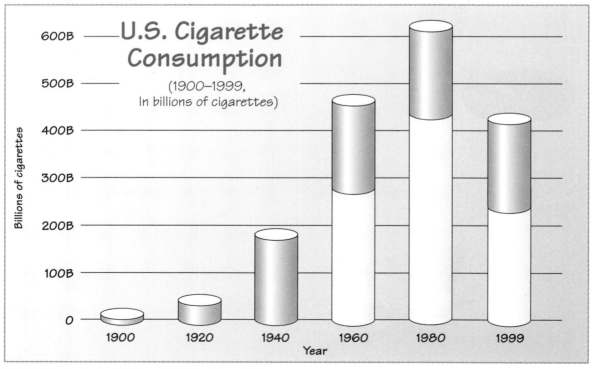

U.S. Cigarette Consumption

(1900–1999, In billions of cigarettes)

Billions of cigarettes

Year

SOURCE: Based on data from U.S. Dept. of Health and Human Services

Profile: Teenage Tobacco Users

Cigarette use is about equal among teen males and females. Teen males, however, make up the vast majority of smokeless tobacco users.

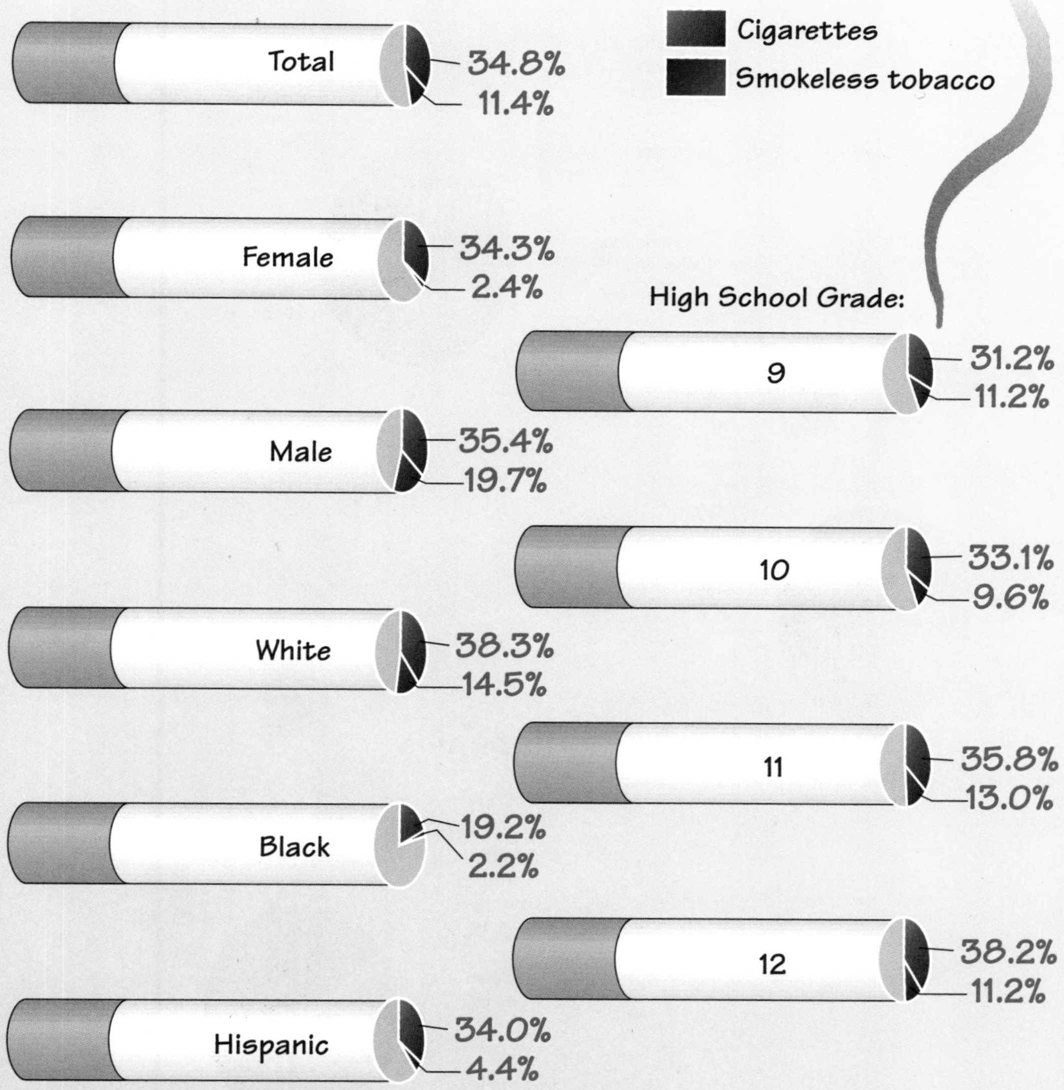

Total — 34.8%
— 11.4%

◼ Cigarettes
◼ Smokeless tobacco

Female — 34.3%
— 2.4%

High School Grade:

9 — 31.2%
— 11.2%

Male — 35.4%
— 19.7%

10 — 33.1%
— 9.6%

White — 38.3%
— 14.5%

11 — 35.8%
— 13.0%

Black — 19.2%
— 2.2%

12 — 38.2%
— 11.2%

Hispanic — 34.0%
— 4.4%

Health

SOURCE: Based on data from U.S. Dept. of Health and Human Services

Health

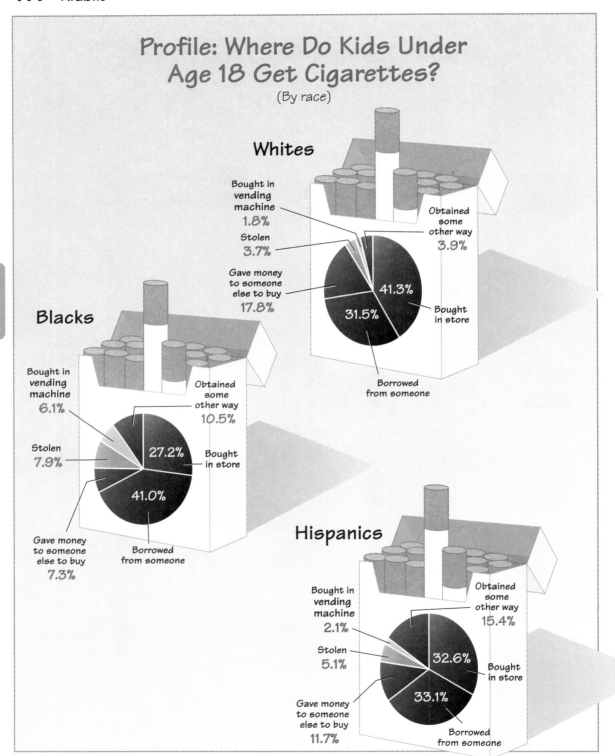

Profile: Where Do Kids Under Age 18 Get Cigarettes?
(By race)

Whites

Bought in vending machine 1.8%

Stolen 3.7%

Gave money to someone else to buy 17.8%

Obtained some other way 3.9%

41.3% Bought in store

31.5%

Borrowed from someone

Blacks

Bought in vending machine 6.1%

Stolen 7.9%

Gave money to someone else to buy 7.3%

Obtained some other way 10.5%

27.2% Bought in store

41.0%

Borrowed from someone

Hispanics

Bought in vending machine 2.1%

Stolen 5.1%

Gave money to someone else to buy 11.7%

Obtained some other way 15.4%

32.6% Bought in store

33.1%

Borrowed from someone

SOURCE: Based on data from U.S. Dept. of Health and Human Services

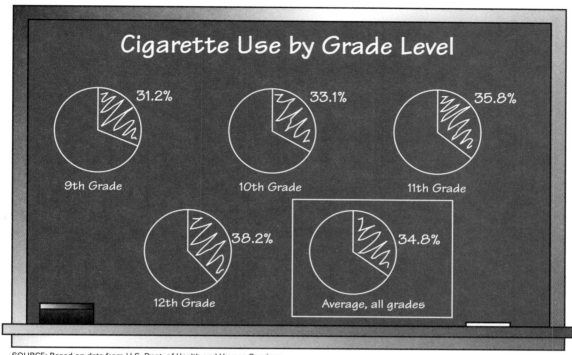

Cigarette Use by Grade Level

31.2%
9th Grade

33.1%
10th Grade

35.8%
11th Grade

38.2%
12th Grade

34.8%
Average, all grades

SOURCE: Based on data from U.S. Dept. of Health and Human Services

Health

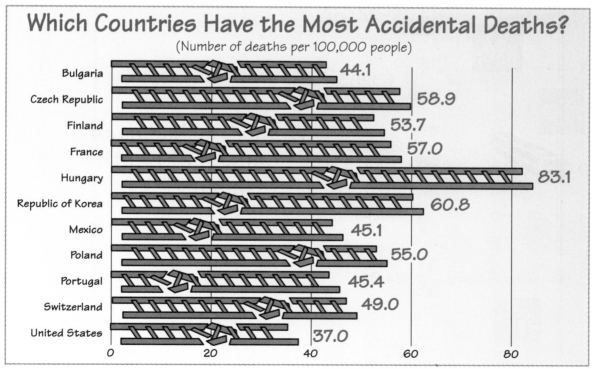

Which Countries Have the Most Accidental Deaths?

(Number of deaths per 100,000 people)

Country	Deaths
Bulgaria	44.1
Czech Republic	58.9
Finland	53.7
France	57.0
Hungary	83.1
Republic of Korea	60.8
Mexico	45.1
Poland	55.0
Portugal	45.4
Switzerland	49.0
United States	37.0

SOURCE: Based on data from World Health Organization

Health

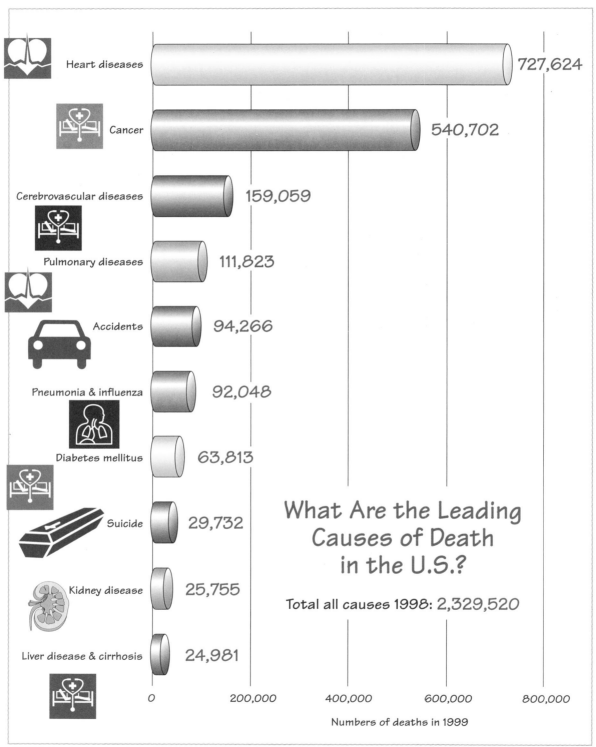

Heart diseases — 727,624

Cancer — 540,702

Cerebrovascular diseases — 159,059

Pulmonary diseases — 111,823

Accidents — 94,266

Pneumonia & influenza — 92,048

Diabetes mellitus — 63,813

Suicide — 29,732

Kidney disease — 25,755

Liver disease & cirrhosis — 24,981

What Are the Leading Causes of Death in the U.S.?

Total all causes 1998: 2,329,520

0   200,000   400,000   600,000   800,000

Numbers of deaths in 1999

SOURCE: Based on data from National Center for Health Statistics, U.S. Dept. of Health and Human Services, 1999

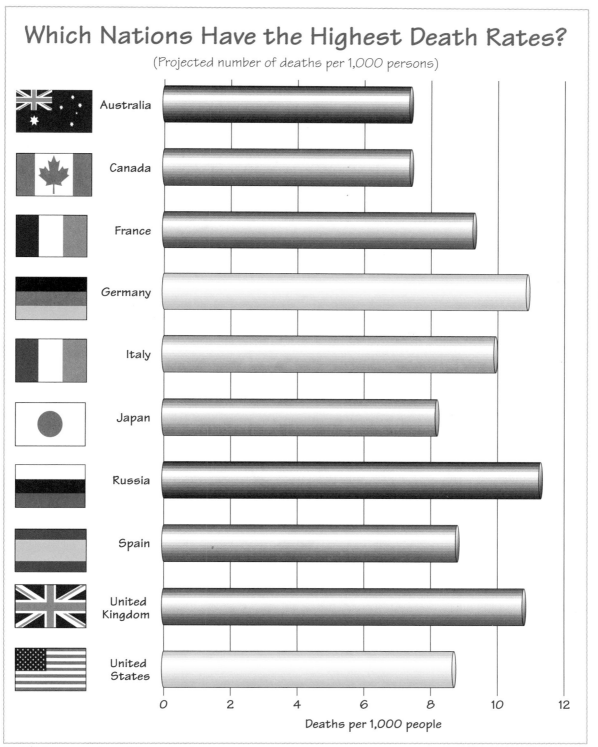

Which Nations Have the Highest Death Rates?

(Projected number of deaths per 1,000 persons)

Australia

Canada

France

Germany

Italy

Japan

Russia

Spain

United Kingdom

United States

Health

0   2   4   6   8   10   12

Deaths per 1,000 people

SOURCE: Based on data from U.S. Bureau of the Census, International Data Base

Health

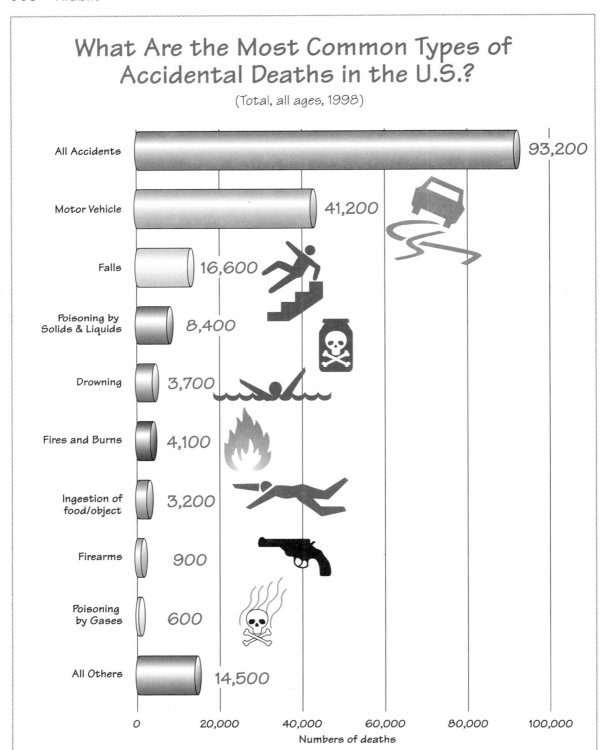

What Are the Most Common Types of Accidental Deaths in the U.S.?

(Total, all ages, 1998)

All Accidents	93,200
Motor Vehicle	41,200
Falls	16,600
Poisoning by Solids & Liquids	8,400
Drowning	3,700
Fires and Burns	4,100
Ingestion of food/object	3,200
Firearms	900
Poisoning by Gases	600
All Others	14,500

0   20,000   40,000   60,000   80,000   100,000

Numbers of deaths

SOURCE: Based on data from National Safety Council

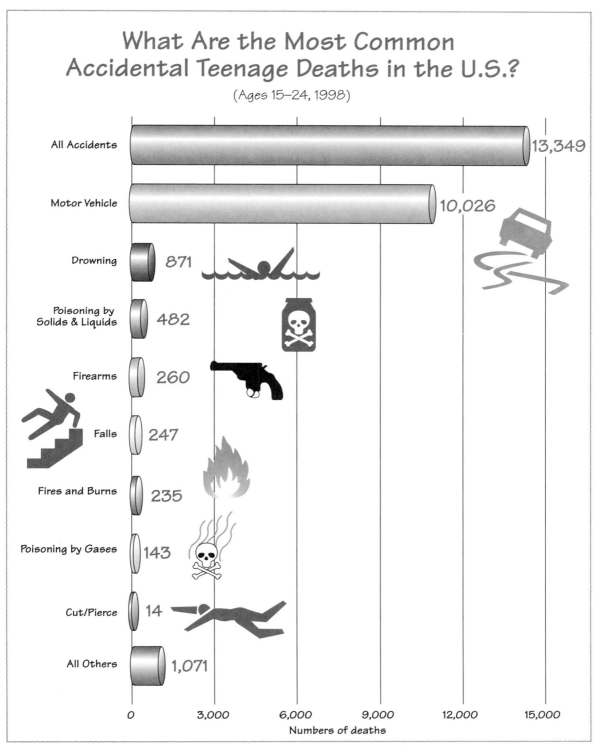

What Are the Most Common Accidental Teenage Deaths in the U.S.?

(Ages 15–24, 1998)

- All Accidents — 13,349
- Motor Vehicle — 10,026
- Drowning — 871
- Poisoning by Solids & Liquids — 482
- Firearms — 260
- Falls — 247
- Fires and Burns — 235
- Poisoning by Gases — 143
- Cut/Pierce — 14
- All Others — 1,071

Numbers of deaths

Health

SOURCE: Based on data from National Safety Council, 1998

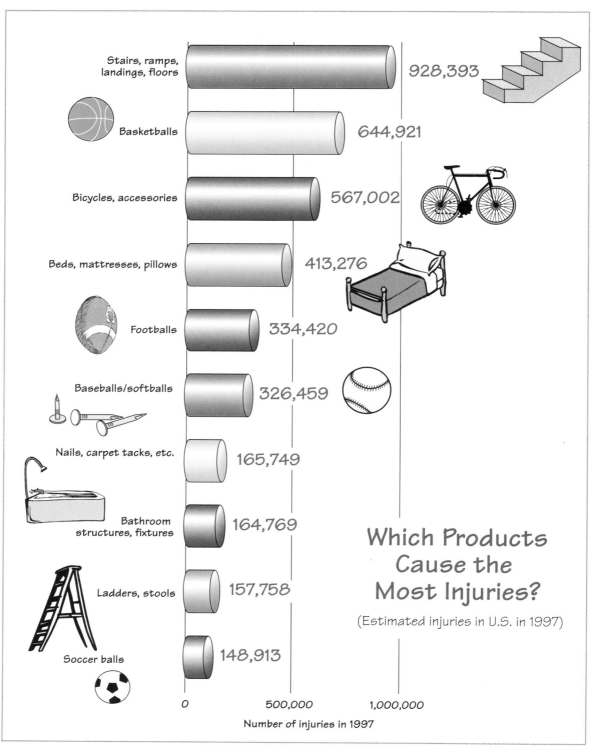

Stairs, ramps, landings, floors — 928,393

Basketballs — 644,921

Bicycles, accessories — 567,002

Beds, mattresses, pillows — 413,276

Footballs — 334,420

Baseballs/softballs — 326,459

Nails, carpet tacks, etc. — 165,749

Bathroom structures, fixtures — 164,769

Ladders, stools — 157,758

Soccer balls — 148,913

Which Products Cause the Most Injuries?

(Estimated injuries in U.S. in 1997)

0 — 500,000 — 1,000,000

Number of injuries in 1997

SOURCE: Based on data from Consumer Product Safety Commission, 1998

Health

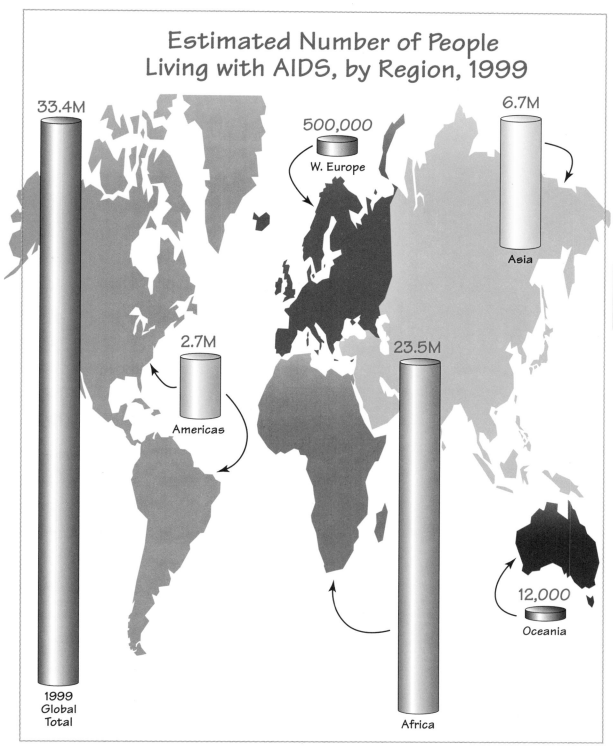

Estimated Number of People Living with AIDS, by Region, 1999

33.4M

500,000
W. Europe

6.7M
Asia

2.7M
Americas

23.5M

12,000
Oceania

1999 Global Total

Africa

Health

SOURCE: Based on data from World Health Organization, Global Programme on AIDS

How Many Kids Have AIDS?

(U.S. patients under 13 years old, as of 1998, with probable cause)

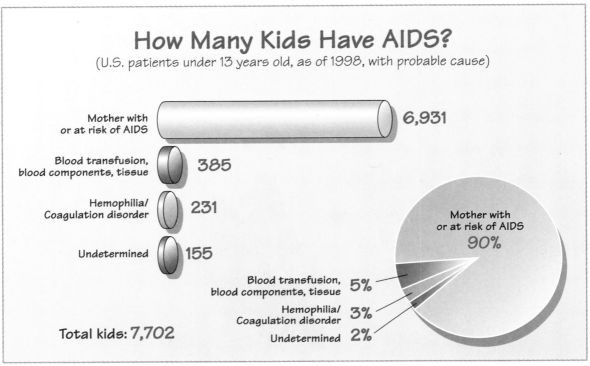

Mother with or at risk of AIDS — 6,931

Blood transfusion, blood components, tissue — 385

Hemophilia/ Coagulation disorder — 231

Undetermined — 155

Mother with or at risk of AIDS 90%

Blood transfusion, blood components, tissue 5%

Hemophilia/ Coagulation disorder 3%

Undetermined 2%

Total kids: 7,702

SOURCE: Based on data from U.S. Dept. of Health and Human Services, 1999

Which Cities Have the Highest AIDS Populations?

(Approximate number of cases)

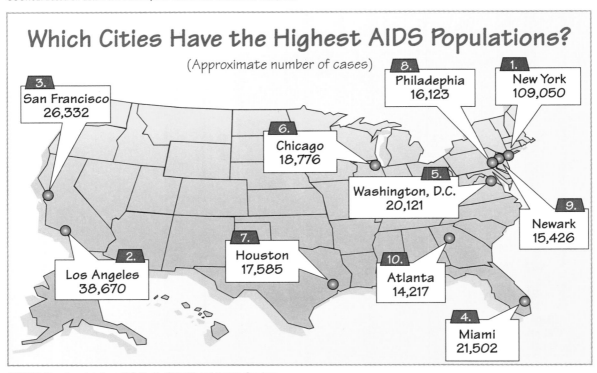

3. San Francisco 26,332

8. Philadephia 16,123

1. New York 109,050

6. Chicago 18,776

5. Washington, D.C. 20,121

9. Newark 15,426

2. Los Angeles 38,670

7. Houston 17,585

10. Atlanta 14,217

4. Miami 21,502

SOURCE: Based on data from U.S. Dept. of Health and Human Services

Estimated Cumulative HIV/AIDS Cases by Region, Mid-1999

(With precentage of adults living with HIV)

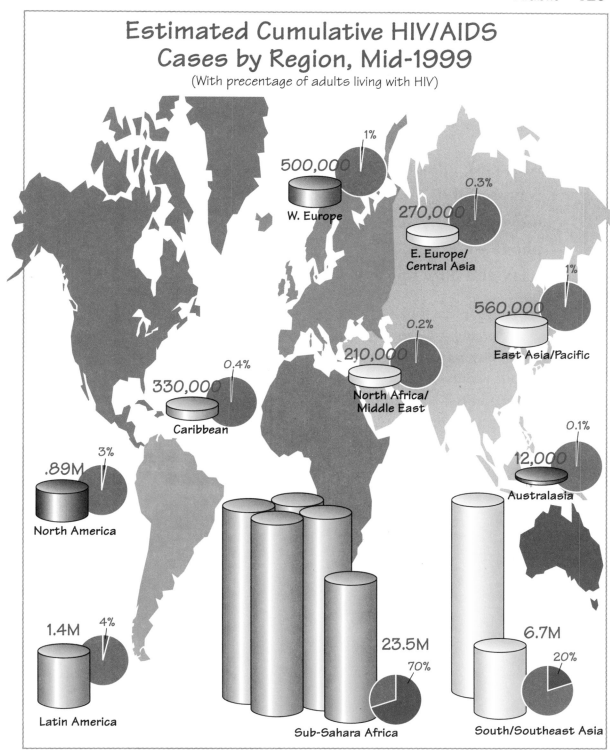

1%
500,000
W. Europe

0.3%
270,000
E. Europe/
Central Asia

1%
560,000
East Asia/Pacific

0.4%
330,000
Caribbean

0.2%
210,000
North Africa/
Middle East

0.1%
12,000
Australasia

3%
.89M
North America

4%
1.4M
Latin America

23.5M
70%
Sub-Sahara Africa

6.7M
20%
South/Southeast Asia

Health

SOURCE: Based on data from UNAIDS Program, United Nations

Recreation

Kids have lots of free time—and lots of cool and exciting ways to fill it! Sports, games, dancing, amusement parks, movies and TV, hanging out with friends, talking on the phone—these are just a few of the things that kids do to relax and have fun.

Some recreational activities are more fun when done as part of a group, and kids are super joiners. About 3.4 million boys belong to the Boy Scouts of America. Almost 2.7 million girls are members of Girl Scouts of the U.S.A. Sports teams, school bands, 4-H clubs, and religious groups are other organizations that attract millions of young people each year.

Taking trips with the family are also popular recreations. In fact, vacations are the best-loved activities of 52% of kids ages 7 to 12! Some vacations include long-distance trips to see famous places such as national parks, historic monuments, and Disney World. Other vacations are highlighted by shorter family activities, such as outings to local beaches or afternoons spent learning how to fish.

Kidbits Tidbits

- A survey of teens in 26 countries found that 93% enjoyed watching TV but only 76% enjoyed playing sports.
- Bowling is among the most popular recreational activities. About 80 million Americans age 5 and older bowl each year.
- Americans spend more than $14 billion a year on boating.
- More than 15 million people visited The Magic Kingdom at Walt Disney World in 1999.

Some activities are more popular with girls than boys, and vice versa. Boys and girls participate in swimming, bowling, and tennis in about equal numbers. But fishing and billiards are much more popular with boys. Horseback riding and volleyball, however, are more popular with girls. Age and finances also play roles in determining people's recreational favorites. More kids than adults play soccer—but more adults than kids can pay the fees required to ski and play golf.

People of all ages can have fun—and get a lot of satisfaction—while helping others. Almost half of the kids in grades 6 through 12 are involved in some kind of volunteer service. For example, a Florida boy organized a program to deliver unused school cafeteria food to poor people. A Boy Scout troop grew vegetables for a homeless shelter. Many teens carry out conservation projects, teach younger kids to read, or assist the elderly and people with disabilities. Teens say that one of the main reasons they lend a helping hand to others is because they feel compassion for people in need.

Of course, not all recreation is for a noble cause. Some of the most popular pastimes in America include going to the movies and watching TV and videos. In fact, about 60% of the U.S. population says they exercise and go to the movies with much of their free time. For kids ages 7–12, movies and TV are ranked behind vacations, outdoor play, and listening to music as favorites.

Kidbits Tidbits

- Symphony orchestra concerts draw over 24 million attendees a year.
- Almost 50% of kids in grades 6 through 12 are involved in some kind of volunteer service.
- Teens who are asked to volunteer are much more likely to do so than teens who aren't asked.
- Each year, Americans donate about 20 billion hours of their time to help each other and their communities.

Recreation

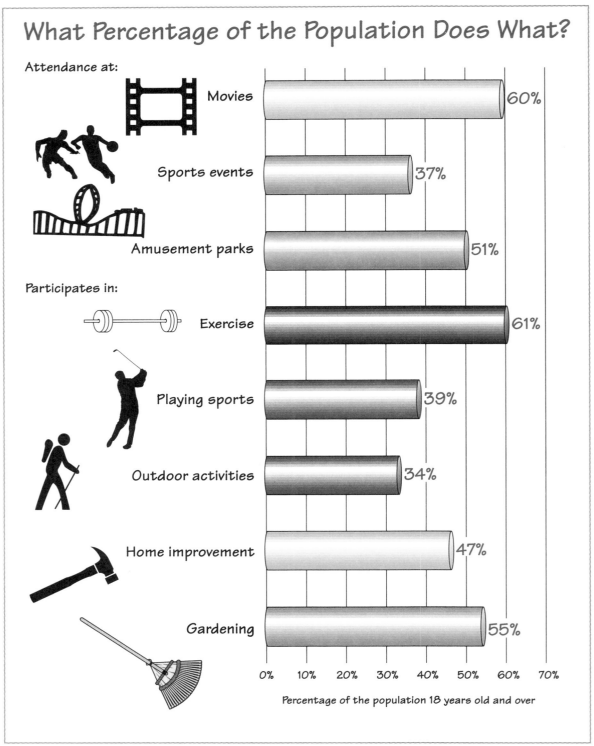

What Percentage of the Population Does What?

Attendance at:

Movies 60%

Sports events 37%

Amusement parks 51%

Participates in:

Exercise 61%

Playing sports 39%

Outdoor activities 34%

Home improvement 47%

Gardening 55%

0% 10% 20% 30% 40% 50% 60% 70%

Percentage of the population 18 years old and over

SOURCE: Based on data from Bureau of the Census, U.S. Dept. of Commerce

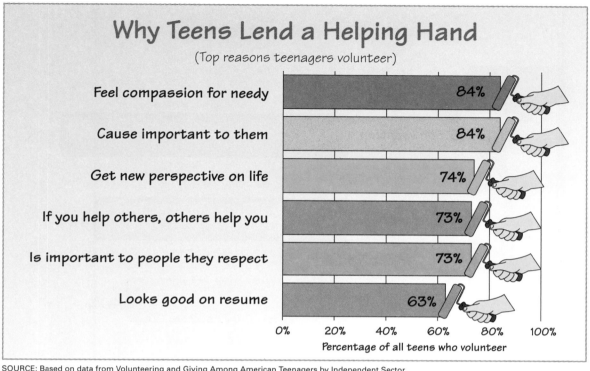

Why Teens Lend a Helping Hand

(Top reasons teenagers volunteer)

Feel compassion for needy	84%
Cause important to them	84%
Get new perspective on life	74%
If you help others, others help you	73%
Is important to people they respect	73%
Looks good on resume	63%

0% 20% 40% 60% 80% 100%

Percentage of all teens who volunteer

SOURCE: Based on data from Volunteering and Giving Among American Teenagers by Independent Sector

Recreation

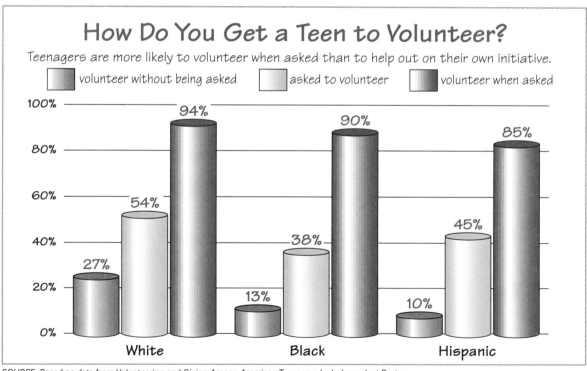

How Do You Get a Teen to Volunteer?

Teenagers are more likely to volunteer when asked than to help out on their own initiative.

■ volunteer without being asked   ■ asked to volunteer   ■ volunteer when asked

	White	Black	Hispanic
volunteer without being asked	27%	13%	10%
asked to volunteer	54%	38%	45%
volunteer when asked	94%	90%	85%

SOURCE: Based on data from Volunteering and Giving Among American Teenagers by Independent Sector

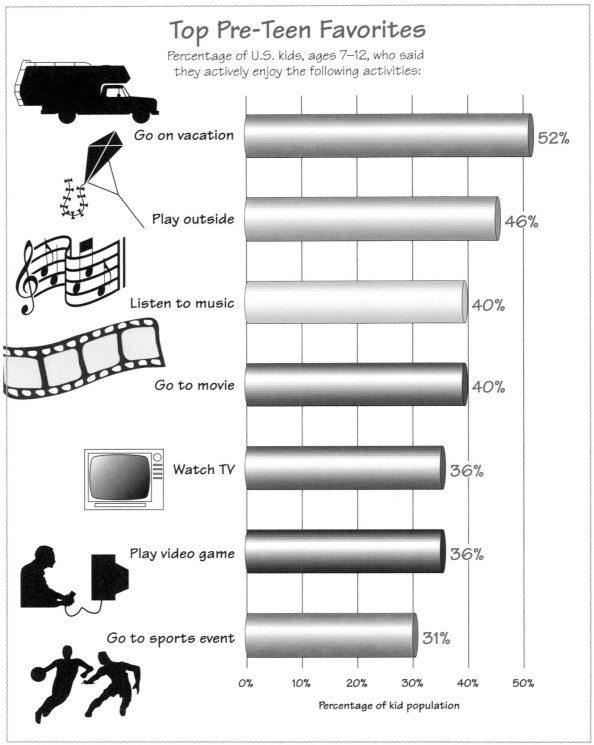

Top Pre-Teen Favorites

Percentage of U.S. kids, ages 7–12, who said
they actively enjoy the following activities:

Recreation

Activity	Percentage
Go on vacation	52%
Play outside	46%
Listen to music	40%
Go to movie	40%
Watch TV	36%
Play video game	36%
Go to sports event	31%

Percentage of kid population

0% 10% 20% 30% 40% 50%

SOURCE: Based on data from A.B.C. Global Kids Study

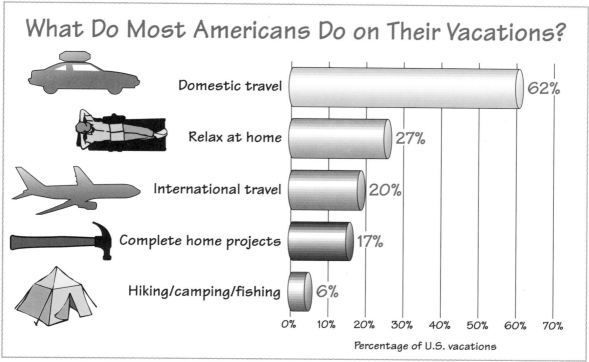

What Do Most Americans Do on Their Vacations?

Domestic travel — 62%

Relax at home — 27%

International travel — 20%

Complete home projects — 17%

Hiking/camping/fishing — 6%

0% 10% 20% 30% 40% 50% 60% 70%

Percentage of U.S. vacations

Recreation

SOURCE: Based on data from Aragon Consulting Group

Membership in the Boy Scouts and Girl Scouts

(In millions)

Members in millions

6M
5M
4M
3M
2M
1M
0

Boy Scouts — 3.4M

Girl Scouts — 2.7M

SOURCE: Based on data from Boy Scouts of America and Girl Scouts of the United States of America, 1999

Recreation

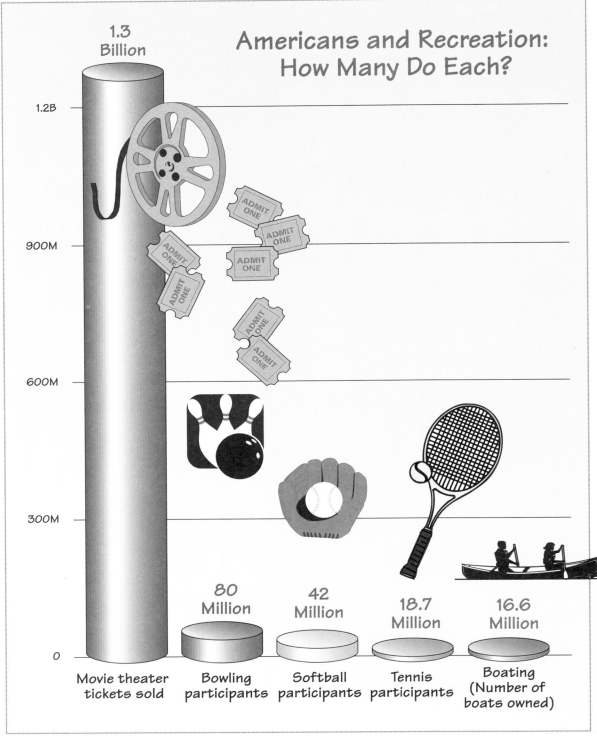

Americans and Recreation: How Many Do Each?

1.3 Billion — Movie theater tickets sold

80 Million — Bowling participants

42 Million — Softball participants

18.7 Million — Tennis participants

16.6 Million — Boating (Number of boats owned)

SOURCES: Based on data from Motion Picture Association of America, Inc.; National Bowling Council; Amateur Softball Association; Tennis Industry Association; National Marine Manufacturers Association

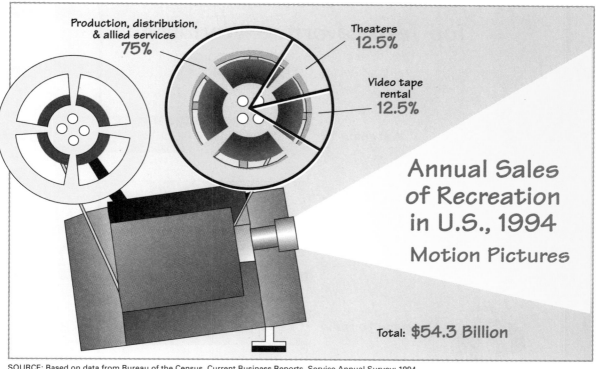

Production, distribution, & allied services
75%

Theaters
12.5%

Video tape rental
12.5%

Annual Sales of Recreation in U.S., 1994

Motion Pictures

Total: **$54.3 Billion**

Recreation

SOURCE: Based on data from Bureau of the Census, Current Business Reports, Service Annual Survey: 1994

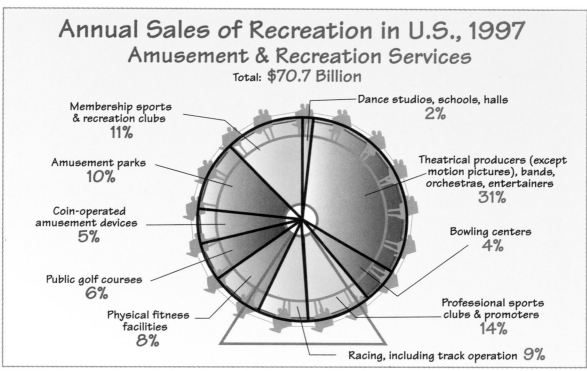

Annual Sales of Recreation in U.S., 1997

Amusement & Recreation Services

Total: **$70.7 Billion**

Membership sports & recreation clubs
11%

Dance studios, schools, halls
2%

Amusement parks
10%

Theatrical producers (except motion pictures), bands, orchestras, entertainers
31%

Coin-operated amusement devices
5%

Bowling centers
4%

Public golf courses
6%

Physical fitness facilities
8%

Professional sports clubs & promoters
14%

Racing, including track operation **9%**

SOURCE: Based on data from Bureau of the Census, Current Business Reports, Service Annual Survey: 1997

Recreation

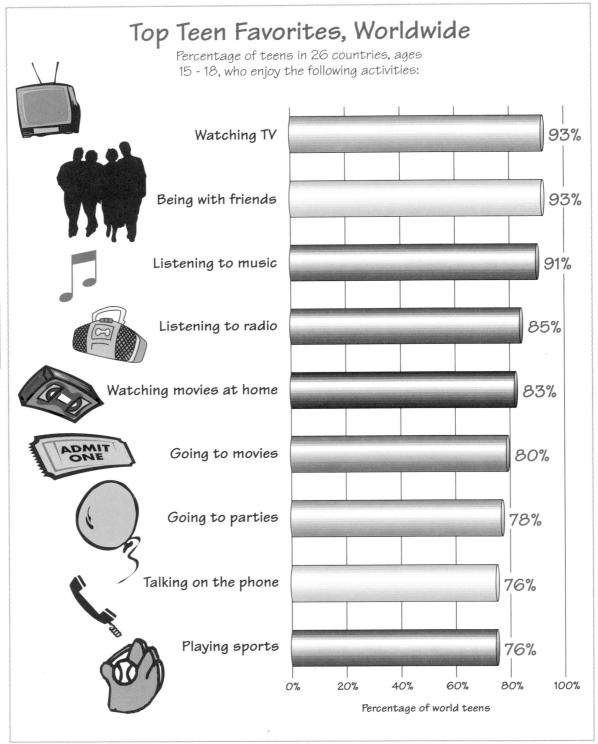

Top Teen Favorites, Worldwide

Percentage of teens in 26 countries, ages
15 - 18, who enjoy the following activities:

Activity	Percentage
Watching TV	93%
Being with friends	93%
Listening to music	91%
Listening to radio	85%
Watching movies at home	83%
Going to movies	80%
Going to parties	78%
Talking on the phone	76%
Playing sports	76%

Percentage of world teens

SOURCE: Based on data from New World Teen Study, The BrainWaves Group

Bike Paths to the Future

Between 1991 and 1997 more than $1 billion in highway taxes was spent on bike paths and walkways in America.
(In millions)

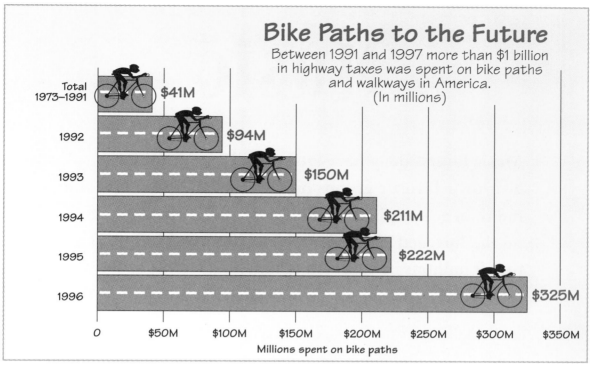

Total 1973–1991	$41M
1992	$94M
1993	$150M
1994	$211M
1995	$222M
1996	$325M

Millions spent on bike paths

SOURCE: Based on data from Bicycle Federation of America

Reel Fun

About 16% of Americans older than 16—some 33 million people—fished in 1998, averaging 18 days of fishing per person. Most common types of fishing by fishers:

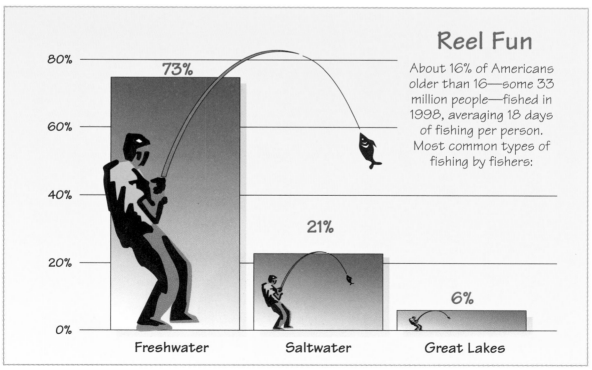

Freshwater 73%
Saltwater 21%
Great Lakes 6%

SOURCE: U.S. Fish and Wildlife Service

Music

Music lovers today have lots of cool opportunities to hear their favorite groups on CDs, videos, television, and radio; in concert halls; and at live music festivals—even on the Internet! These days, it's not unusual for a CD to sell millions of copies in a matter of weeks, or for a concert to attract upwards of 100,000 fans!

Rock is by far the most popular type of music among young people, but many other kinds of music also enjoy wide appeal. Country, rap, pop, hip-hop, rhythm-and-blues, folk, gospel, jazz, and even classical all have solid followings. Some of American kids' favorite musicians are very close to their own age group. They're teenagers such as pop sensation Britney Spears, blues singer Jonny Lang, and the heart-throb group 'N Sync, for example.

Americans spent a whopping $14.3 billion on recorded music in 2000. Out of that, American teens are the biggest customers: people ages 15 to 19 accounted for 17.2% of total sales; kids age 10 to 14 added another 7.9%. CDs are the most popular recorded music format, with 89.3% of 2000 sales. Cassettes were second with 4.9%.

Kidbits Tidbits

- In 1999, kids 15–19 accounted for 12.6% of all recorded music sales; kids 10–14 added another 8.5%.
- In 1999, rock was the most popular type of music sold, accounting for 25.2% of all sales. Country was next, with 10.8%.
- In the 1960s, about 45 new albums were released each week. By the late 1990s, an average of 710 CDs were released weekly.
- In 2000, the RIAA announced that Garth Brooks was the fastest-selling solo artist in music history. He sold 100 million albums from 1990 to 2000.

Young people's favorites constantly change. What's "hot" with kids today won't be "cool" with kids tomorrow. But, while some musicians are one-hit wonders, others keep going for years and years. For example, Elvis Presley records are still selling strong more than 20 years after his death. As of the end of 1999, the best-selling albums of all time in the U.S. were Michael Jackson's *Thriller* (25 million copies) and *Their Greatest Hits* from the Eagles (24 million). And, though the Rolling Stones have been around for over 30 years, they managed to pull off the top grossing tour of 1999; their "No Security" tour took in $89.2 million.

There are more than 576 million radios in the U.S., including 367 million in homes and 142 million in cars. Each weekday, 95% of Americans over age 12 listen to radio for an average of 3 hours. There are over 12,000 radio stations, with country music stations the most common (2,525).

Enjoying music isn't always a couch potato activity. Millions of kids sing and play instruments. And when music has a good beat, everyone wants to jump up and dance. Dance crazes come and go. The '70s was disco. The 80's was slam-dancing. The mid-1990s was macarena time. Any guesses which dances kids will be doing 10 years from now and what kind of music will be #1 on the charts?

Kidbits Tidbits

- About half of all music albums are bought in record stores; about one-third are bought in discount stores such as Wal-Mart and K-Mart.
- Elvis Presley's records have sold more than 1 billion copies, making him the most successful solo recording artist ever.
- The best-selling single of all time is Elton John's *Candle in the Wind*, re-released when Princess Diana died.
- There were 10,394 commercial radio stations in 1998. Some 23% played country music, while 14% played adult contemporary.
- Radios are everywhere: nearly every car in America has one and 98% of American homes own at least one.

Music

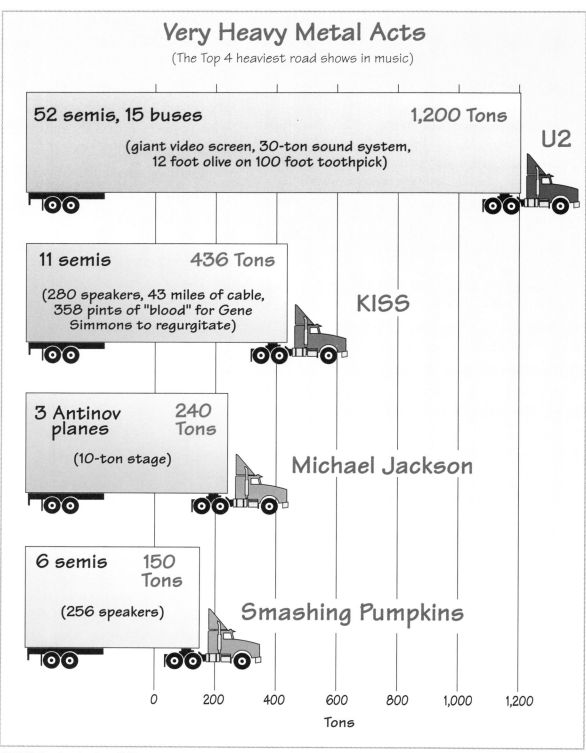

Very Heavy Metal Acts
(The Top 4 heaviest road shows in music)

52 semis, 15 buses   1,200 Tons

(giant video screen, 30-ton sound system,
12 foot olive on 100 foot toothpick)

U2

11 semis   436 Tons

(280 speakers, 43 miles of cable,
358 pints of "blood" for Gene
Simmons to regurgitate)

KISS

3 Antinov planes   240 Tons

(10-ton stage)

Michael Jackson

6 semis   150 Tons

(256 speakers)

Smashing Pumpkins

0   200   400   600   800   1,000   1,200

Tons

SOURCE: Based on data from LIVE!

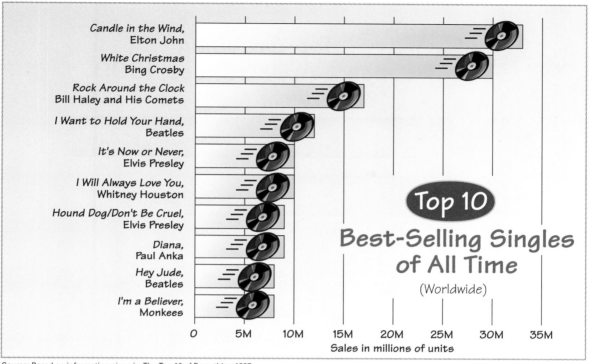

Top 10

Best-Selling Singles of All Time

(Worldwide)

Sales in millions of units

Source: Based on information given in *The Top 10 of Everything 1997*

Music

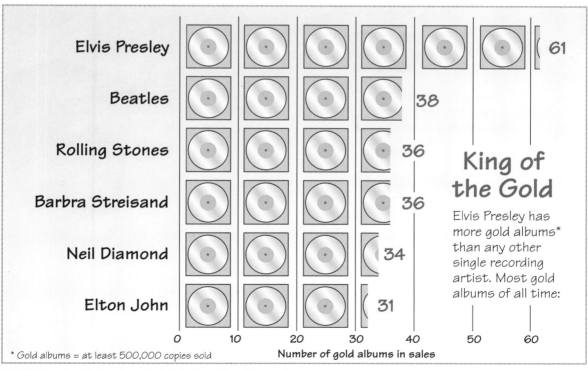

King of the Gold

Elvis Presley has more gold albums* than any other single recording artist. Most gold albums of all time:

* Gold albums = at least 500,000 copies sold

Number of gold albums in sales

SOURCE: Based on data from Recording Industry Association of America, Inc.

Music

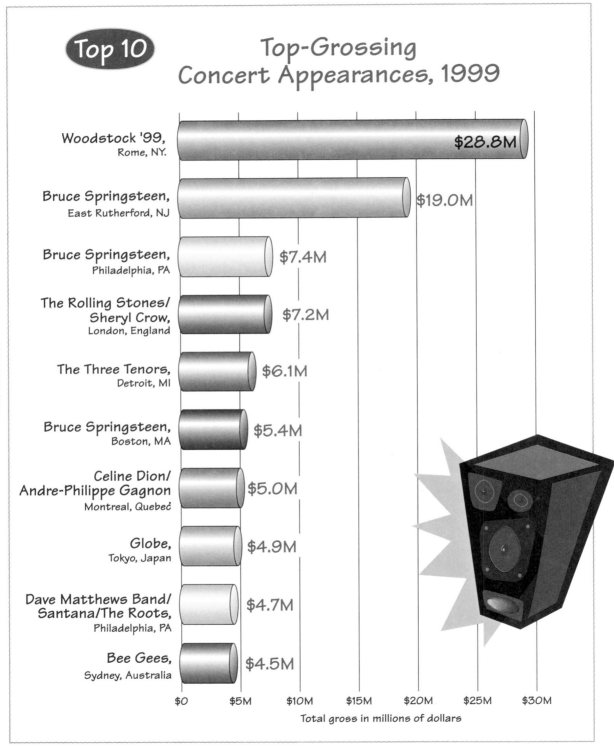

Top 10

Top-Grossing Concert Appearances, 1999

Artist	Total gross
Woodstock '99, Rome, NY.	$28.8M
Bruce Springsteen, East Rutherford, NJ	$19.0M
Bruce Springsteen, Philadelphia, PA	$7.4M
The Rolling Stones/ Sheryl Crow, London, England	$7.2M
The Three Tenors, Detroit, MI	$6.1M
Bruce Springsteen, Boston, MA	$5.4M
Celine Dion/ Andre-Philippe Gagnon, Montreal, Quebec	$5.0M
Globe, Tokyo, Japan	$4.9M
Dave Matthews Band/ Santana/The Roots, Philadelphia, PA	$4.7M
Bee Gees, Sydney, Australia	$4.5M

$0 $5M $10M $15M $20M $25M $30M

Total gross in millions of dollars

SOURCE: Based on data from Amusement Business

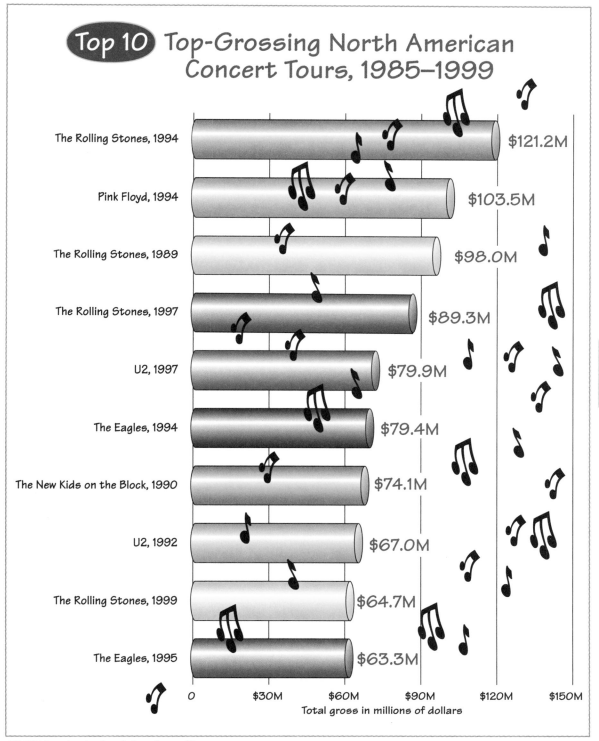

Top 10 Top-Grossing North American Concert Tours, 1985–1999

Artist	Total gross
The Rolling Stones, 1994	$121.2M
Pink Floyd, 1994	$103.5M
The Rolling Stones, 1989	$98.0M
The Rolling Stones, 1997	$89.3M
U2, 1997	$79.9M
The Eagles, 1994	$79.4M
The New Kids on the Block, 1990	$74.1M
U2, 1992	$67.0M
The Rolling Stones, 1999	$64.7M
The Eagles, 1995	$63.3M

Total gross in millions of dollars

0   $30M $60M $90M $120M $150M

Music

SOURCE: Based on data from Pollstar, Fresno, CA

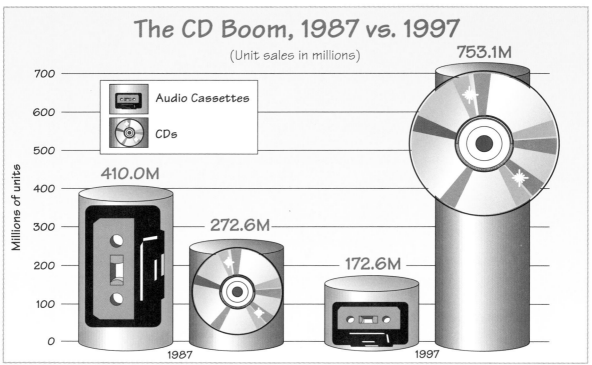

The CD Boom, 1987 vs. 1997
(Unit sales in millions)

753.1M

410.0M

272.6M

172.6M

Millions of units

700
600
500
400
300
200
100
0

Audio Cassettes

CDs

1987   1997

SOURCE: Based on data from Recording Industry Association of America, 1998

Music

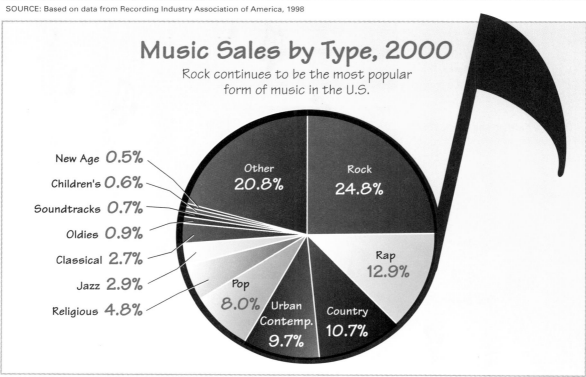

Music Sales by Type, 2000
Rock continues to be the most popular
form of music in the U.S.

New Age 0.5%
Children's 0.6%
Soundtracks 0.7%
Oldies 0.9%
Classical 2.7%
Jazz 2.9%
Religious 4.8%

Other 20.8%

Rock 24.8%

Rap 12.9%

Pop 8.0%

Urban Contemp. 9.7%

Country 10.7%

SOURCE: Based on data from Recording Industry Association of America, 2001

Music Sales by Format, 2000

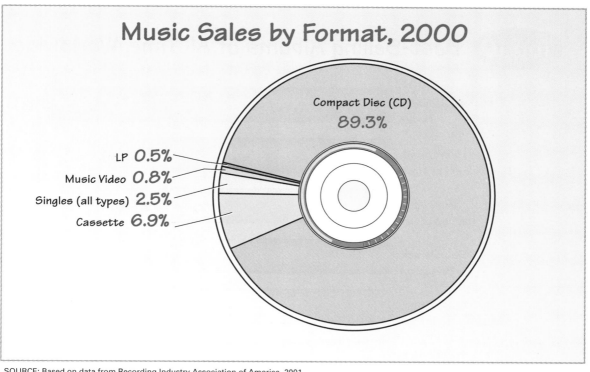

Compact Disc (CD)
89.3%

LP 0.5%
Music Video 0.8%
Singles (all types) 2.5%
Cassette 6.9%

SOURCE: Based on data from Recording Industry Association of America, 2001

How Much Music Do Kids Buy?

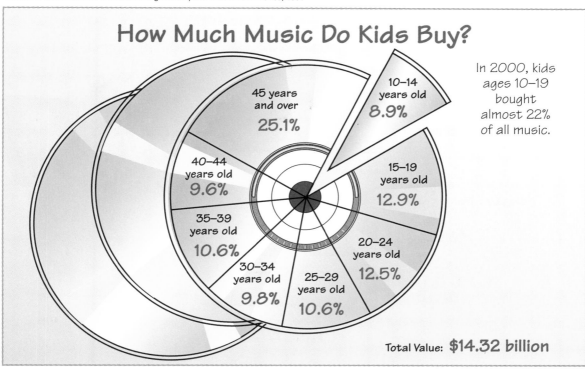

45 years
and over
25.1%

10–14
years old
8.9%

In 2000, kids
ages 10–19
bought
almost 22%
of all music.

40–44
years old
9.6%

15–19
years old
12.9%

35–39
years old
10.6%

30–34
years old
9.8%

25–29
years old
10.6%

20–24
years old
12.5%

Total Value: **$14.32 billion**

SOURCE: Based on data from Recording Industry Association of America, 2000

Music

Music

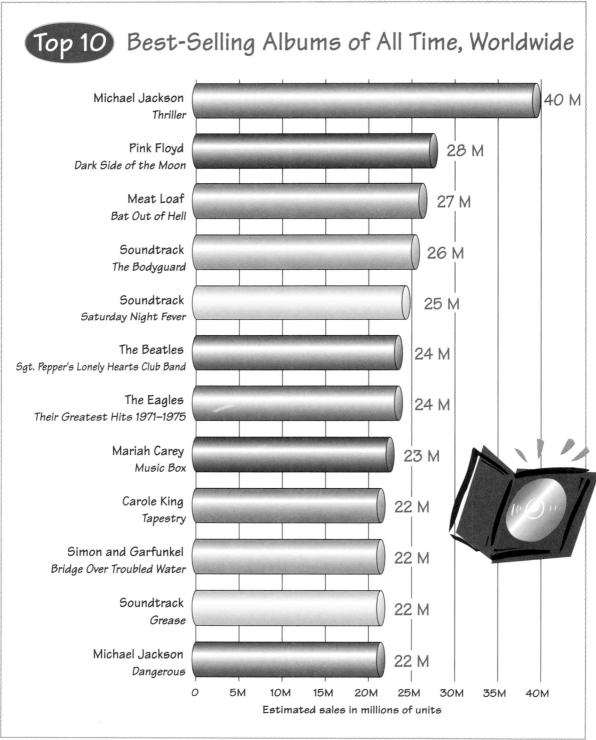

Top 10 Best-Selling Albums of All Time, Worldwide

Artist / Album	Sales
Michael Jackson — *Thriller*	40 M
Pink Floyd — *Dark Side of the Moon*	28 M
Meat Loaf — *Bat Out of Hell*	27 M
Soundtrack — *The Bodyguard*	26 M
Soundtrack — *Saturday Night Fever*	25 M
The Beatles — *Sgt. Pepper's Lonely Hearts Club Band*	24 M
The Eagles — *Their Greatest Hits 1971–1975*	24 M
Mariah Carey — *Music Box*	23 M
Carole King — *Tapestry*	22 M
Simon and Garfunkel — *Bridge Over Troubled Water*	22 M
Soundtrack — *Grease*	22 M
Michael Jackson — *Dangerous*	22 M

Estimated sales in millions of units

0   5M   10M   15M   20M   25M   30M   35M   40M

SOURCE: Based on information from the Recording Industry Association of America

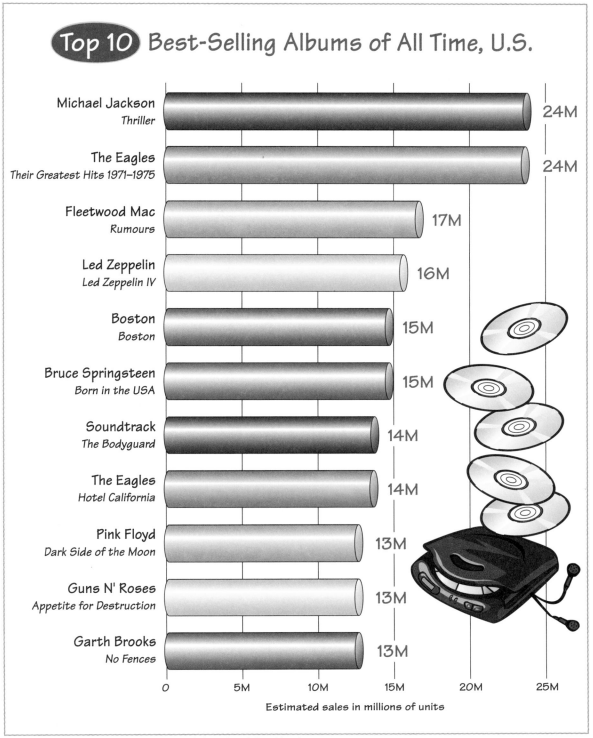

Top 10 Best-Selling Albums of All Time, U.S.

Artist	Album	Sales
Michael Jackson	*Thriller*	24M
The Eagles	*Their Greatest Hits 1971–1975*	24M
Fleetwood Mac	*Rumours*	17M
Led Zeppelin	*Led Zeppelin IV*	16M
Boston	*Boston*	15M
Bruce Springsteen	*Born in the USA*	15M
Soundtrack	*The Bodyguard*	14M
The Eagles	*Hotel California*	14M
Pink Floyd	*Dark Side of the Moon*	13M
Guns N' Roses	*Appetite for Destruction*	13M
Garth Brooks	*No Fences*	13M

Estimated sales in millions of units

Music

SOURCE: Based on information from the Recording Industry Association of America

Music

Top 10 Best-Selling Country Albums of All Time in the U.S.

	Artist	Title	Year
1	Garth Brooks	*No Fences*	1990
2	Garth Brooks	*Ropin' the Wind*	1991
3	Billy Ray Cyrus	*Some Gave All*	1992
4	Garth Brooks	*In Pieces*	1993
5	Garth Brooks	*Garth Brooks*	1990
6	Garth Brooks	*The Hits*	1995
7	Garth Brooks	*The Chase*	1992
8	Patsy Cline	*Greatest Hits*	1987
9	Brooks & Dunn	*Brand New Man*	1991
10	Alabama	*Feels So Right*	1981

Source: Based on information given in *The Top 10 of Everything 1997*

Top 5 Most Popular Kinds of U.S. Radio Stations

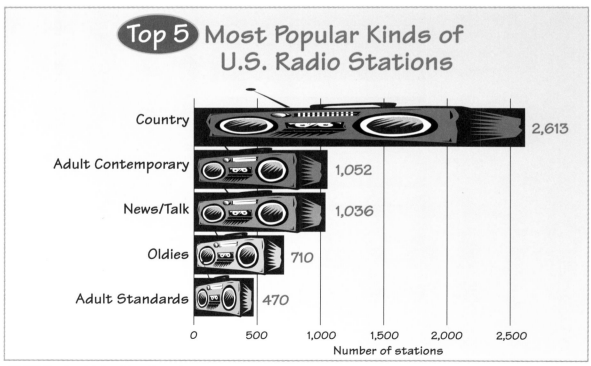

Kind	Number of stations
Country	2,613
Adult Contemporary	1,052
News/Talk	1,036
Oldies	710
Adult Standards	470

Number of stations

SOURCE: Based on data from Interep Research

Top Teen Radio Station Formats

(By percentage of teens who listed format as "favorite")

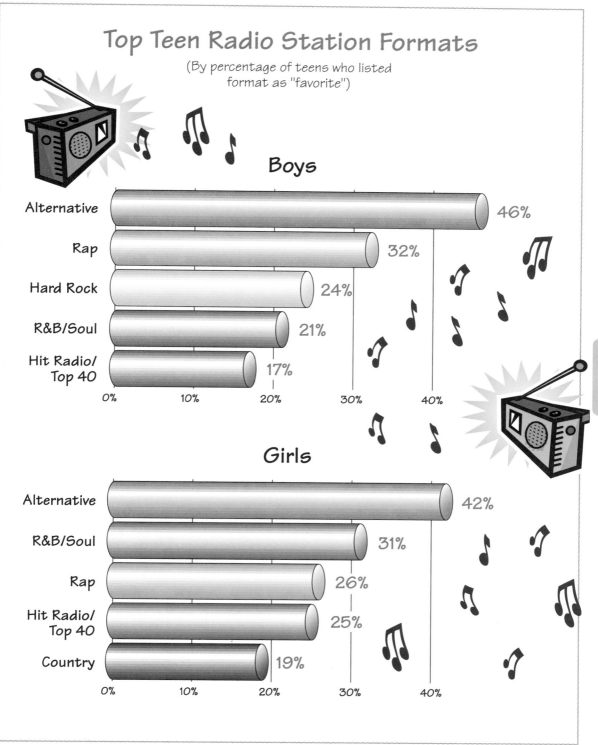

Boys

Format	%
Alternative	46%
Rap	32%
Hard Rock	24%
R&B/Soul	21%
Hit Radio/Top 40	17%

0% 10% 20% 30% 40%

Girls

Format	%
Alternative	42%
R&B/Soul	31%
Rap	26%
Hit Radio/Top 40	25%
Country	19%

0% 10% 20% 30% 40%

Music

SOURCE: Based on data from Teenage Research Unlimited, Inc.

Music

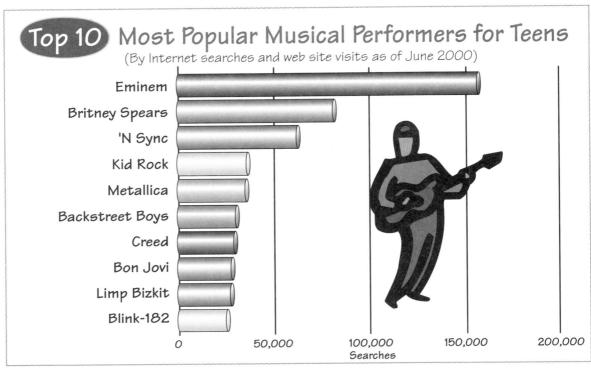

Top 10 Most Popular Musical Performers for Teens
(By Internet searches and web site visits as of June 2000)

Eminem
Britney Spears
'N Sync
Kid Rock
Metallica
Backstreet Boys
Creed
Bon Jovi
Limp Bizkit
Blink-182

0   50,000   100,000   150,000   200,000
Searches

SOURCE: Based on data from Listen.com

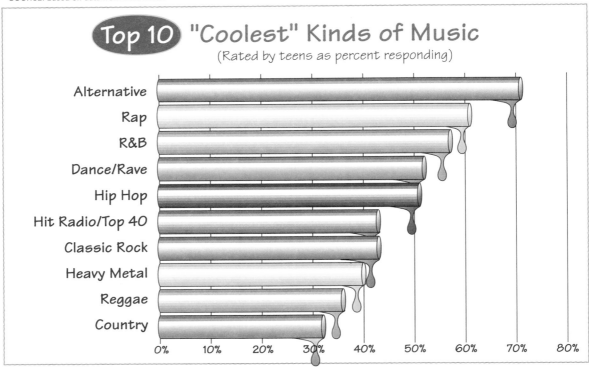

Top 10 "Coolest" Kinds of Music
(Rated by teens as percent responding)

Alternative
Rap
R&B
Dance/Rave
Hip Hop
Hit Radio/Top 40
Classic Rock
Heavy Metal
Reggae
Country

0%   10%   20%   30%   40%   50%   60%   70%   80%

SOURCE: Based on data from Teenage Research Unlimited, Inc.

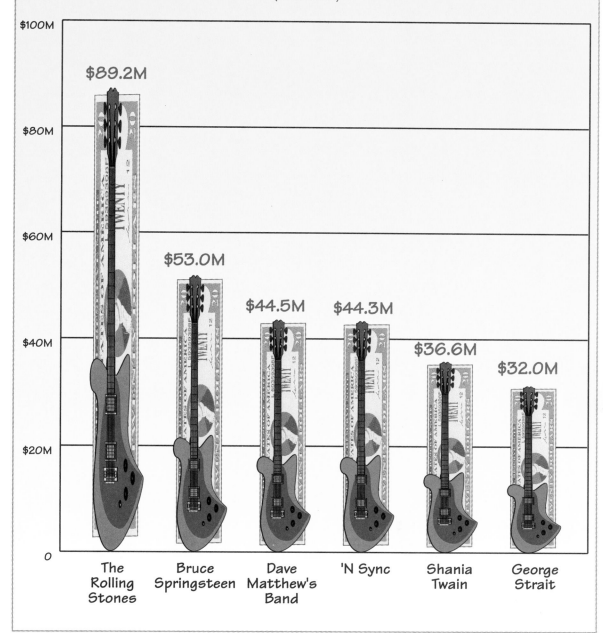

Top Worldwide Tour Moneymakers, 1999

Top-name music groups collectively brought in more than $1 billion in revenues from touring in 1999.

(In millions)

SOURCE: Based on data from Amusement Business

Music

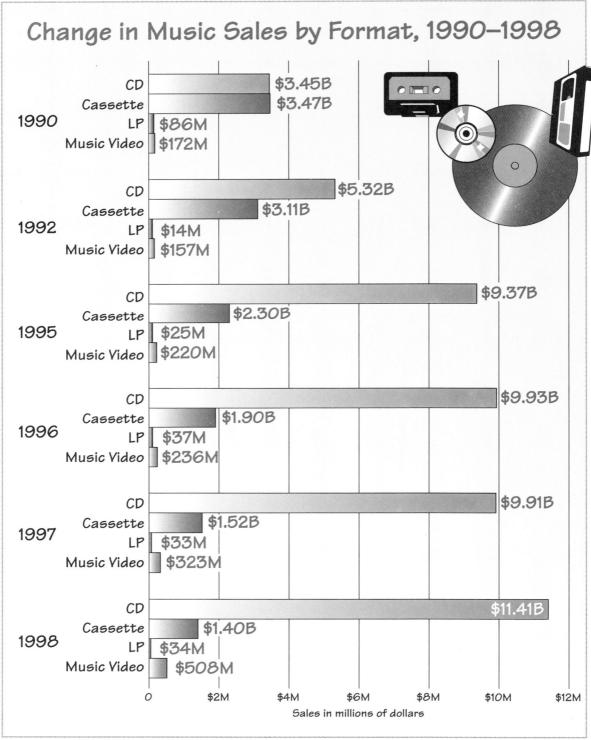

Change in Music Sales by Format, 1990–1998

1990
- CD — $3.45B
- Cassette — $3.47B
- LP — $86M
- Music Video — $172M

1992
- CD — $5.32B
- Cassette — $3.11B
- LP — $14M
- Music Video — $157M

1995
- CD — $9.37B
- Cassette — $2.30B
- LP — $25M
- Music Video — $220M

1996
- CD — $9.93B
- Cassette — $1.90B
- LP — $37M
- Music Video — $236M

1997
- CD — $9.91B
- Cassette — $1.52B
- LP — $33M
- Music Video — $323M

1998
- CD — $11.41B
- Cassette — $1.40B
- LP — $34M
- Music Video — $508M

0   $2M $4M $6M $8M $10M $12M

Sales in millions of dollars

Music

SOURCE: Based on data from Recording Industry Association of America

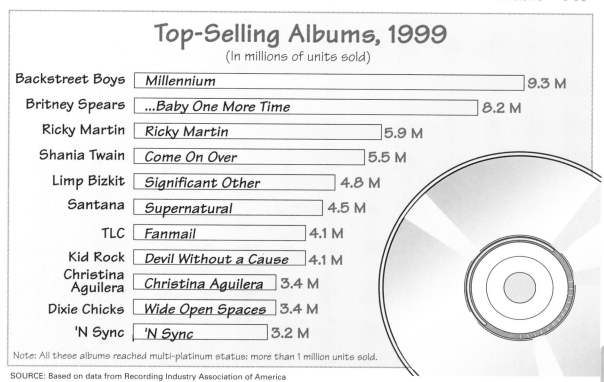

Top-Selling Albums, 1999

(In millions of units sold)

Backstreet Boys	Millennium	9.3 M
Britney Spears	...Baby One More Time	8.2 M
Ricky Martin	Ricky Martin	5.9 M
Shania Twain	Come On Over	5.5 M
Limp Bizkit	Significant Other	4.8 M
Santana	Supernatural	4.5 M
TLC	Fanmail	4.1 M
Kid Rock	Devil Without a Cause	4.1 M
Christina Aguilera	Christina Aguilera	3.4 M
Dixie Chicks	Wide Open Spaces	3.4 M
'N Sync	'N Sync	3.2 M

Note: All these albums reached multi-platinum status: more than 1 million units sold.

SOURCE: Based on data from Recording Industry Association of America

Music

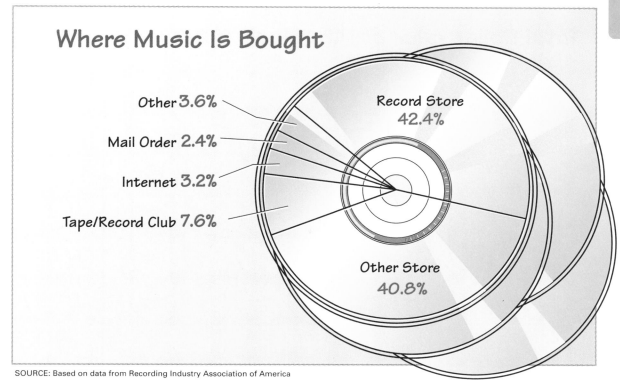

Where Music Is Bought

Other 3.6%

Mail Order 2.4%

Internet 3.2%

Tape/Record Club 7.6%

Record Store 42.4%

Other Store 40.8%

SOURCE: Based on data from Recording Industry Association of America

Music

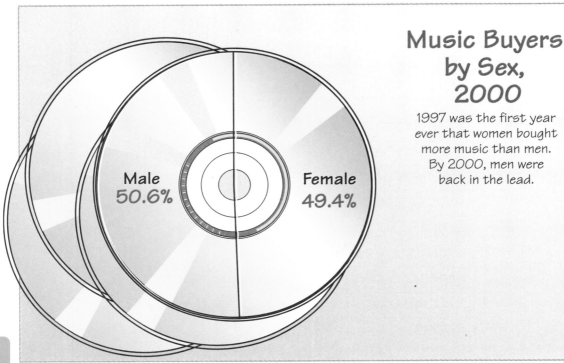

Music Buyers by Sex, 2000

1997 was the first year ever that women bought more music than men. By 2000, men were back in the lead.

Male 50.6%

Female 49.4%

SOURCE: Based on data from Recording Industry Association of America, 2000

Total Dollar Value of U.S. Music Sales, 1991-2000

(In billions of dollars)

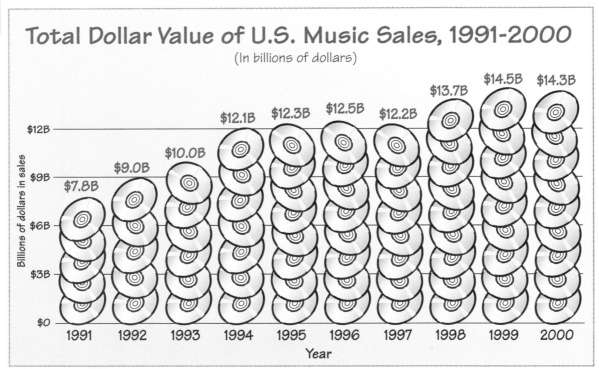

Billions of dollars in sales

$12B — $9B — $6B — $3B — $0

Year	1991	1992	1993	1994	1995	1996	1997	1998	1999	2000
	$7.8B	$9.0B	$10.0B	$12.1B	$12.3B	$12.5B	$12.2B	$13.7B	$14.5B	$14.3B

Year

SOURCE: Based on data from Recording Industry Association of America, 2000

Selected MTV Video Music Awards, 1990-2000
Best Video

Year	Artist	Video
2000	Eminem	The Real Slim Shady
1999	Lauryn Hill	Doo-Wop (That Thing)
1998	Madonna	Ray of Light
1997	Jamiroquai	Virtual Insanity
1996	Smashing Pumpkins	Tonight, Tonight
1995	TLC	Waterfalls
1994	Aerosmith	Cryin'
1993	Pearl Jam	Jeremy
1992	Van Halen	Right Now
1991	R.E.M.	Losing My Religion
1990	Sinead O'Connor	Nothing Compares to You

SOURCE: Based on data from Press Department, MTV Networks

Music

Selected MTV Video Music Awards, 1990-2000
Best Male Video

Year	Artist	Video
2000	Eminem	The Real Slim Shady
1999	Will Smith	Miami
1998	Will Smith	Just the Two of Us
1997	Beck	Devil's Haircut
1996	Beck	Where It's At
1995	Tom Petty and the Heartbreakers	You Don't Know How it Feels
1994	Tom Petty and the Heartbreakers	Mary Jane's Last Dance
1993	Lenny Kravitz	Are You Gonna Go My Way
1992	Eric Clapton	Tears in Heaven
1991	Chris Isaak	Wicked Game
1990	Don Henley	End of the Innocence

SOURCE: Based on data from Press Department, MTV Networks

Music

Selected MTV Video Music Awards, 1990-2000
Best Female Video

Year	Artist	Video
2000	Aaliyah	Try Again
1999	Lauryn Hill	Doo-Wop (That Thing)
1998	Madonna	Ray of Light
1997	Jewel	You Were Meant For Me
1996	Alanis Morissette	Ironic
1995	Madonna	Take a Bow
1994	Janet Jackson	If
1993	k.d. lang	Constant Craving
1992	Annie Lennox	Why
1991	Janet Jackson	Love Will Never Do Without You
1990	Sinead O'Connor	Nothing Compares to You

SOURCE: Based on data from Press Department, MTV Networks

Selected MTV Video Music Awards, 1990-2000
Best Group Video

Year	Artist	Video
2000	Blink-182	All the Small Things
1999	TLC	No Secrets
1998	Backstreet Boys	Everybody
1997	No Doubt	Don't Speak
1996	Foo Fighters	Big Me
1995	TLC	Waterfalls
1994	Aerosmith	Cryin'
1993	Pearl Jam	Jeremy
1992	U2	Even Better Than the Real Thing
1991	R.E.M.	Losing My Religion
1990	B-52s	Love Shack

SOURCE: Based on data from Press Department, MTV Networks

Selected MTV Video Music Awards, 1990-2000
Best New Artist in a Video

Year	Artist	Video
2000	Macy Gray	I Try
1999	Eminem	My Name Is
1998	Natalie Imbruglia	Torn
1997	Fiona Apple	Sleep to Dream
1996	Alanis Morissette	Ironic
1995	Hootie & the Blowfish	Hold My Hand
1994	Counting Crows	Mr. Jones
1993	Stone Temple Pilots	Plush
1992	Nirvana	Smells Like Teen Spirit
1991	Jesus Jones	Right Here, Right Now
1990	Michael Penn	No Myth

SOURCE: Based on data from Press Department, MTV Networks

Music

Selected Grammy Winners, 1990–2000
Record of the Year

Year	Artist	Record
2000	U2	Beautiful Day
1999	Santana	Smooth
1998	Celine Dion	My Heart Will Go On
1997	Shawn Colvin	Sunny Came Home
1996	Eric Clapton	Change the World
1995	Seal	Kiss From a Rose
1994	Sheryl Crow	All I Wanna Do
1993	Whitney Houston	I Will Always Love You
1992	Eric Clapton	Tears in Heaven
1991	Natalie Cole	Unforgettable
1990	Phil Collins	Another Day in Paradise

SOURCE: Based on data from National Academy of Recording Arts and Sciences

Music

Selected Grammy Winners, 1990–2000
Album of the Year

Year	Artist	Album
2000	Steely Dan	Two Against Nature
1999	Santana	Supernatural
1998	Lauryn Hill	The Miseducation of Lauryn Hill
1997	Bob Dylan	Time Out of Mind
1996	Celine Dion	Falling Into You
1995	Alanis Morissette	Jagged Little Pill
1994	Tony Bennett	MTV Unplugged
1993	Whitney Houston	The Bodyguard
1992	Eric Clapton	MTV Unplugged
1991	Natalie Cole	Unforgettable
1990	Quincy Jones	Back on the Block

SOURCE: Based on data from National Academy of Recording Arts and Sciences

Selected Grammy Winners, 1990–2000
Song of the Year

Year	Artist	Song
2000	U2	Beautiful Day
1999	Itaal Shur and Rob Thomas	Smooth
1998	Will Jennings	My Heart Will Go On
1997	Shawn Colvin	Sunny Came Home
1996	Wayne Kirkpatrick & Tommy Sims	Change the World
1995	Seal	Kiss From a Rose
1994	Bruce Springsteen	Streets of Philadelphia
1993	Alan Menken & Tim Rice	A Whole New World (Aladdin's Theme)
1992	Eric Clapton	Tears in Heaven
1991	Irving Gordon	Unforgettable
1990	Julie Gold	From a Distance

SOURCE: Based on data from National Academy of Recording Arts and Sciences

Selected Grammy Winners, 1990–2000
Best Male Vocal Performance

Year	Artist	Performance
2000	Sting	She Walks This Earth (Soberana Rosa)
1999	Sting	Brand New Day
1998	Eric Clapton	My Father's Eyes
1997	Elton John	Candle in the Wind 1997
1996	Eric Clapton	Change the World
1995	Seal	Kiss From a Rose
1994	Elton John	Can You Feel the Love Tonight
1993	Sting	If I Ever Lose My Faith in You
1992	Eric Clapton	Tears in Heaven
1991	Michael Bolton	When a Man Loves a Woman
1990	Roy Orbison	Oh, Pretty Woman

SOURCE: Based on data from National Academy of Recording Arts and Sciences

Selected Grammy Winners, 1990–2000
Best Female Vocal Performance

Year	Artist	Performance
2000	Macy Gray	I Try
1999	Sarah McLachlan	I Will Remember You
1998	Celine Dion	My Heart Will Go On
1997	Sarah McLachlan	Building a Mystery
1996	Toni Braxton	Unbreak My Heart
1995	Annie Lennox	No More "I Love Yous"
1994	Sheryl Crow	All I Wanna Do
1993	Whitney Houston	I Will Always Love You
1992	k.d. lang	Constant Craving
1991	Bonnie Raitt	Something to Talk About
1990	Mariah Carey	Vision of Love

SOURCE: Based on data from National Academy of Recording Arts and Sciences

Music

Television

Almost every U.S. home has at least one color television set. Most have two or more sets. And these sets are busy! On average, a home has at least one TV on for more than 7 hours every day. The typical American watches about 4 hours of television daily. On average, adults watch more TV than children do.

Most viewing time is spent watching shows on the major networks, such as ABC, CBS, FOX, and NBC. Cable networks, such as ESPN and CNN, haven't been around as long, but they have been growing in popularity. By 1999, a total of 68% of U.S. homes with television sets subscribed to basic cable services. Of those, the top pay channel—by far—is HBO. The next big thing in television is high-definition television, or HDTV. This technology brings wide-screen, super-sharp pictures into the average home, complete with six-channel "surround sound."

Kids enjoy all kinds of programs, including comedies, cartoons, movies, and animal shows. Sports—from football games to ice-skating competitions—are among the most popular shows. If a show includes young people, so much the better. Nickelodeon's

Kidbits Tidbits

- 98% of U.S. homes have at least one color TV set.
- In 1999, about 91% of U.S. homes had at least one VCR.
- Children ages 2 to 11 watch about 3 hours of television a day. Those ages 12 to 17 watch almost as much.
- In early 1998, "E.R." was the #1 show among whites, but ranked #18 with blacks. "Between Brothers" was the most popular show among blacks, and #107 among whites.

series "The Secret Life of Alex Mack" became a hit because of its 16-year-old star, Larisa Oleynik. And Rosie O'Donnell's show drew lots of young viewers when Justin Miller—who published his first cookbook in 1997 at age 7—was on the air whipping up a batch of cookies.

Television use is monitored by the A.C. Nielsen Company. If a show has a Nielsen rating of 12, it was watched by 12% of all television owners. During the 1999–00 season, America's top-rated show was "Who Wants to Be a Millionaire." It had a rating of 18.6. It was followed by "E.R." at 16.9 and "Frasier" at 14.0.

Most TV programs are paid for by companies that buy advertising time. The bigger the audience a program gets, the more companies are willing to pay to advertise their products during its commercial breaks. For example, it cost an average of $1.3 million for a 30-second ad during the 1998 Super Bowl, an event that drew as many as 140 million viewers. Why do companies pay so much? Can you think of another way to get the attention of 140 million people all at once for 30 seconds?

In addition to TVs, the great majority of U.S. homes have at least one VCR. Most people use their VCRs to watch rental videos. But Americans also bought a total of 392 million blank cassettes in 1996—to record TV shows, family parties, vacations, high school games, and so on.

Kidbits Tidbits

- Basic cable systems had more than 67 million subscribers in 1999.
- The pay-cable service with the most subscribers in 1999 was Home Box Office. The Disney Channel was second.
- In 1980, the average monthly cable bill was $7.69. In 1999, it was $26.48.
- HDTV uses digital signals, just like a computer. Conventional TVs use analog waves for broadcasting.
- About 40% of children ages 6–11 have a television in their bedroom. Boys, on average, watch TV for 50 hours more than girls each year.

Television

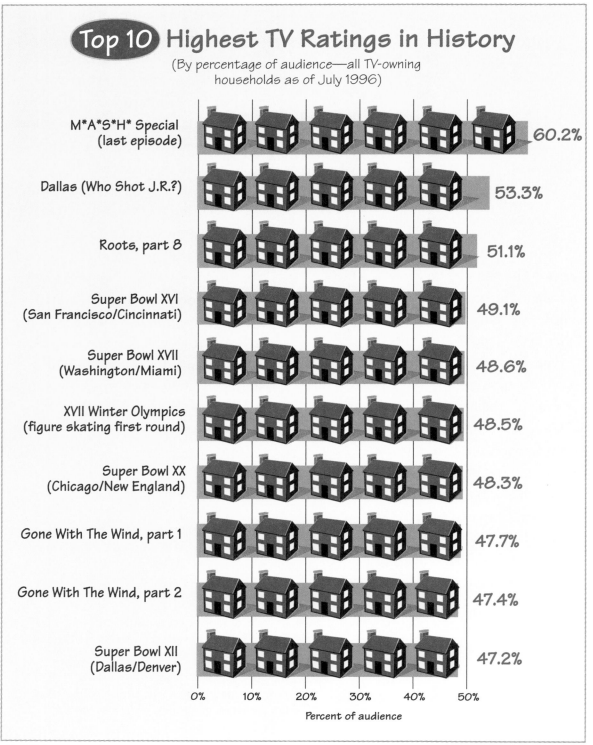

Top 10 Highest TV Ratings in History

(By percentage of audience—all TV-owning households as of July 1996)

	Percent of audience
M*A*S*H* Special (last episode)	60.2%
Dallas (Who Shot J.R.?)	53.3%
Roots, part 8	51.1%
Super Bowl XVI (San Francisco/Cincinnati)	49.1%
Super Bowl XVII (Washington/Miami)	48.6%
XVII Winter Olympics (figure skating first round)	48.5%
Super Bowl XX (Chicago/New England)	48.3%
Gone With The Wind, part 1	47.7%
Gone With The Wind, part 2	47.4%
Super Bowl XII (Dallas/Denver)	47.2%

0% 10% 20% 30% 40% 50%

Percent of audience

SOURCE: Based on data from Nielsen Media Research

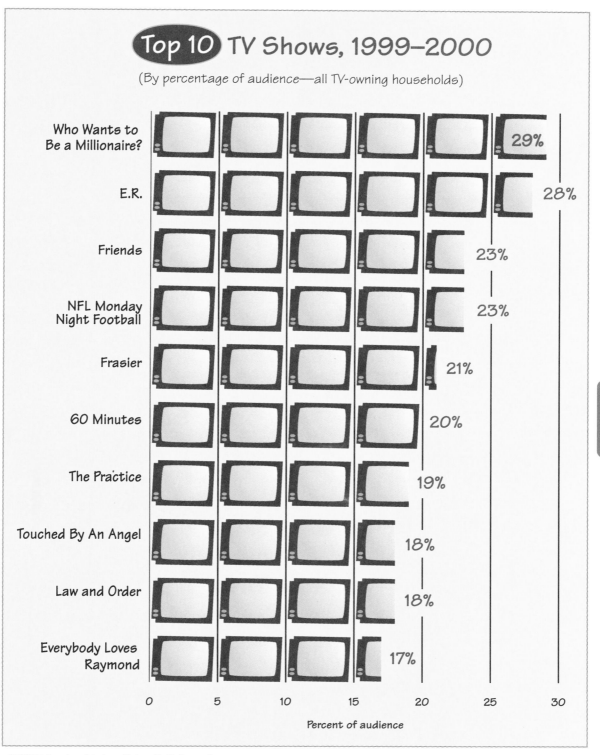

Top 10 TV Shows, 1999–2000

(By percentage of audience—all TV-owning households)

Show	Percent
Who Wants to Be a Millionaire?	29%
E.R.	28%
Friends	23%
NFL Monday Night Football	23%
Frasier	21%
60 Minutes	20%
The Practice	19%
Touched By An Angel	18%
Law and Order	18%
Everybody Loves Raymond	17%

Percent of audience

Television

SOURCE: Based on data from Nielsen Media Research

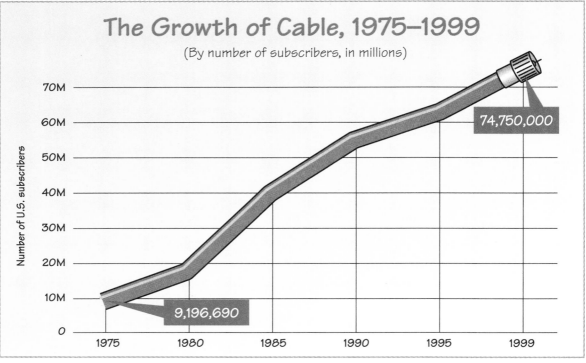

The Growth of Cable, 1975–1999
(By number of subscribers, in millions)

Number of U.S. subscribers

70M — 60M — 50M — 40M — 30M — 20M — 10M — 0

1975   1980   1985   1990   1995   1999

74,750,000

9,196,690

SOURCE: Based on data from National Cable Television Association

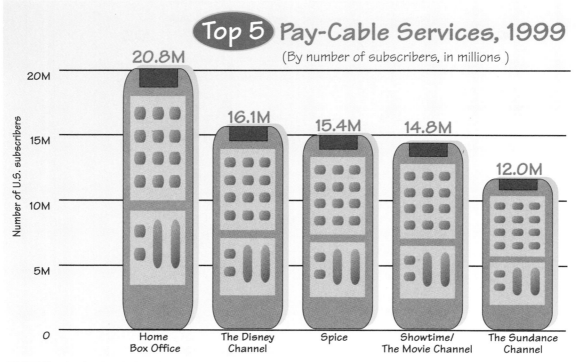

Top 5 Pay-Cable Services, 1999
(By number of subscribers, in millions)

Number of U.S. subscribers

20M — 15M — 10M — 5M — 0

Home Box Office	The Disney Channel	Spice	Showtime/ The Movie Channel	The Sundance Channel
20.8M	16.1M	15.4M	14.8M	12.0M

SOURCE: Based on data from National Cable Television Association

Top 10 Cable TV Networks, 1999

Network	Number of subscribers (In millions)
1. TBS Superstation	78.0
2. The Discovery Channel	77.4
3. USA Network	77.2
4. ESPN	77.1
5. C-SPAN	77.0
6. Cable Network News (CNN)	77.0
7. Turner Network Television	76.8
8. Nickelodeon	76.0
9. Fox Family Channel	75.7
10. Lifetime Television	75.0

SOURCE: Based on data from National Cable Television Association

Average Kids and Teens TV Viewing Time
(Per week)

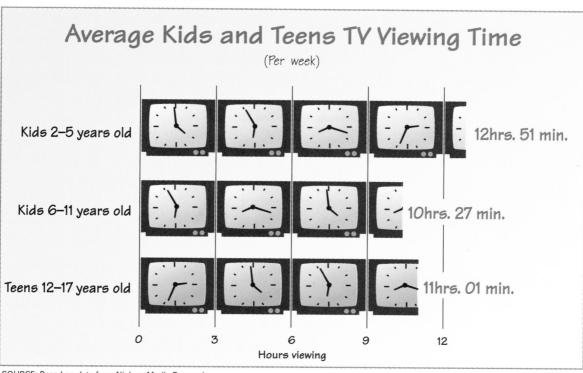

Kids 2–5 years old — 12hrs. 51 min.

Kids 6–11 years old — 10hrs. 27 min.

Teens 12–17 years old — 11hrs. 01 min.

0 3 6 9 12
Hours viewing

SOURCE: Based on data from Nielsen Media Research

Television

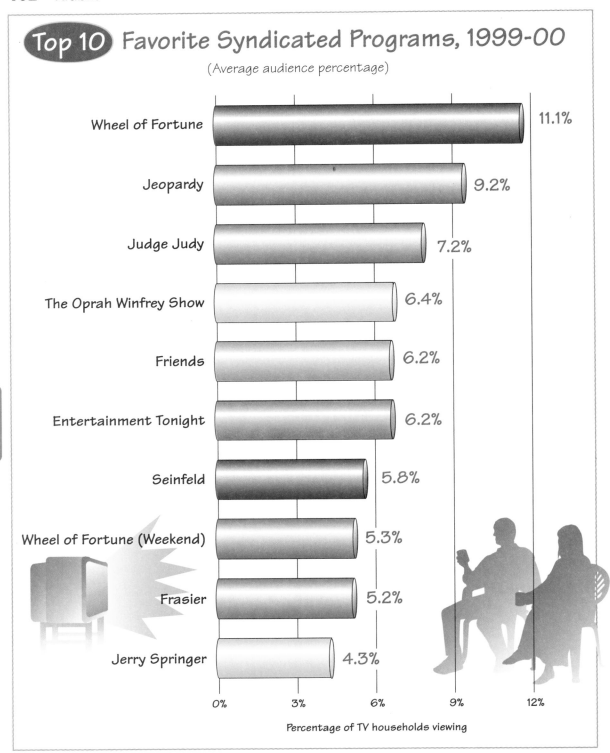

Top 10 Favorite Syndicated Programs, 1999-00

(Average audience percentage)

Television

Program	Percentage
Wheel of Fortune	11.1%
Jeopardy	9.2%
Judge Judy	7.2%
The Oprah Winfrey Show	6.4%
Friends	6.2%
Entertainment Tonight	6.2%
Seinfeld	5.8%
Wheel of Fortune (Weekend)	5.3%
Frasier	5.2%
Jerry Springer	4.3%

0%   3%   6%   9%   12%

Percentage of TV households viewing

SOURCE: Based on data from Nielsen Media Research

Getting Wired: U.S. Households With Cable TV

(Percentage of homes with TVs getting cable 1977–1996)

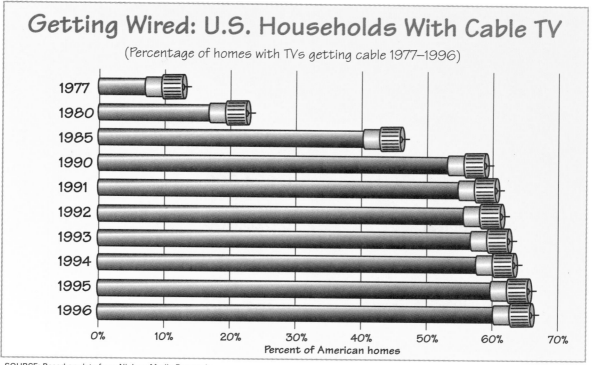

SOURCE: Based on data from Nielsen Media Research

Top 10 Most Popular Cartoon Charactors for 6–11-Year-Olds

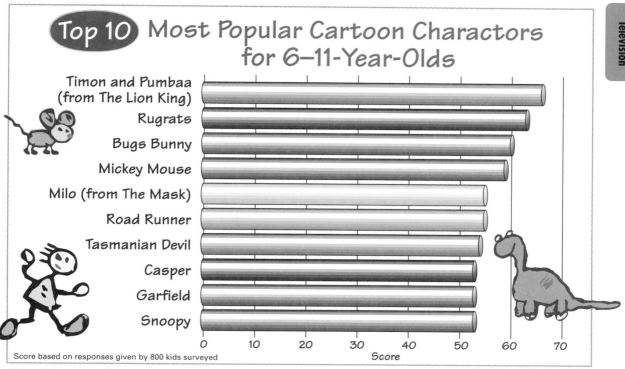

Score based on responses given by 800 kids surveyed

SOURCE: Based on data from Marketing Evaluations/TVQ

Television

Top 5 Most-Watched U.S. Daytime Soap Operas

Program	Number of Households viewing	Percentage of Households viewing
The Young and the Restless	8,084,000	8.6%
All My Children	6,204,000	6.6%
General Hospital	5,828,000	6.2%
The Bold and the Beautiful	5,730,000	6.1%
As the World Turns	5,452,000	5.8%

SOURCE: Based on data from Nielsen Media Research

Top 5 Most Watched U.S. Sports Events of All Time

Program	Number of Households viewing	Percentage of Households viewing
Super Bowl XVI San Francisco vs. Cincinnati	40,020,000	49.1%
Super Bowl XVII Washington vs. Miami	40,500,000	48.6%
XVII Winter Olympics	45,690,000	48.5%
Super Bowl XX Chicago vs. New England	41,490,000	48.3%
Super Bowl XII Dallas vs. Denver	34,410,000	47.2%

SOURCE: Based on data from Nielsen Media Research

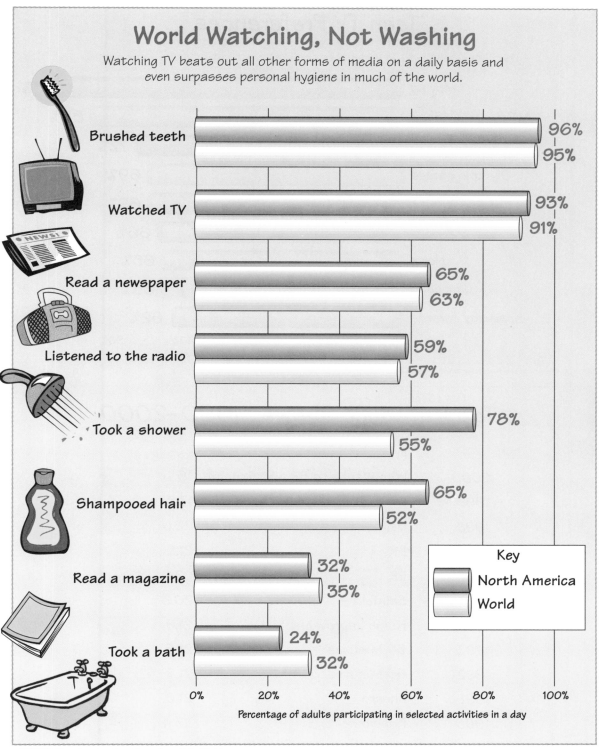

World Watching, Not Washing

Watching TV beats out all other forms of media on a daily basis and even surpasses personal hygiene in much of the world.

Activity	North America	World
Brushed teeth	96%	95%
Watched TV	93%	91%
Read a newspaper	65%	63%
Listened to the radio	59%	57%
Took a shower	78%	55%
Shampooed hair	65%	52%
Read a magazine	32%	35%
Took a bath	24%	32%

Key
North America
World

0%   20%   40%   60%   80%   100%

Percentage of adults participating in selected activities in a day

Television

SOURCE: Based on data from Roper Starch Worldwide

Television

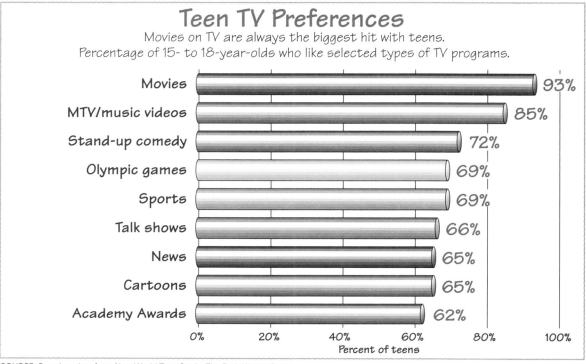

Teen TV Preferences

Movies on TV are always the biggest hit with teens.
Percentage of 15- to 18-year-olds who like selected types of TV programs.

Program	Percent
Movies	93%
MTV/music videos	85%
Stand-up comedy	72%
Olympic games	69%
Sports	69%
Talk shows	66%
News	65%
Cartoons	65%
Academy Awards	62%

Percent of teens

SOURCE: Based on data from New World Teen Study, The BrainWaves Group

Top Rated TV Shows, 1990–2000

Year	Program	Rating
2000	Who Wants to Be a Millionaire	18.6
1999	ER	17.8
1998	Seinfeld	22.0
1997	ER	21.2
1996	ER	22.0
1995	Seinfeld	20.5
1994	Home Improvement	21.9
1993	60 Minutes	21.6
1992	60 Minutes	21.7
1991	Cheers	21.6
1990	Roseanne	23.4

SOURCE: Nielsen Media Research

Top 10 Favorite Programs for Younger Viewers
(All hours, 1998–99)

Rank	Program	Network
1	Wild Thornberries	Nickelodeon
2	Rugrats	Nickelodeon
3	Cousin Skeeter	Nickelodeon
4	Hey Arnold	Nickelodeon
5	Disney's Saturday Morning 3	ABC
6	Disney's Saturday Morning 4	ABC
7	Saturday Nicktoons TV	Nickelodeon
8	Disney's Saturday Morning 2	ABC
9	Kenan & Kel	Nickelodeon
10	Angry Beavers	Nickelodeon

SOURCE: Based on data from Nielsen Media Research

Who Watches the Most Sports?
(Percentage of broadcast markets)

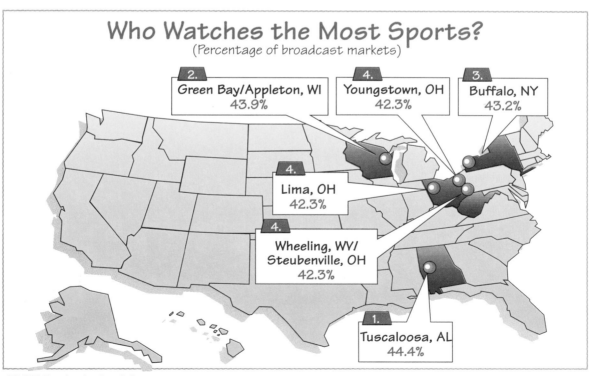

2. Green Bay/Appleton, WI 43.9%

4. Youngstown, OH 42.3%

3. Buffalo, NY 43.2%

4. Lima, OH 42.3%

4. Wheeling, WV/ Steubenville, OH 42.3%

1. Tuscaloosa, AL 44.4%

SOURCE: Based on data from Polk

TV Tidbits

Number of violent acts children see on TV before the age of 18: 200,000.

Number of 30-second commercials the average child sees in a year: 20,000.

Percentage of parents who would like to limit their children's time in front of the TV: 73%

By the time a child is 70, he or she will have spent 9 years watching TV.

Some 66% of homes have three or more TV sets.

Americans watch 250 billion hours of TV a year.

Americans rent 6 million videos a day.

About 70% of daycare centers run a TV during part of the day.

By age 65, the average person has seen 2 million commercials.

About 66% of families watch TV while eating dinner.

Television

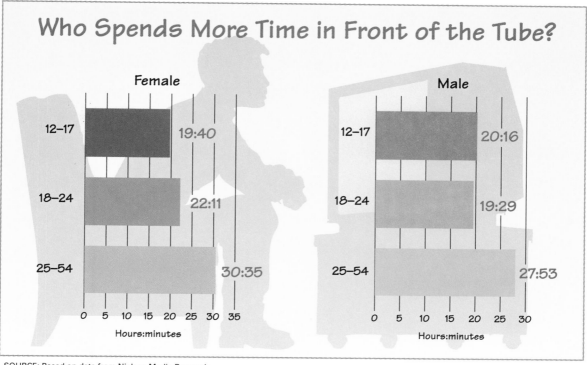

Who Spends More Time in Front of the Tube?

Female

Age	Time
12–17	19:40
18–24	22:11
25–54	30:35

0 5 10 15 20 25 30 35

Hours:minutes

Male

Age	Time
12–17	20:16
18–24	19:29
25–54	27:53

0 5 10 15 20 25 30

Hours:minutes

SOURCE: Based on data from Nielsen Media Research

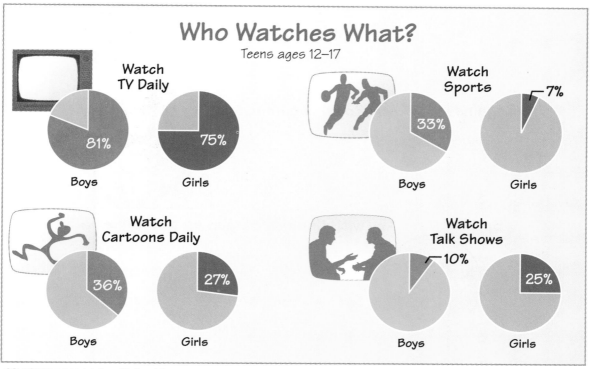

Who Watches What?

Teens ages 12–17

Watch TV Daily

Boys 81% Girls 75%

Watch Sports

Boys 33% Girls 7%

Watch Cartoons Daily

Boys 36% Girls 27%

Watch Talk Shows

Boys 10% Girls 25%

SOURCE: Based on data from Mediawatch

Television

Television

Teens Top 5 Least-Favorite TV Commercials

| Mentos | Any Mentos commercial |

| McDonald's | Arch Deluxe commercial |

| Budweiser | Budweiser frog commercials |

| Rogaine | Any Rogaine commercial |

| Sprint | Any with Candice Bergen as the "Dime Lady" |

SOURCE: Based on data from Teenage Research Unlimited, Inc.

Favorite Teen TV Commercials

75% of teens' favorite commercials are for food products.

Budweiser — Frog commercials

Pepsi — Goldfish plays dead for Pepsi

Milk — Man gets called by radio station ("Aaron Burr")

M&M's — With Red and Yellow M&M characters

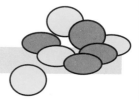

Television

McDonald's — Baby in swing cries when can't see McDonald's sign

Edy's Ice Cream — Baby boy gets up and starts dancing for Edy's Ice Cream

Nike — Lil' Penny

Polaroid — Dog takes picture of cat getting into garbage can

SOURCE: Based on data from Teenage Research Unlimited, Inc.

Television

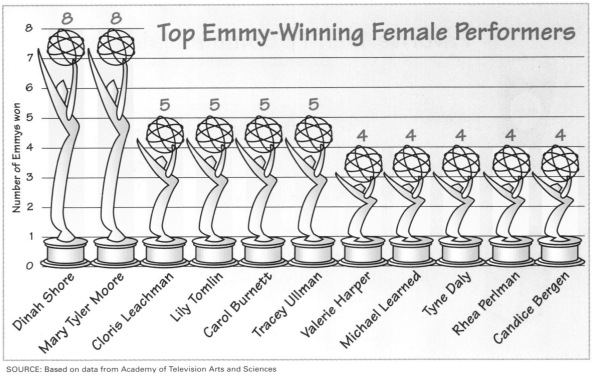

Top Emmy-Winning Female Performers

Number of Emmys won

SOURCE: Based on data from Academy of Television Arts and Sciences

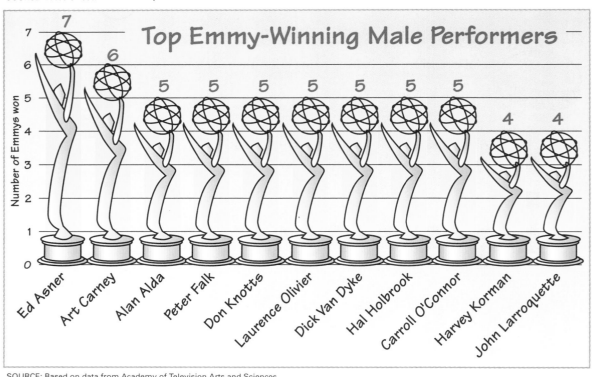

Top Emmy-Winning Male Performers

Number of Emmys won

SOURCE: Based on data from Academy of Television Arts and Sciences

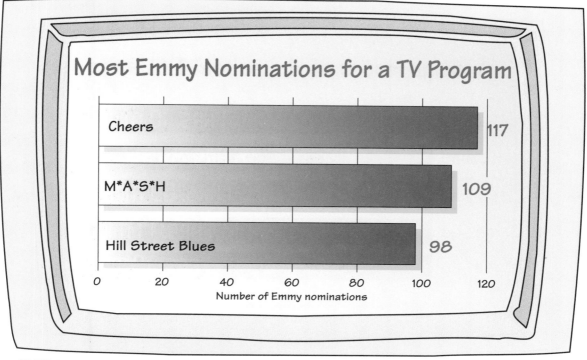

Most Emmy Nominations for a TV Program

Cheers — 117
M*A*S*H — 109
Hill Street Blues — 98

Number of Emmy nominations

SOURCE: Based on data from Academy of Television Arts and Sciences

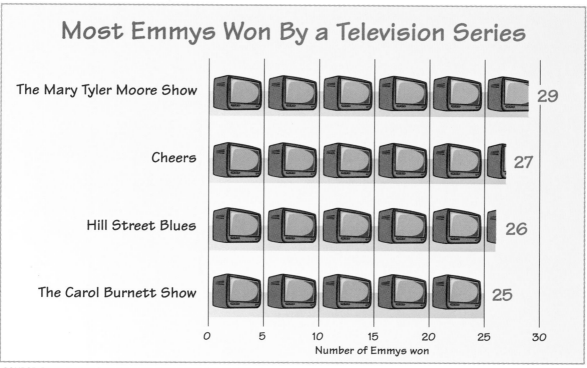

Most Emmys Won By a Television Series

The Mary Tyler Moore Show — 29
Cheers — 27
Hill Street Blues — 26
The Carol Burnett Show — 25

Number of Emmys won

SOURCE: Based on data from Academy of Television Arts and Sciences

Television

Television

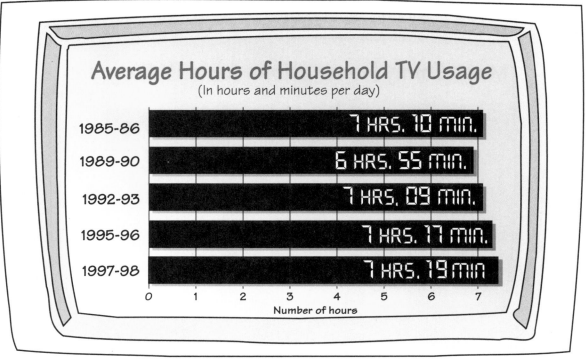

Average Hours of Household TV Usage
(In hours and minutes per day)

1985-86	7 HRS. 10 min.
1989-90	6 HRS. 55 min.
1992-93	7 HRS. 09 min.
1995-96	7 HRS. 17 min.
1997-98	7 HRS. 19 min

Number of hours

SOURCE: Based on data from Nielsen Media Research

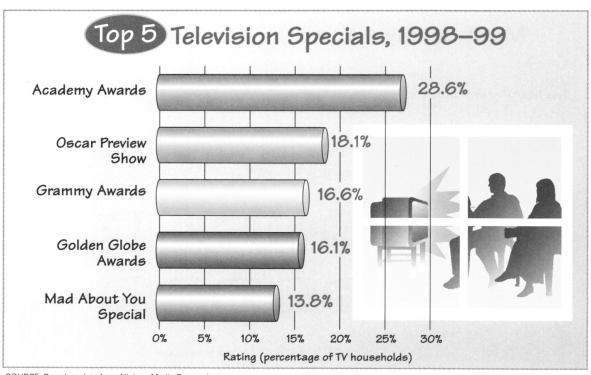

Top 5 Television Specials, 1998–99

Special	Rating
Academy Awards	28.6%
Oscar Preview Show	18.1%
Grammy Awards	16.6%
Golden Globe Awards	16.1%
Mad About You Special	13.8%

Rating (percentage of TV households)

SOURCE: Based on data from Nielsen Media Research

Who Watches What?

(Average audience)

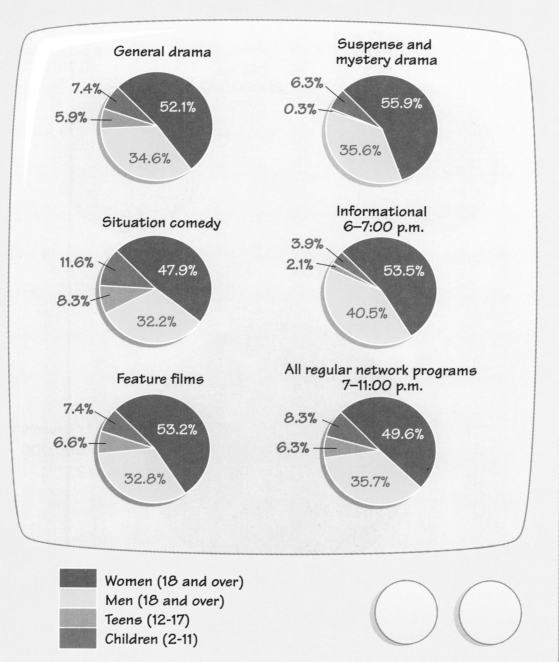

General drama
- 52.1%
- 34.6%
- 7.4%
- 5.9%

Suspense and mystery drama
- 55.9%
- 35.6%
- 6.3%
- 0.3%

Situation comedy
- 47.9%
- 32.2%
- 11.6%
- 8.3%

Informational 6–7:00 p.m.
- 53.5%
- 40.5%
- 3.9%
- 2.1%

Feature films
- 53.2%
- 32.8%
- 7.4%
- 6.6%

All regular network programs 7–11:00 p.m.
- 49.6%
- 35.7%
- 8.3%
- 6.3%

Women (18 and over)
Men (18 and over)
Teens (12-17)
Children (2-11)

Television

SOURCE: Based on data from Nielsen Media Research

U.S. Television Ownership, 1997
(By household)

Color TV sets
82,350,000
85%

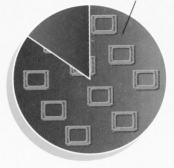

One set
25,220,000
27%

2 or more sets
71,780,000
73%

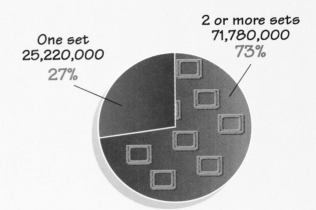

Television

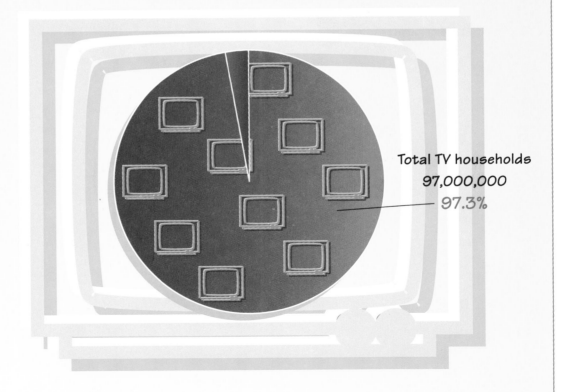

Total TV households
97,000,000
97.3%

SOURCE: Based on data from Nielsen Media Research

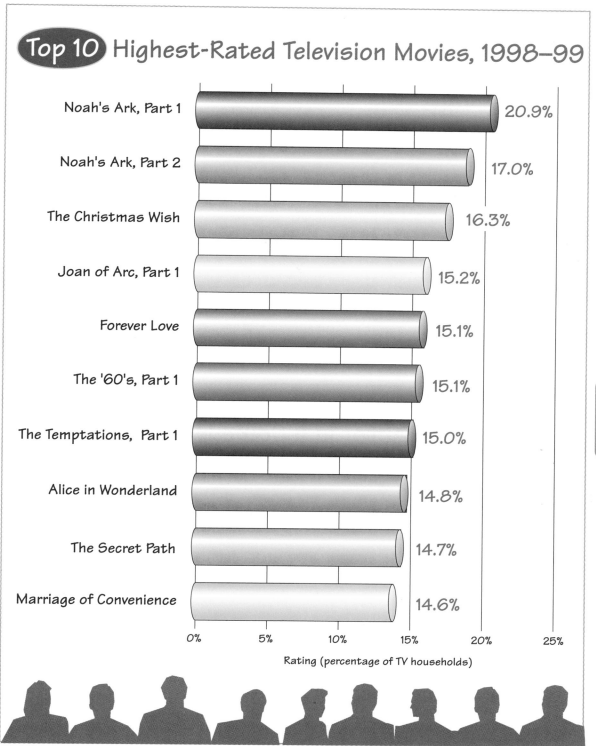

Top 10 Highest-Rated Television Movies, 1998–99

Movie	Rating
Noah's Ark, Part 1	20.9%
Noah's Ark, Part 2	17.0%
The Christmas Wish	16.3%
Joan of Arc, Part 1	15.2%
Forever Love	15.1%
The '60's, Part 1	15.1%
The Temptations, Part 1	15.0%
Alice in Wonderland	14.8%
The Secret Path	14.7%
Marriage of Convenience	14.6%

Rating (percentage of TV households)

Television

SOURCE: Based on data from Nielsen Media Research

Emmy Winners, 1990-2000
Lead Actress in a Comedy Series

Year	Actress	Character	Program
2000	Patricia Heaton	Debra Barone	Everybody Loves Raymond
1999	Helen Hunt	Jamie Buchman	Mad About You
1998	Helen Hunt	Jamie Buchman	Mad About You
1997	Helen Hunt	Jamie Buchman	Mad About You
1996	Helen Hunt	Jamie Buchman	Mad About You
1995	Candice Bergen	Murphy Brown	Murphy Brown
1994	Candice Bergen	Murphy Brown	Murphy Brown
1993	Roseanne	Roseanne Arnold	Roseanne
1992	Candice Bergen	Murphy Brown	Murphy Brown
1991	Kirstie Alley	Rebecca Howe	Cheers
1990	Candice Bergen	Murphy Brown	Murphy Brown

SOURCE: Based on data from Academy of Television Arts and Sciences

Television

Emmy Winners, 1990–2000
Lead Actor in a Comedy Series

Year	Actor	Character	Program
2000	Michael J. Fox	Mike Flaherty	Spin City
1999	John Lithgow	Dick Solomon	3rd Rock from the Sun
1998	Kelsey Grammer	Dr. Frasier Crane	Frasier
1997	John Lithgow	Dick Solomon	3rd Rock From the Sun
1996	John Lithgow	Dick Solomon	3rd Rock From the Sun
1995	Kelsey Grammer	Dr. Frasier Crane	Frasier
1994	Kelsey Grammer	Dr. Frasier Crane	Frasier
1993	Ted Danson	Sam Malone	Cheers
1992	Craig T. Nelson	Hayden Fox	Coach
1991	Burt Reynolds	Wood Newton	Evening Shade
1990	Ted Danson	Sam Malone	Cheers

SOURCE: Based on data from Academy of Television Arts and Sciences

Emmy Winners, 1990–2000
Lead Actress in a Drama Series

Year	Actress	Character	Program
2000	Sela Ward	Lily Manning	Once and Again
1999	Edie Falco	Carmella Soprano	The Sopranos
1998	Christine Lahti	Dr. Kathryn Austin	Chicago Hope
1997	Gillian Anderson	Agent Dana Scully	The X-Files
1996	Kathy Baker	Jill Brock	Picket Fences
1995	Kathy Baker	Jill Brock	Picket Fences
1994	Sela Ward	Teddy Reed	Sisters
1993	Kathy Baker	Jill Brock	Picket Fences
1992	Dana Delany	Colleen McMurphy	China Beach
1991	Patricia Wettig	Nancy Weston	Thirtysomething
1990	Patricia Wettig	Nancy Weston	Thirtysomething

SOURCE: Based on data from Academy of Television Arts and Sciences

Emmy Winners, 1990–2000
Lead Actor in a Drama Series

Year	Actor	Character	Program
2000	James Gandolfini	Tony Soprano	The Sopranos
1999	Dennis Franz	Detective Andy Sipowicz	NYPD Blue
1998	Andre Braugher	Detective Frank Pembleton	Homicide
1997	Dennis Franz	Detective Andy Sipowicz	NYPD Blue
1996	Dennis Franz	Detective Andy Sipowicz	NYPD Blue
1995	Mandy Patinkin	Dr. Jeffrey Geiger	Chicago Hope
1994	Dennis Franz	Detective Andy Sipowicz	NYPD Blue
1993	Tom Skerritt	Jimmy Brock	Picket Fences
1992	Christopher Lloyd	Alistair Dimple	Avonlea
1991	James Earl Jones	Gabriel Bird	Gabriel's Fire
1990	Peter Falk	Lieutenant Columbo	Columbo

SOURCE: Based on data from Academy of Television Arts and Sciences

Television

Emmy Winners, 1990–2000
Best Comedy Series

Year	Program
2000	Will & Grace
1999	Ally McBeal
1998	Frasier
1997	Frasier
1996	Frasier
1995	Frasier
1994	Frasier
1993	Seinfeld
1992	Murphy Brown
1991	Cheers
1990	Murphy Brown

SOURCE: Based on data from Academy of Television Arts and Sciences

Emmy Winners, 1990–2000
Best Drama Series

Year	Program
2000	The West Wing
1999	The Practice
1998	The Practice
1997	Law & Order
1996	E.R.
1995	NYPD Blue
1994	Picket Fences
1993	Picket Fences
1992	Northern Exposure
1991	L.A. Law
1990	L.A. Law

SOURCE: Based on data from Academy of Television Arts and Sciences

Emmy Winners, 1990–2000
Supporting Actor in a Comedy Series

Year	Actor	Character	Program
2000	Sean Hayes	Jack McFarland	Will & Grace
1999	David Hyde Pierce	Dr. Niles Crane	Frasier
1998	David Hyde Pierce	Dr. Niles Crane	Frasier
1997	Michael Richards	Kramer	Seinfeld
1996	Rip Torn	Arthur	The Larry Sanders Show
1995	David Hyde Pierce	Dr. Niles Crane	Frasier
1994	Michael Richards	Kramer	Seinfeld
1993	Michael Richards	Kramer	Seinfeld
1992	Michael Jeter	Herman Stiles	Evening Shade
1991	Jonathon Winters	Gunny Davies	Davis Rules
1990	Jay Thomas	Jerry Gold	Murphy Brown

SOURCE: Based on data from Academy of Television Arts and Sciences

Emmy Winners, 1990–2000
Supporting Actress in a Comedy Series

Year	Actress	Character	Program
2000	Megan Mullally	Karen Walker	Will & Grace
1999	Kristen Johnston	Sally Solomon	3rd Rock From the Sun
1998	Lisa Kudrow	Phoebe Buffay	Friends
1997	Kristen Johnston	Sally Solomon	3rd Rock From the Sun
1996	Julia Louis-Dreyfus	Elaine Benes	Seinfeld
1995	Christine Baranski	Maryann Thorpe	Cybill
1994	Laurie Metcalf	Jackie Harris	Roseanne
1993	Laurie Metcalf	Jackie Harris	Roseanne
1992	Laurie Metcalf	Jackie Harris	Roseanne
1991	Bebe Neuwirth	Dr. Lillith Sternin-Crane	Cheers
1990	Bebe Neuwirth	Dr. Lillith Sternin-Crane	Cheers

SOURCE: Based on data from Academy of Television Arts and Sciences

Television

Movies and Videos

• • • • • • • • • • •

About 400 new films are released in the United States each year. Some disappear quickly. Others remain popular for years and years—not only in cinemas and on video, but in the spin-offs and merchandise they create: toys and games, clothing, and recordings of their musical scores.

Americans spend about $6 billion a year on movie tickets, with an average admission charge of $4.42. As 2001 began, the film that held the U.S. record for making the most money at the box office was *Star Wars*, a 1977 movie that had sold $460 million worth of tickets. Worldwide, the record was held by the 1993 film *Jurassic Park*, which had pulled in a total of $913 million. But on March 1, 1998, the 1997 film *Titanic* became the first film to surpass $1 billion worldwide. It also became the first movie to tie the all-time record for Oscar nominations, with 14 total. On Oscar night in March 1998, it also became the first movie to tie the all-time record for Oscar wins: the film tied the 1959 epic *Ben-Hur* with 11 awards.

Kidbits Tidbits

● The American Film Institute has rated *Citizen Kane* the best movie of all time.

● In 1997, *Titanic* became the most expensive movie ever made. It cost $200 million.

● North America's top grossing movie in 1999 was *Star Wars: Episode 1—The Phantom Menace,* with $430 million.

● *Ben-Hur,* a 1959 movie, held the Oscar record of 11 Academy Awards for 39 years, until *Titanic* tied in 1998.

Teenagers make up a hefty portion of the movie audience, in part because they have more leisure time than older people. In a recent study, 48% of 12- to 17-year-olds said they see a movie at least once a month, as compared with only 26% of people age 18 and older. Also, unlike adults, teenagers will see a movie over and over again if they like it. To some degree, boys and girls have different theatrical tastes—young males like action films while young women prefer romantic tales. But just about every teenager loves a spooky horror movie, or a film with dazzling computer-generated special effects, such as enormous stalking dinosaurs and cataclysmic natural disasters.

In addition to viewing movies in cinemas, kids watch lots of movies at home. More than 81% of U.S. homes have VCRs—a higher percentage than in any other country in the world. Most of these homes rent at least one movie a month.

Of all the categories of movies being rented, action films and comedies are the favorites. In 1996, rental income from action films was about $631 million, with comedies close behind at $611.5 million.

Films are given a rating by the Motion Picture Association of America. The rating is a reflection of a movie's violence and sexual content. The majority of the films released each year receive an "R" rating, which means that people under age 17 can be admitted only if accompanied by a parent or adult guardian. Other ratings include G (general audience), PG (parental guidance advised), PG-13 (may not be suitable for preteens), and NC-17 (persons under age 17 not admitted).

Movies and Videos

Kidbits Tidbits

● In 2000, about 7% of rental income was from DVDs.

● The top-selling video of all time is *The Lion King.* The #1 rental video of all time is *Top Gun.*

● Movies often reinforce misleading images of society. For example, one survey of top-grossing films of the 1990s found that 80% of the male leads smoked.

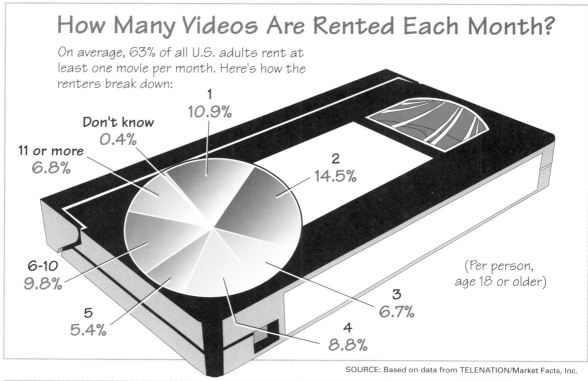

How Many Videos Are Rented Each Month?

On average, 63% of all U.S. adults rent at least one movie per month. Here's how the renters break down:

Don't know 0.4%

11 or more 6.8%

1 10.9%

2 14.5%

3 6.7%

4 8.8%

5 5.4%

6-10 9.8%

(Per person, age 18 or older)

SOURCE: Based on data from TELENATION/Market Facts, Inc.

Top 10 Top-Selling Videos of All Time
(Worldwide)

1   The Lion King
2   Aladdin
3   Beauty and the Beast
4   Snow White and the Seven Dwarfs
5   Forrest Gump
6   101 Dalmations
7   Jurassic Park
8   The Little Mermaid
9   Pinocchio
10 E.T.: The Extra-Terrestrial

Movies and Videos

SOURCE: Based on data from Alexander & Associates

Top 10 Top-Renting Videos of All Time
(In U.S.)

1   Top Gun
2   Pretty Woman
3   The Little Mermaid
4   Home Alone
5   Ghost
6   Beauty and the Beast
7   The Lion King
8   Terminator II: Judgement Day
9   Forrest Gump
10 Dances with Wolves

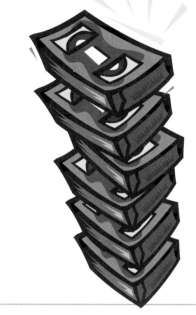

SOURCE: Based on data from Alexander & Associates (2000)

U.S. Box-Office Revenues, 1926–99

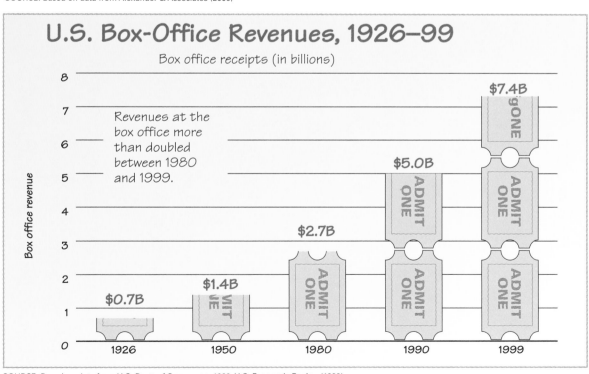

Box office receipts (in billions)

Revenues at the box office more than doubled between 1980 and 1999.

$0.7B — 1926
$1.4B — 1950
$2.7B — 1980
$5.0B — 1990
$7.4B — 1999

SOURCE: Based on data from U.S. Dept. of Commerce; 1999 *U.S. Economic Review* (1999)

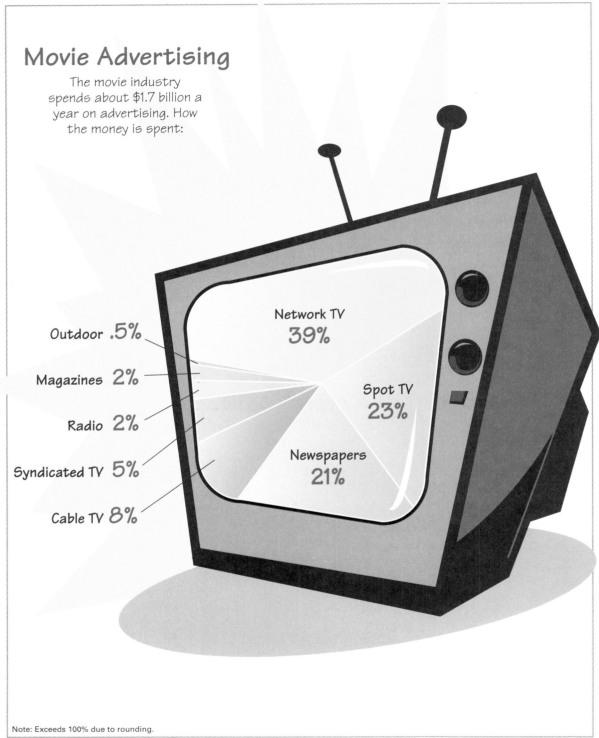

Movie Advertising

The movie industry spends about $1.7 billion a year on advertising. How the money is spent:

Outdoor .5%

Magazines 2%

Radio 2%

Syndicated TV 5%

Cable TV 8%

Network TV
39%

Spot TV
23%

Newspapers
21%

Movies and Videos

Note: Exceeds 100% due to rounding.

SOURCE: Based on data from Competitive Media Reporting

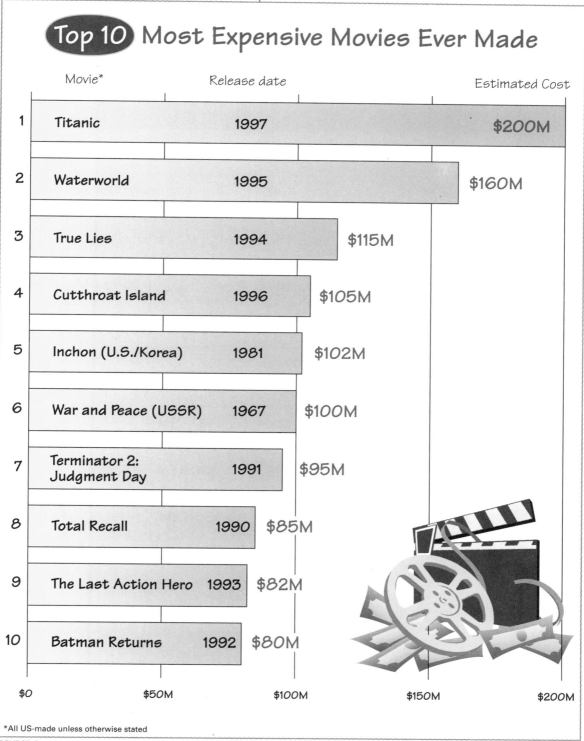

Top 10 Most Expensive Movies Ever Made

	Movie*	Release date	Estimated Cost
1	Titanic	1997	$200M
2	Waterworld	1995	$160M
3	True Lies	1994	$115M
4	Cutthroat Island	1996	$105M
5	Inchon (U.S./Korea)	1981	$102M
6	War and Peace (USSR)	1967	$100M
7	Terminator 2: Judgment Day	1991	$95M
8	Total Recall	1990	$85M
9	The Last Action Hero	1993	$82M
10	Batman Returns	1992	$80M

$0 $50M $100M $150M $200M

*All US-made unless otherwise stated

SOURCE: Based partially on information given in *The Top 10 of Everything 1997*

Movies and Videos

Top 10 Highest-Grossing Movies in the U.S.

(In box-office revenues, not adjusted for inflation)

Title	Release date	Gross (millions)
Titanic*	1997	$471.0M
Star Wars	1977	$461.0M
E.T.: The Extra-Terrestrial	1982	$399.8M
Jurassic Park	1993	$356.8M
Forrest Gump	1994	$329.7M
The Lion King	1994	$312.9M
Return of the Jedi	1983	$309.2M
Independence Day	1996	$306.2M
The Empire Strikes Back	1980	$290.3M
Home Alone	1990	$285.0M

$0 $100M $200M $300M $400M

*As of March 1998

Movies and Videos

SOURCE: Based partially on data from Exhibitor Relations Co. Inc.

Top 10 Highest-Grossing Movies in the U.S.
(In box-office revenues, adjusted for inflation)

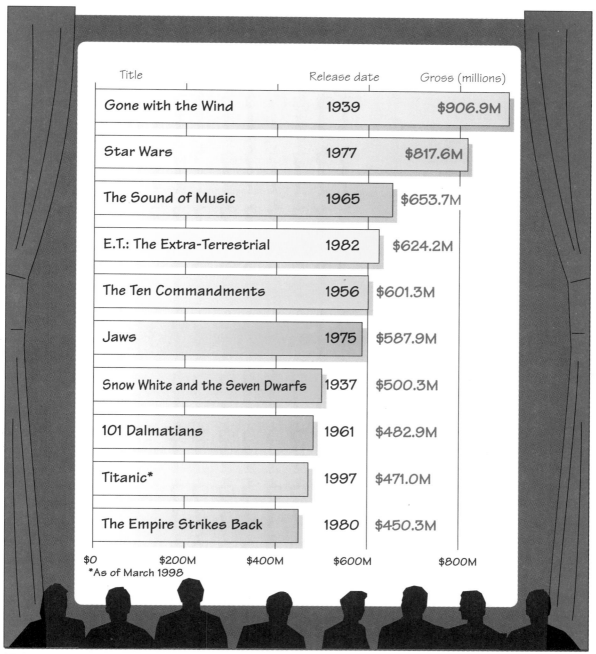

Title	Release date	Gross (millions)
Gone with the Wind	1939	$906.9M
Star Wars	1977	$817.6M
The Sound of Music	1965	$653.7M
E.T.: The Extra-Terrestrial	1982	$624.2M
The Ten Commandments	1956	$601.3M
Jaws	1975	$587.9M
Snow White and the Seven Dwarfs	1937	$500.3M
101 Dalmatians	1961	$482.9M
Titanic*	1997	$471.0M
The Empire Strikes Back	1980	$450.3M

$0 $200M $400M $600M $800M

*As of March 1998

Movies and Videos

SOURCE: Based partially on data from Exhibitor Relations Co. Inc.

Top Oscar Winners

Movie	Year		Awards
Titanic	1998		11
Ben-Hur	1959		11
West Side Story	1961		10
Gigi	1958		9
The Last Emperor	1987		9
Gone with the Wind	1939		8
From Here to Eternity	1953		8
On the Waterfront	1954		8
My Fair Lady	1964		8
Cabaret	1972		8
Gandhi	1982		8
Amadeus	1984		8

Movies and Videos

Oscar® is a registered trademark of the
Academy of Motion Pictures Arts and Sciences

SOURCE: Based partially on information given in *The Top 10 of Everything 1997; Academy of Motion Picture Arts & Sciences*

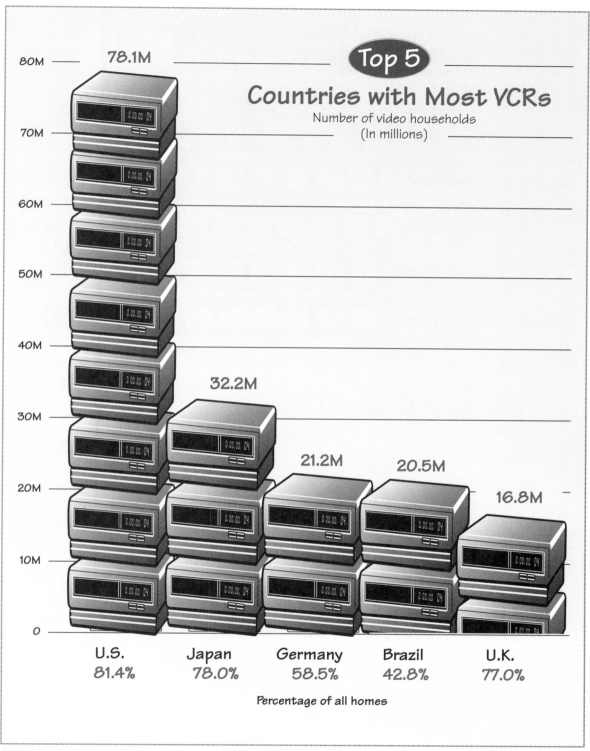

Top 5

Countries with Most VCRs

Number of video households
(In millions)

80M — 78.1M

70M

60M

50M

40M

32.2M

30M

21.2M   20.5M

20M   16.8M

10M

0

| U.S. | Japan | Germany | Brazil | U.K. |
| 81.4% | 78.0% | 58.5% | 42.8% | 77.0% |

Percentage of all homes

Movies and Videos

SOURCE: Based on information given in *The Top 10 of Everything 1997*

Million Dollar Movie Days

Steven Spielberg's *The Lost World*, sequel to *Jurassic Park*, did a record $90.1 million at the box office in its first 5 days. It is the fastest movie to gross $100 million:

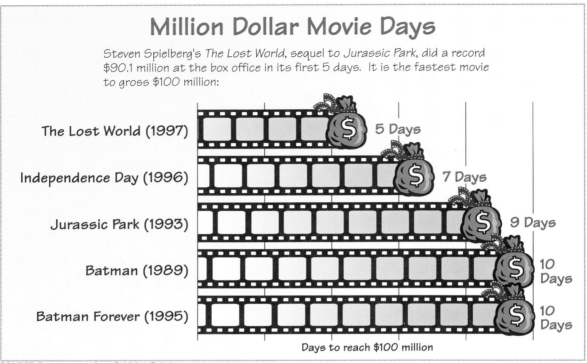

The Lost World (1997) — 5 Days

Independence Day (1996) — 7 Days

Jurassic Park (1993) — 9 Days

Batman (1989) — 10 Days

Batman Forever (1995) — 10 Days

Days to reach $100 million

SOURCE: Based on data from Exhibitor Relations

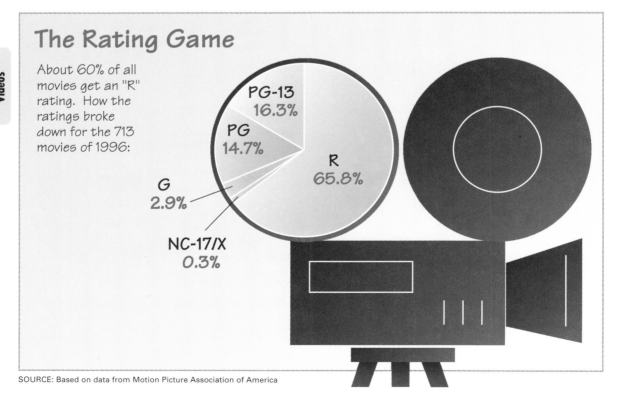

The Rating Game

About 60% of all movies get an "R" rating. How the ratings broke down for the 713 movies of 1996:

PG-13 16.3%

PG 14.7%

R 65.8%

G 2.9%

NC-17/X 0.3%

Movies and Videos

SOURCE: Based on data from Motion Picture Association of America

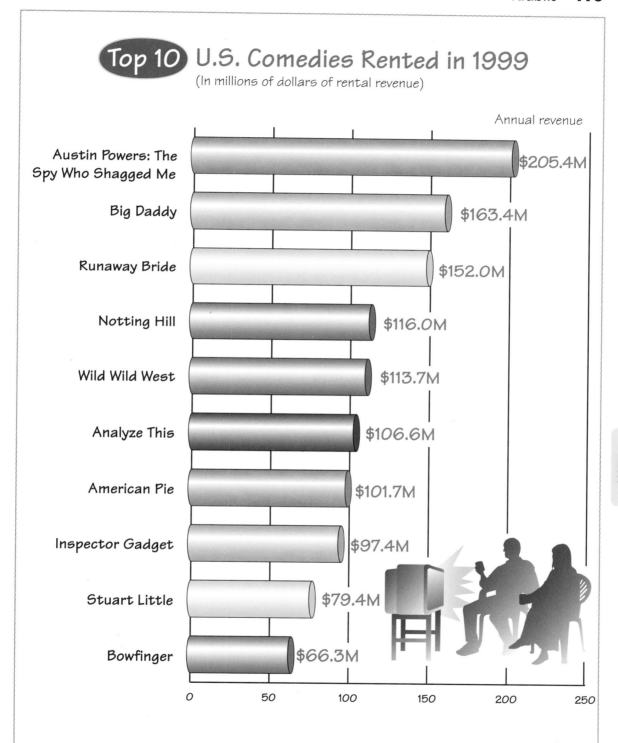

Top 10 U.S. Comedies Rented in 1999

(In millions of dollars of rental revenue)

Annual revenue

Austin Powers: The Spy Who Shagged Me	$205.4M
Big Daddy	$163.4M
Runaway Bride	$152.0M
Notting Hill	$116.0M
Wild Wild West	$113.7M
Analyze This	$106.6M
American Pie	$101.7M
Inspector Gadget	$97.4M
Stuart Little	$79.4M
Bowfinger	$66.3M

0   50   100   150   200   250

Movies and Videos

SOURCE: Based on data from *Video Store Magazine*

Top 10 Best-Selling U.S. Videos

(In millions of dollars of sales)

Title	Release date	Sales
The Lion King	Mar. 3, 1995	$27.5M
Snow White and the Seven Dwarfs	Oct. 28, 1994	$27.5M
Aladdin	Oct. 1. 1993	$25.0M
Independence Day	Nov. 19, 1996	$22.0M
Jurassic Park	Oct. 4, 1994	$21.5M
Toy Story	Oct. 29, 1996	$21.0M
Beauty and the Beast	Oct. 30, 1992	$20.0M
Pocahontas	Feb. 26, 1996	$18.0M
Star Wars Trilogy	Aug. 29, 1995	$15.3M
Forrest Gump	Apr. 27, 1995	$14.8M

$0 $5M $10M $15M $20M $25M $30M

Movies and Videos

SOURCE: Based on data from *Video Store Magazine*

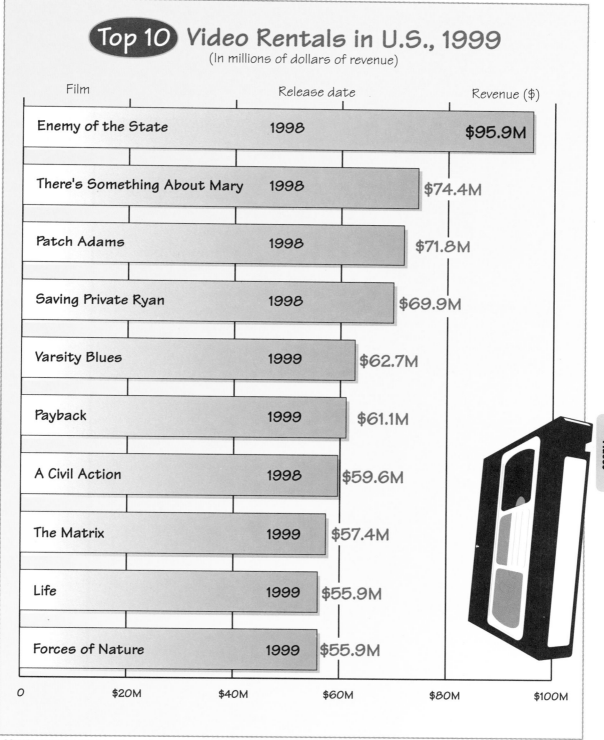

Top 10 Video Rentals in U.S., 1999

(In millions of dollars of revenue)

Film	Release date	Revenue ($)
Enemy of the State	1998	$95.9M
There's Something About Mary	1998	$74.4M
Patch Adams	1998	$71.8M
Saving Private Ryan	1998	$69.9M
Varsity Blues	1999	$62.7M
Payback	1999	$61.1M
A Civil Action	1998	$59.6M
The Matrix	1999	$57.4M
Life	1999	$55.9M
Forces of Nature	1999	$55.9M

0   $20M $40M $60M $80M $100M

Movies and Videos

SOURCE: Based on data from *Screen Source*.

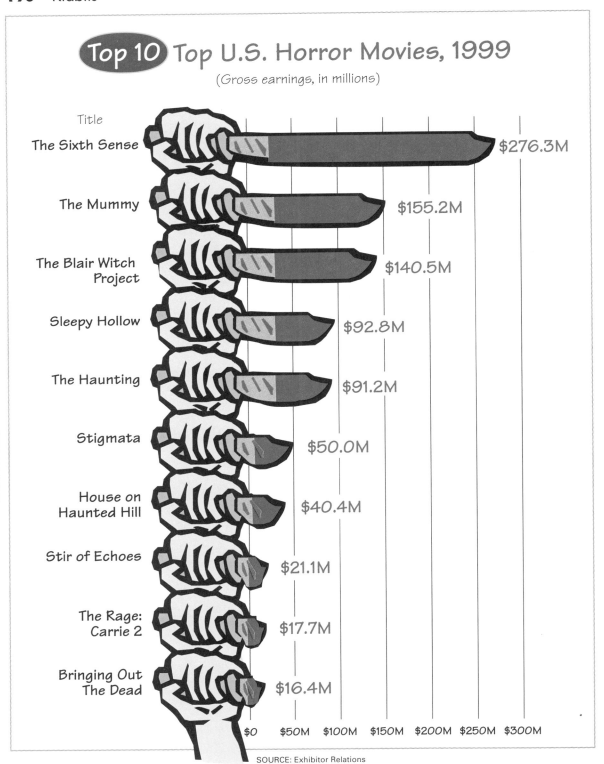

Top 10 Top U.S. Horror Movies, 1999

(Gross earnings, in millions)

Movies and Videos

Title	
The Sixth Sense	$276.3M
The Mummy	$155.2M
The Blair Witch Project	$140.5M
Sleepy Hollow	$92.8M
The Haunting	$91.2M
Stigmata	$50.0M
House on Haunted Hill	$40.4M
Stir of Echoes	$21.1M
The Rage: Carrie 2	$17.7M
Bringing Out The Dead	$16.4M

$0 $50M $100M $150M $200M $250M $300M

SOURCE: Exhibitor Relations

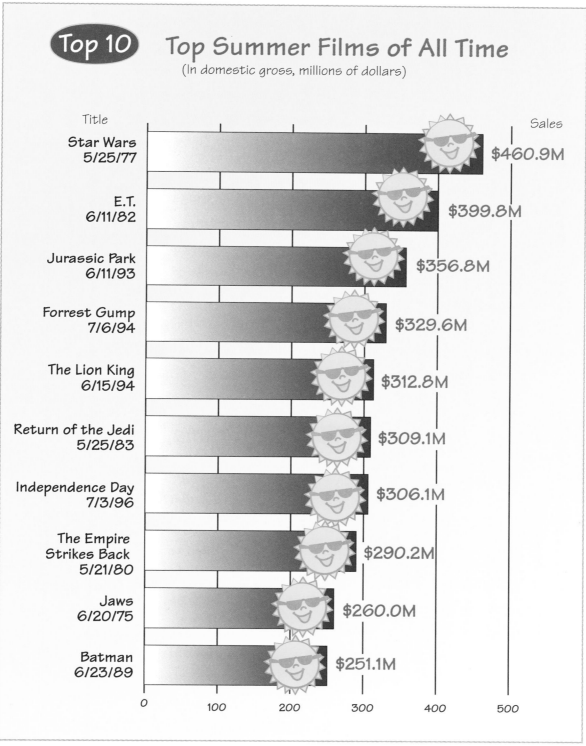

Top 10 — Top Summer Films of All Time
(In domestic gross, millions of dollars)

Title	Sales
Star Wars 5/25/77	$460.9M
E.T. 6/11/82	$399.8M
Jurassic Park 6/11/93	$356.8M
Forrest Gump 7/6/94	$329.6M
The Lion King 6/15/94	$312.8M
Return of the Jedi 5/25/83	$309.1M
Independence Day 7/3/96	$306.1M
The Empire Strikes Back 5/21/80	$290.2M
Jaws 6/20/75	$260.0M
Batman 6/23/89	$251.1M

0   100   200   300   400   500

Movies and Videos

SOURCE: Exhibitor Relations

Golden Globe Awards for "Best Performance by an Actor in a Motion Picture—Drama," 1990–2000

Year	Actor	Film
2000	Denzel Washington	The Hurricane
1999	Jim Carrey	The Truman Show
1998	Peter Fonda	Ulee's Gold
1997	Geoffrey Rush	Shine
1996	Nicolas Cage	Leaving Las Vegas
1995	Tom Hanks	Forrest Gump
1994	Tom Hanks	Philadelphia
1993	Al Pacino	Scent of a Woman
1992	Nick Nolte	The Prince of Tides
1991	Jeremy Irons	Reversal of Fortune
1990	Tom Cruise	Born on the Fourth of July

SOURCE: Based on data from Motion Picture Association of America

Golden Globe Awards For "Best Performance by an Actress in a Motion Picture—Drama," 1990–2000

Year	Actress	Film
2000	Hilary Swank	Boys Don't Cry
1999	Cate Blanchett	Elizabeth
1998	Judi Dench	Mrs. Brown
1997	Brenda Blethyn	Secrets and Lies
1996	Sharon Stone	Casino
1995	Jessica Lange	Blue Sky
1994	Holly Hunter	The Piano
1993	Emma Thompson	Howard's End
1992	Jodie Foster	The Silence of the Lambs
1991	Kathy Bates	Misery
1990	Michelle Pfeiffer	The Fabulous Baker Boys

SOURCE: Based on data from Motion Picture Association of America

Movies and Videos

Golden Globe Awards for "Best Performance by an Actor in a Motion Picture—Musical or Comedy," 1990–2000

Year	Actor and Film
2000	Jim Carrey in *Man on the Moon*
1999	Michael Caine in *Little Voice*
1998	Jack Nicholson in *As Good As It Gets*
1997	Tom Cruise in *Jerry Maguire*
1996	John Travolta in *Get Shorty*
1995	Hugh Grant in *Four Weddings and a Funeral*
1994	Robin Williams in *Mrs. Doubtfire*
1993	Tim Robbins in *The Player*
1992	Robin Williams in *The Fisher King*
1991	Gerard Depardieu in *Green Card*
1990	Morgan Freeman in *Driving Miss Daisy*

SOURCE: Based on statistics from E! Online and the Academy of Motion Picture Arts and Sciences

Golden Globe Awards for "Best Performance by an Actress in a Motion Picture—Musical or Comedy," 1990–2000

Year	Actress and Film
2000	Janet McTeer in *Tumbleweeds*
1999	Gwyneth Paltrow in *Shakespeare in Love*
1998	Helen Hunt in *As Good As It Gets*
1997	Madonna in *Evita*
1996	Nicole Kidman in *To Die For*
1995	Jamie Lee Curtis in *True Lies*
1994	Angela Bassett in *What's Love Got To Do With It?*
1993	Miranda Richardson in *Enchanted April*
1992	Bette Midler in *For the Boys*
1991	Julia Roberts in *Pretty Woman*
1990	Jessica Tandy in *Driving Miss Daisy*

SOURCE: Based on statistics from E! Online and the Academy of Motion Picture Arts and Sciences

Movies and Videos

Golden Globe Awards for "Best Motion Picture—Musical or Comedy," 1990–2000

Year	Film
2000	American Beauty
1999	Shakespeare in Love
1998	As Good As It Gets
1997	Evita
1996	Babe
1995	The Lion King
1994	Mrs. Doubtfire
1993	The Player
1992	Beauty and the Beast
1991	Green Card
1990	Driving Miss Daisy

SOURCE: Based on statistics from E! Online and the Academy of Motion Picture Arts and Sciences

The Top Oscar-Nominated Movies of All Time

Year	Film	Nominations
1997	Titanic	14
1950	All About Eve	14
1939	Gone with the Wind	13
1953	From Here to Eternity	13
1964	Mary Poppins	13
1966	Who's Afraid of Virginia Woolf?	13
1994	Forrest Gump	13

Oscar® is a registered trademark of the Academy of Motion Picture Arts and Sciences

SOURCE: Based on statistics from E! Online and the Academy of Motion Picture Arts and Sciences

Movies and Videos

Best Picture Oscars: 1991–2001

Year	Film
2001	Gladiator
2000	American Beauty
1999	Shakespeare in Love
1998	Titanic
1997	The English Patient
1996	Braveheart
1995	Forrest Gump
1994	Schindler's List
1993	Unforgiven
1992	The Silence of the Lambs
1991	Dances with Wolves

SOURCE: Based on data from Motion Picture Association of America

Best Director Oscars: 1991–2001

Year	Director	Film
2001	Steven Soderbergh	Traffic
2000	Sam Mendes	American Beauty
1999	Stephen Spielberg	Saving Private Ryan
1998	James Cameron	Titanic
1997	Anthony Minghella	The English Patient
1996	Mel Gibson	Braveheart
1995	Robert Zemeckis	Forrest Gump
1994	Steven Spielberg	Schindler's List
1993	Clint Eastwood	Unforgiven
1992	Jonathan Demme	The Silence of the Lambs
1991	Kevin Costner	Dances with Wolves

Movies and Videos

SOURCE: Based on data from Motion Picture Association of America

Best Actress Oscars: 1991–2001

Year	Actress
2001	Julia Roberts (*Erin Brockovich*)
2000	Hilary Swank (*Boys Don't Cry*)
1999	Gwyneth Paltrow (*Shakespeare in Love*)
1998	Helen Hunt (*As Good As It Gets*)
1997	Frances McDormand (*Fargo*)
1996	Susan Sarandon (*Dead Man Walking*)
1995	Jessica Lange (*Blue Sky*)
1994	Holly Hunter (*The Piano*)
1993	Emma Thompson (*Howard's End*)
1992	Jodie Foster (*The Silence of the Lambs*)
1991	Kathy Bates (*Misery*)

SOURCE: Based on data from Motion Picture Association of America

Best Actor Oscars: 1991–2001

Year	Actor
2001	Russell Crowe (*Gladiator*)
2000	Kevin Spacey (*American Beauty*)
1999	Roberto Benigni (*Life Is Beautiful*)
1998	Jack Nicholson (*As Good As It Gets*)
1997	Geoffrey Rush (*Shine*)
1996	Nicolas Cage (*Leaving Las Vegas*)
1995	Tom Hanks (*Forrest Gump*)
1994	Tom Hanks (*Philadelphia*)
1993	Al Pacino (*Scent of a Woman*)
1992	Anthony Hopkins (*The Silence of the Lambs*)
1991	Jeremy Irons (*Reversal of Fortune*)

Movies and Videos

SOURCE: Based on data from Motion Picture Association of America

Best Supporting Actress Oscars: 1991–2001

Year	Actress
2001	Marcia Gay Harden (*Pollock*)
2000	Angelina Jolie (*Girl, Interrupted*)
1999	Judi Dench (*Shakespeare in Love*)
1998	Kim Basinger (*L.A. Confidential*)
1997	Juliette Binoche (*The English Patient*)
1996	Mira Sorvino (*Mighty Aphrodite*)
1995	Dianne Wiest (*Bullets Over Broadway*)
1994	Anna Paquin (*The Piano*)
1993	Marisa Tomei (*My Cousin Vinny*)
1992	Mercedes Ruehl (*The Fisher King*)
1991	Whoopi Goldberg (*Ghost*)

SOURCE: Based on data from Motion Picture Association of America

Best Supporting Actor Oscars: 1991–2001

Year	Actor
2001	Benicio Del Toro (*Traffic*)
2000	Michael Caine (*Cider House Rules*)
1999	James Coburn (*Affliction*)
1998	Robin Williams (*Good Will Hunting*)
1997	Cuba Gooding Jr. (*Jerry Maguire*)
1996	Kevin Spacey (*The Usual Suspects*)
1995	Martin Landau (*Ed Wood*)
1994	Tommy Lee Jones (*The Fugitive*)
1993	Gene Hackman (*Unforgiven*)
1992	Jack Palance (*City Slickers*)
1991	Joe Pesci (*Goodfellas*)

Movies and Videos

SOURCE: Based on data from Motion Picture Association of America

Pro Sports

Even very young children love to follow professional sports. By the time they enter middle school and high school, millions of kids are fanatics! They root for their favorite team, collect trading cards that picture their favorite players, and wear sweatshirts and caps with team logos. Many dream of the day when they, too, might become pro players. Of course, very few children realize these dreams. Very few develop the skills needed to compete at a professional level. But for those who are successful, the payoff can be enormous.

Top professionals earn millions of dollars each year, not only in salaries but also from their endorsements of clothing, video games, cereals, and other products. Professionals are paid for their endorsements because companies know that they'll sell more merchandise—especially to young people—if it carries Michael Jordan's picture or Tiger Wood's name.

This wasn't always true. Professional sports have changed tremendously over the years. In 1959, members of the

Kidbits
Tidbits

- Formula 1 Race car driver Michael Schumacher is one of the highest paid athletes of 2000, earning $36 million per season.
- The highest paid football player in 1998 was Deion Sanders, who received $7.57 million.
- Under the 2003-2004 NBA agreement, teams cannot pay players more than $14 million each, and cannot spend more than $34 million on the team as a whole.

Professional Bowlers Association competed in three tournaments for prizes worth a total of $49,500; by 1997 they were competing in four seasonal tours for more than $8 million in prize money. When Babe Ruth played baseball, there were no night games, no domed ballparks, no coast-to-coast travel, no million-dollar salaries—and no black players in the major leagues. When Ray Harroun won the first Indianapolis 500 in 1911, he drove at an average speed of less than 75 mph; when Kenny Brack won in 1999, his average speed was 153.1 mph!

Today, the media—particularly TV—spends big bucks on sports. These dollars help pay for salaries. In return, the media has a large part in deciding everything from the starting times of games to playing dates.

Another big change has been the growth of women's professional sports. For example, the 1990s saw the beginning of the Women's National Basketball Association and other pro leagues. Much of the credit for this change belongs to the passage of a federal law in 1972. The law—called Title IX—outlaws discrimination in school sports on the basis of gender. The law meant that girls could have equal opportunities to develop as athletes. As a result, many girls have grown up to be strong, skilled professional athletes. Women's winnings and salaries, however, still do not equal those of men. For example, the #1 woman golfer in 2000 earned $1,865,053. The #1 male golfer earned $8,412,232.

Kidbits
Tidbits

- In 1997, at the ripe old age of 21, Tiger Woods became the youngest golfer ever to win the Masters.
- The most valuable NFL franchise in 2000 was the Washington Redskins ($741 million). The most valuable MLB franchise was the New York Yankees ($491 million).
- The final game in the 1999 Women's World Cup drew more than 90,000 spectators—the largest audience for any women's sporting event.

Pro Sports

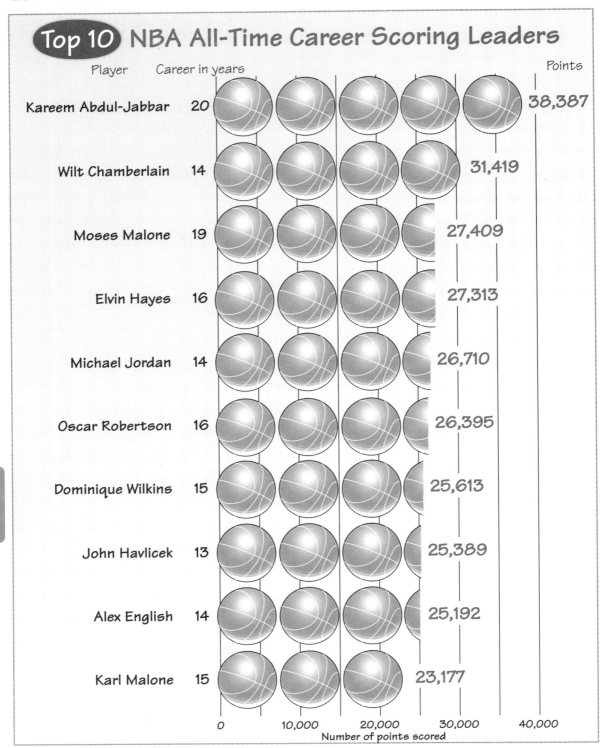

Top 10 NBA All-Time Career Scoring Leaders

Player	Career in years	Points
Kareem Abdul-Jabbar	20	38,387
Wilt Chamberlain	14	31,419
Moses Malone	19	27,409
Elvin Hayes	16	27,313
Michael Jordan	14	26,710
Oscar Robertson	16	26,395
Dominique Wilkins	15	25,613
John Havlicek	13	25,389
Alex English	14	25,192
Karl Malone	15	23,177

Number of points scored: 0 — 10,000 — 20,000 — 30,000 — 40,000

Pro Sports

SOURCE: Based on data from National Basketball Association

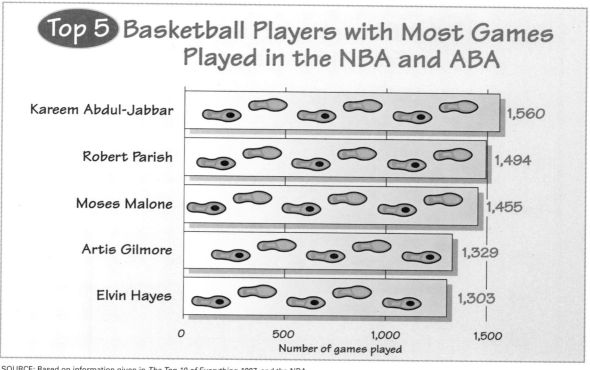

Top 5 Basketball Players with Most Games Played in the NBA and ABA

Player	Number of games played
Kareem Abdul-Jabbar	1,560
Robert Parish	1,494
Moses Malone	1,455
Artis Gilmore	1,329
Elvin Hayes	1,303

SOURCE: Based on information given in *The Top 10 of Everything 1997,* and the NBA

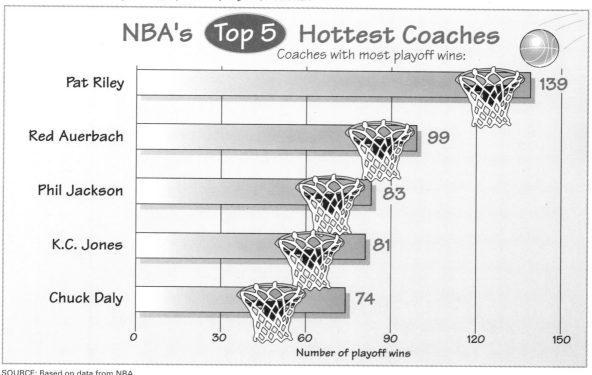

NBA's Top 5 Hottest Coaches

Coaches with most playoff wins:

Coach	Number of playoff wins
Pat Riley	139
Red Auerbach	99
Phil Jackson	83
K.C. Jones	81
Chuck Daly	74

SOURCE: Based on data from NBA

Pro Sports

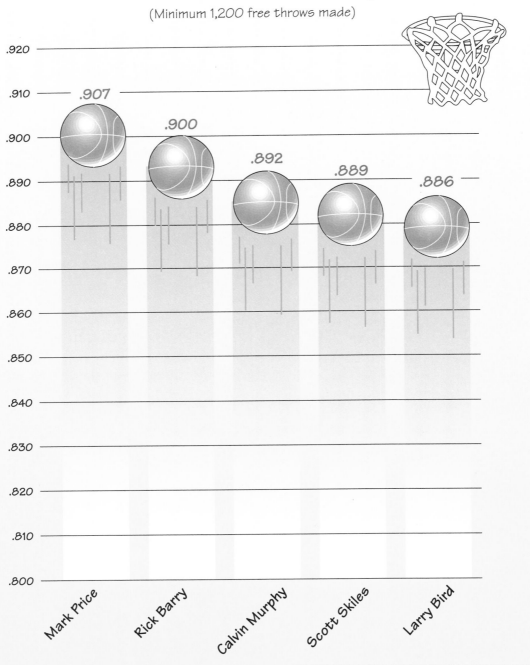

Top 5 Basketball Players, by Free Throw Percentages

(Minimum 1,200 free throws made)

- Mark Price — .907
- Rick Barry — .900
- Calvin Murphy — .892
- Scott Skiles — .889
- Larry Bird — .886

Pro Sports

SOURCE: Based on statistics from the NBA

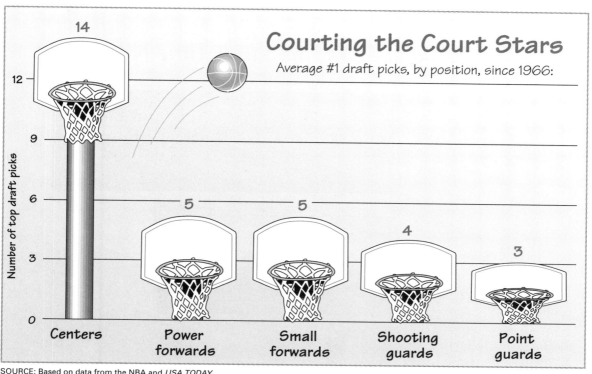

Courting the Court Stars

Average #1 draft picks, by position, since 1966:

Number of top draft picks

Centers	Power forwards	Small forwards	Shooting guards	Point guards
14	5	5	4	3

SOURCE: Based on data from the NBA and *USA TODAY*

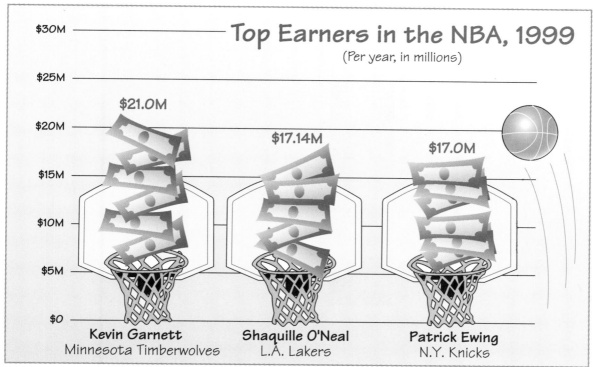

Top Earners in the NBA, 1999

(Per year, in millions)

Kevin Garnett Minnesota Timberwolves	Shaquille O'Neal L.A. Lakers	Patrick Ewing N.Y. Knicks
$21.0M	$17.14M	$17.0M

Pro Sports

SOURCE: Based on data from *USA TODAY*

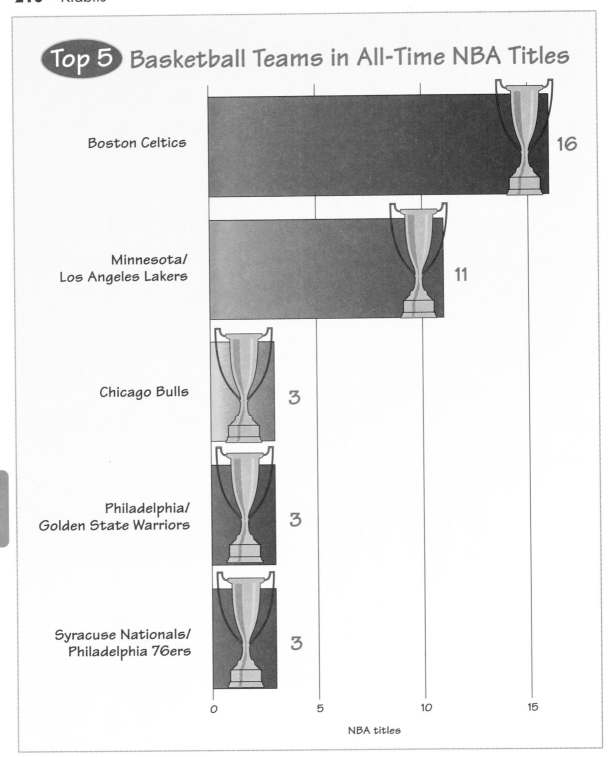

Top 5 Basketball Teams in All-Time NBA Titles

Boston Celtics — 16

Minnesota/ Los Angeles Lakers — 11

Chicago Bulls — 3

Philadelphia/ Golden State Warriors — 3

Syracuse Nationals/ Philadelphia 76ers — 3

NBA titles

Pro Sports

SOURCE: Based on data from *World Almanac*, NBA

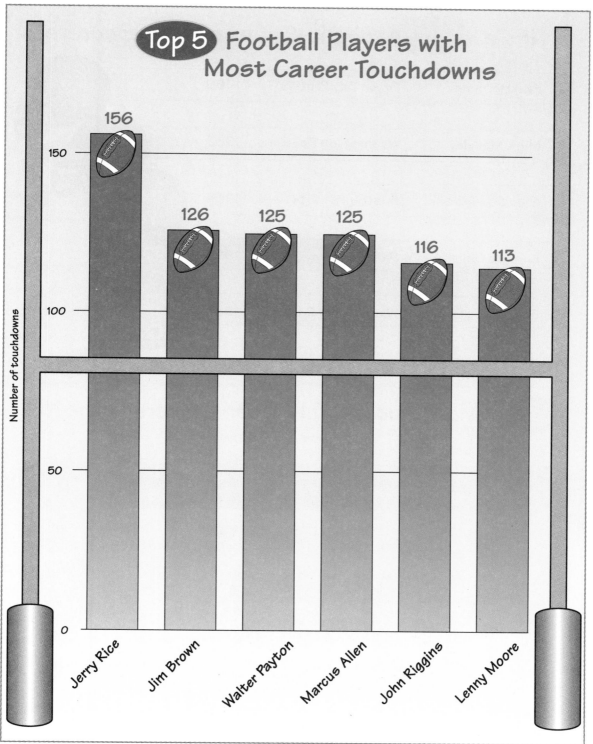

Top 5 Football Players with Most Career Touchdowns

Number of touchdowns

156 — Jerry Rice
126 — Jim Brown
125 — Walter Payton
125 — Marcus Allen
116 — John Riggins
113 — Lenny Moore

Pro Sports

SOURCE: Based on information from *World Almanac*, NFL

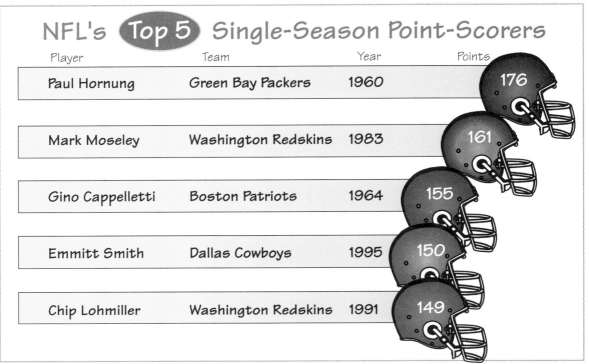

NFL's (Top 5) Single-Season Point-Scorers

Player	Team	Year	Points
Paul Hornung	Green Bay Packers	1960	176
Mark Moseley	Washington Redskins	1983	161
Gino Cappelletti	Boston Patriots	1964	155
Emmitt Smith	Dallas Cowboys	1995	150
Chip Lohmiller	Washington Redskins	1991	149

SOURCE: Based on information given in *The Top 10 of Everything 1997*

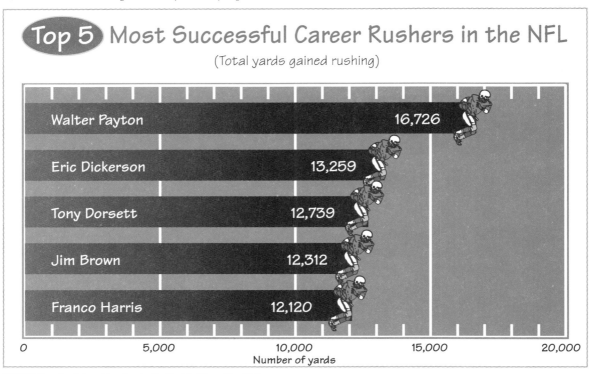

(Top 5) Most Successful Career Rushers in the NFL

(Total yards gained rushing)

Player	Number of yards
Walter Payton	16,726
Eric Dickerson	13,259
Tony Dorsett	12,739
Jim Brown	12,312
Franco Harris	12,120

0   5,000   10,000   15,000   20,000
Number of yards

SOURCE: Based on information given in *The Top 10 of Everything 1997*

Top All-Time Passing Records in the NFL

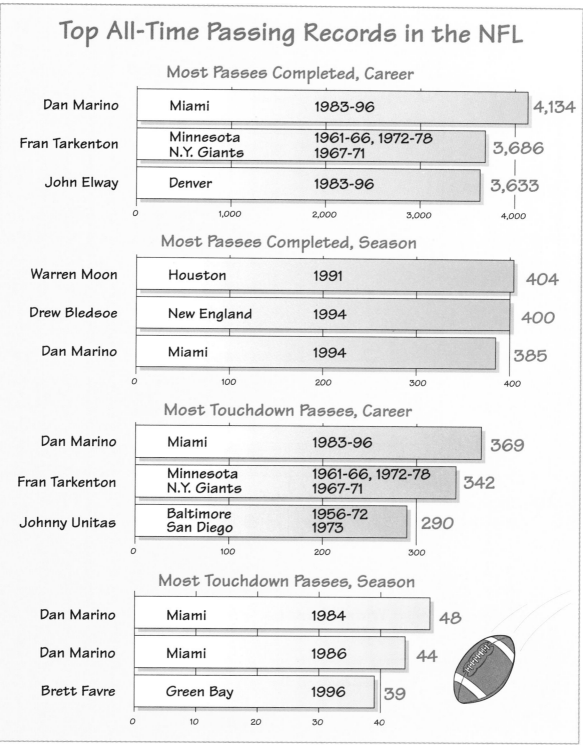

Most Passes Completed, Career

Player	Team	Years	
Dan Marino	Miami	1983-96	4,134
Fran Tarkenton	Minnesota / N.Y. Giants	1961-66, 1972-78 / 1967-71	3,686
John Elway	Denver	1983-96	3,633

Scale: 0, 1,000, 2,000, 3,000, 4,000

Most Passes Completed, Season

Player	Team	Year	
Warren Moon	Houston	1991	404
Drew Bledsoe	New England	1994	400
Dan Marino	Miami	1994	385

Scale: 0, 100, 200, 300, 400

Most Touchdown Passes, Career

Player	Team	Years	
Dan Marino	Miami	1983-96	369
Fran Tarkenton	Minnesota / N.Y. Giants	1961-66, 1972-78 / 1967-71	342
Johnny Unitas	Baltimore / San Diego	1956-72 / 1973	290

Scale: 0, 100, 200, 300

Most Touchdown Passes, Season

Player	Team	Year	
Dan Marino	Miami	1984	48
Dan Marino	Miami	1986	44
Brett Favre	Green Bay	1996	39

Scale: 0, 10, 20, 30, 40

Pro Sports

SOURCE: Based on data from *The Wall Street Journal Almanac 1998*

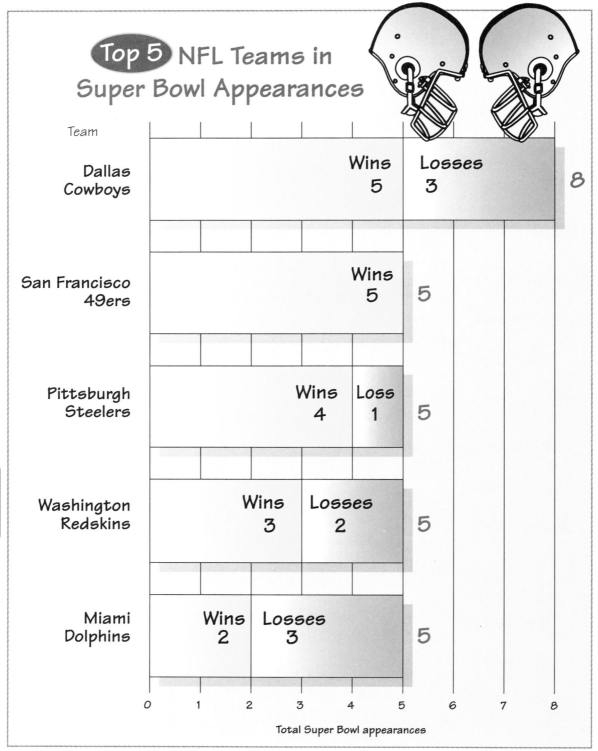

Top 5 NFL Teams in Super Bowl Appearances

Team

Dallas Cowboys — Wins 5 | Losses 3 | 8

San Francisco 49ers — Wins 5 | 5

Pittsburgh Steelers — Wins 4 | Loss 1 | 5

Washington Redskins — Wins 3 | Losses 2 | 5

Miami Dolphins — Wins 2 | Losses 3 | 5

0 1 2 3 4 5 6 7 8

Total Super Bowl appearances

Pro Sports

SOURCE: Based on data from National Football League

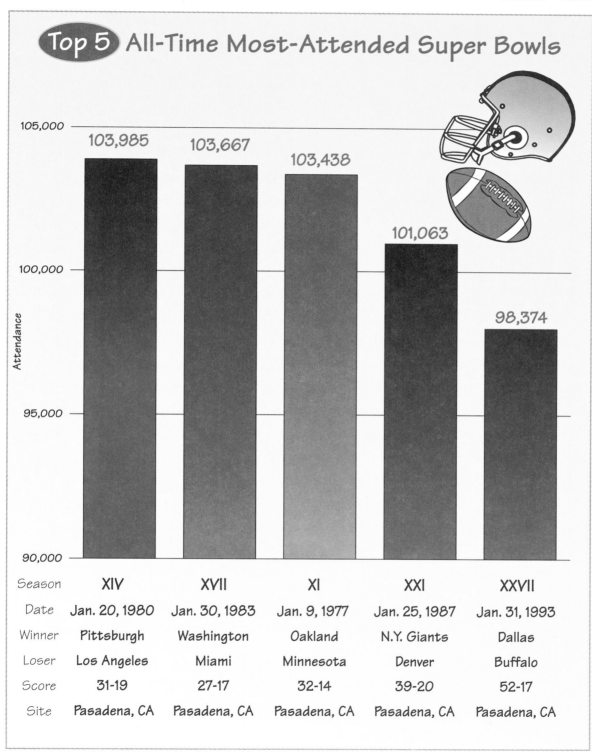

Top 5 All-Time Most-Attended Super Bowls

Attendance

103,985	103,667	103,438	101,063	98,374

Season	XIV	XVII	XI	XXI	XXVII
Date	Jan. 20, 1980	Jan. 30, 1983	Jan. 9, 1977	Jan. 25, 1987	Jan. 31, 1993
Winner	Pittsburgh	Washington	Oakland	N.Y. Giants	Dallas
Loser	Los Angeles	Miami	Minnesota	Denver	Buffalo
Score	31-19	27-17	32-14	39-20	52-17
Site	Pasadena, CA	Pasadena, CA	Pasadena, CA	Pasadena, CA	Pasadena, CA

Pro Sports

SOURCE: Based on data from National Football League

Top 5 Draft Suppliers to the NFL

Colleges and universities who have had the most
first-round draft players since 1936:

Number of first-round draft picks

Notre Dame	57
Southern Cal.	55
Ohio State	48
Michigan	34
Univ. of Miami, Fla.	31

Pro Sports

SOURCE: Based on data from NFL

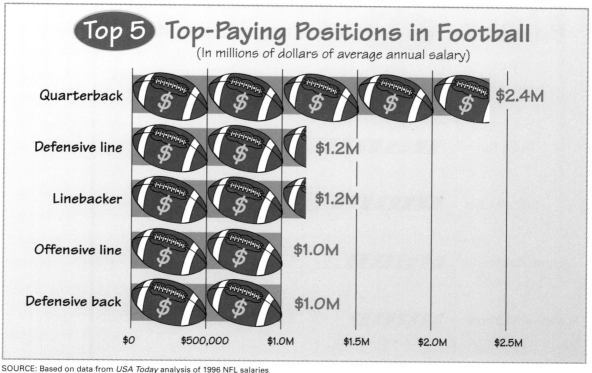

Top 5 Top-Paying Positions in Football

(In millions of dollars of average annual salary)

Quarterback	$2.4M
Defensive line	$1.2M
Linebacker	$1.2M
Offensive line	$1.0M
Defensive back	$1.0M

$0 $500,000 $1.0M $1.5M $2.0M $2.5M

SOURCE: Based on data from *USA Today* analysis of 1996 NFL salaries

Top Earners in NFL, 1998

(In millions)

	Deion Sanders Dallas Cowboys	Dan Marino Miami Dolphins	Drew Bledsoe New England Patriots
	$7.57M	$7.57M	$7.09M

$8M $7M $6M $5M $4M $3M $2M $1M 0

SOURCE: Based on data from *USA TODAY*

Pro Sports

Pro Sports

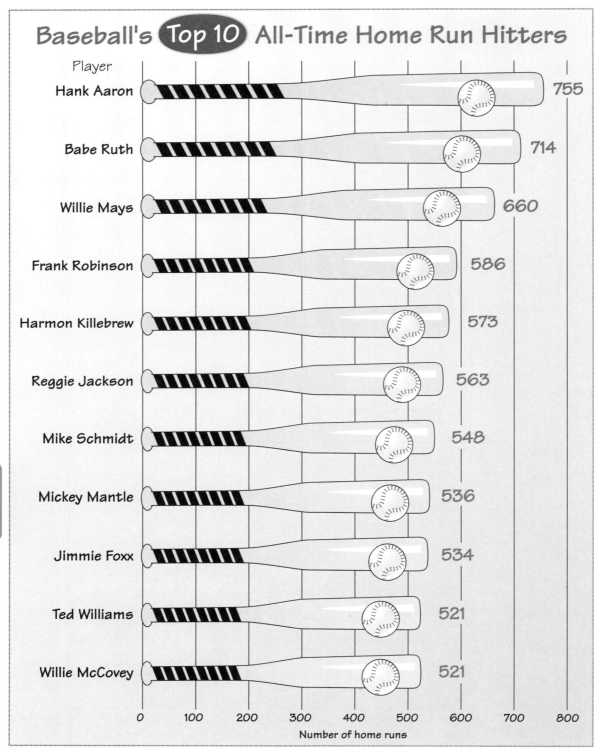

Baseball's Top 10 All-Time Home Run Hitters

Player

Player	Number of home runs
Hank Aaron	755
Babe Ruth	714
Willie Mays	660
Frank Robinson	586
Harmon Killebrew	573
Reggie Jackson	563
Mike Schmidt	548
Mickey Mantle	536
Jimmie Foxx	534
Ted Williams	521
Willie McCovey	521

0   100   200   300   400   500   600   700   800

Number of home runs

SOURCE: Based on data from *Total Baseball, the Official Encyclopedia of Major League Baseball*

Top Baseball Players with Highest Career Batting Averages

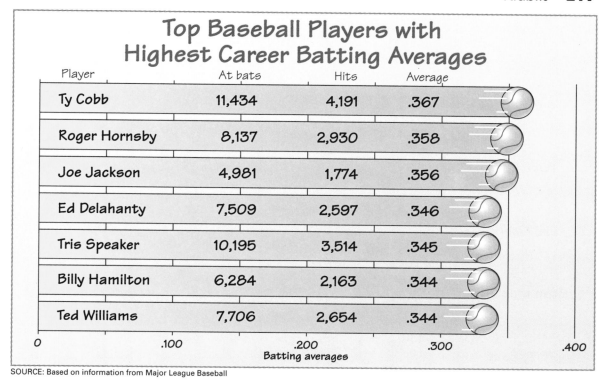

Player	At bats	Hits	Average
Ty Cobb	11,434	4,191	.367
Roger Hornsby	8,137	2,930	.358
Joe Jackson	4,981	1,774	.356
Ed Delahanty	7,509	2,597	.346
Tris Speaker	10,195	3,514	.345
Billy Hamilton	6,284	2,163	.344
Ted Williams	7,706	2,654	.344

0   .100   .200   .300   .400

Batting averages

SOURCE: Based on information from Major League Baseball

Top 5 Baseball Players with Most Career Games

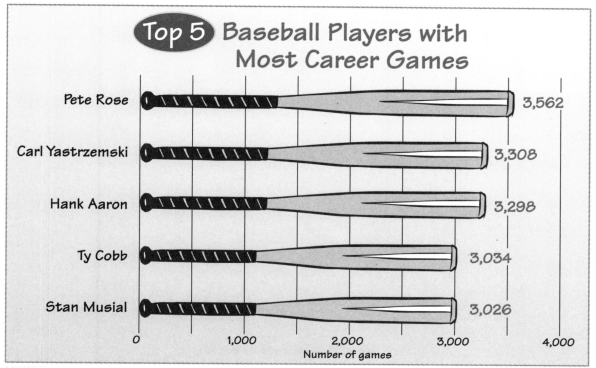

Player	Number of games
Pete Rose	3,562
Carl Yastrzemski	3,308
Hank Aaron	3,298
Ty Cobb	3,034
Stan Musial	3,026

0   1,000   2,000   3,000   4,000

Number of games

SOURCE: Based on information from Major League Baseball.

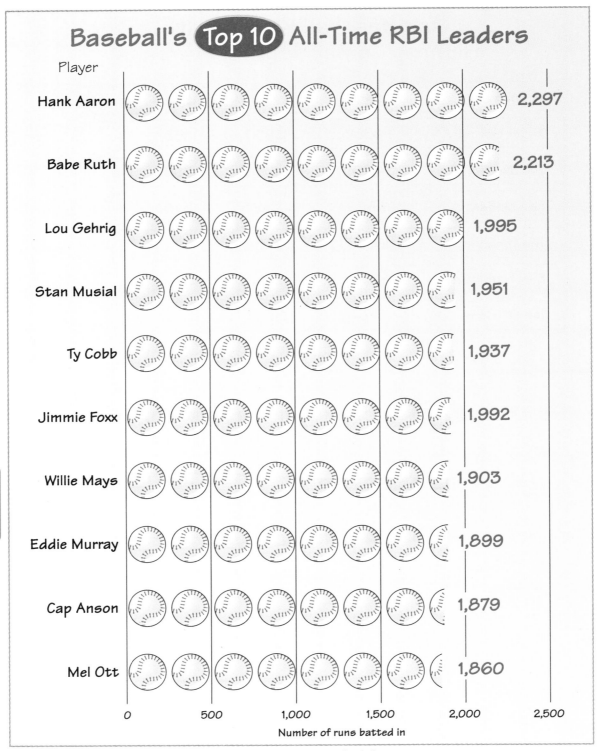

Baseball's Top 10 All-Time RBI Leaders

Player

Hank Aaron	2,297
Babe Ruth	2,213
Lou Gehrig	1,995
Stan Musial	1,951
Ty Cobb	1,937
Jimmie Foxx	1,992
Willie Mays	1,903
Eddie Murray	1,899
Cap Anson	1,879
Mel Ott	1,860

0   500   1,000   1,500   2,000   2,500

Number of runs batted in

Pro Sports

SOURCE: Based on data from *Total Baseball, the Official Encyclopedia of Major League Baseball*

Baseball's Top 10 All-Time Base Stealers

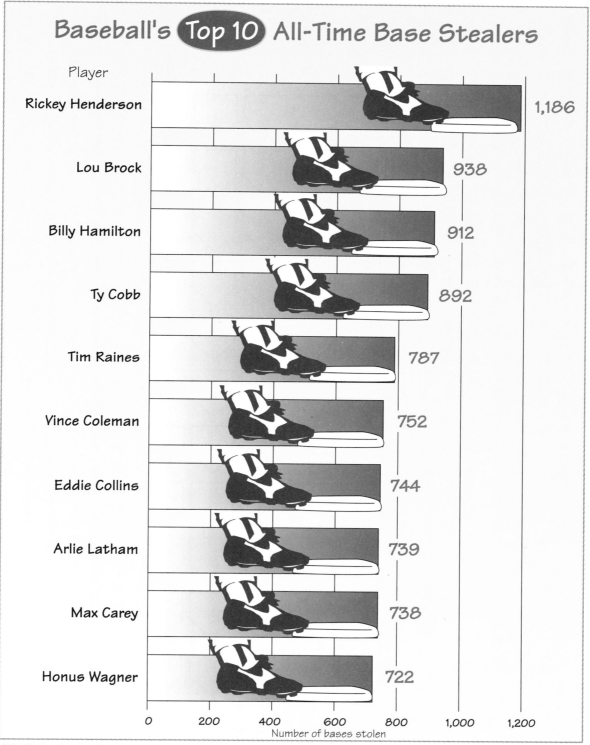

Player

Player	Number of bases stolen
Rickey Henderson	1,186
Lou Brock	938
Billy Hamilton	912
Ty Cobb	892
Tim Raines	787
Vince Coleman	752
Eddie Collins	744
Arlie Latham	739
Max Carey	738
Honus Wagner	722

0   200   400   600   800   1,000   1,200

Number of bases stolen

SOURCE: Based on data from *Total Baseball, the Official Encyclopedia of Major League Baseball*

Pro Sports

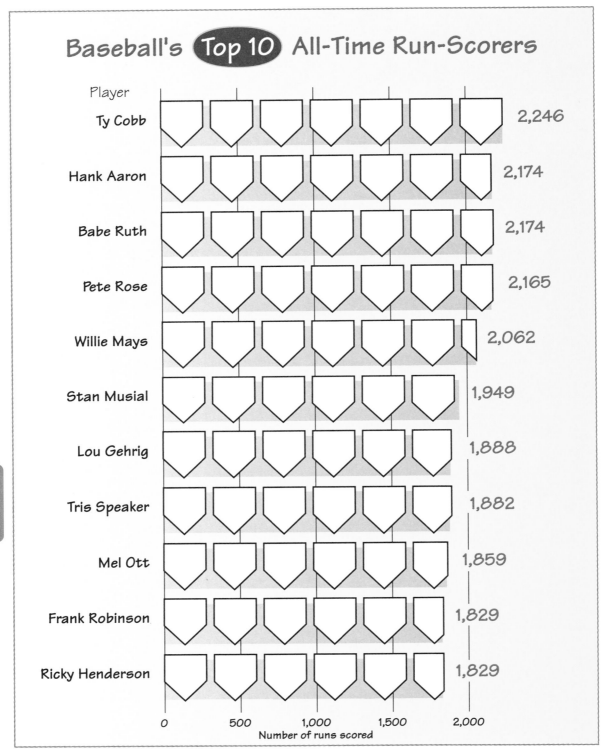

Baseball's (Top 10) All-Time Run-Scorers

Player

Player	Runs
Ty Cobb	2,246
Hank Aaron	2,174
Babe Ruth	2,174
Pete Rose	2,165
Willie Mays	2,062
Stan Musial	1,949
Lou Gehrig	1,888
Tris Speaker	1,882
Mel Ott	1,859
Frank Robinson	1,829
Ricky Henderson	1,829

Number of runs scored: 0   500   1,000   1,500   2,000

Pro Sports

SOURCE: Based on data from *Total Baseball, the Official Encyclopedia of Major League Baseball*

Top Earners in Major League Baseball, 1999

(In millions)

$11.95M

$11.0M

$10.7M

$10M

$8M

$6M

$4M

$2M

$0

Albert Belle
Chicago White Sox

Pedro Martinez
Boston Red Sox

Kevin Brown
L.A. Dodgers

SOURCE: Based on data from *USA TODAY*

Top 5 Oldest U.S. Baseball Stadiums

(Still in use)

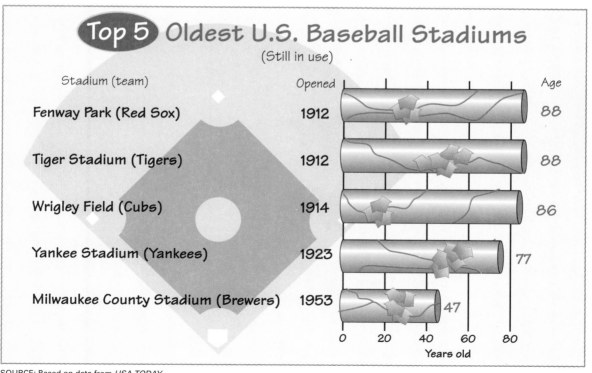

Stadium (team)	Opened		Age
Fenway Park (Red Sox)	1912		88
Tiger Stadium (Tigers)	1912		88
Wrigley Field (Cubs)	1914		86
Yankee Stadium (Yankees)	1923		77
Milwaukee County Stadium (Brewers)	1953		47

0   20   40   60   80

Years old

SOURCE: Based on data from *USA TODAY*

Pro Sports

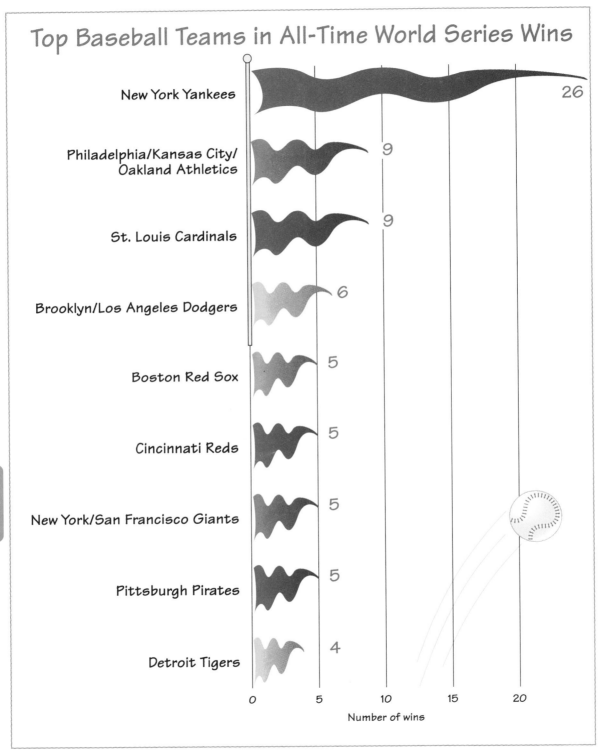

Top Baseball Teams in All-Time World Series Wins

Team	Wins
New York Yankees	26
Philadelphia/Kansas City/Oakland Athletics	9
St. Louis Cardinals	9
Brooklyn/Los Angeles Dodgers	6
Boston Red Sox	5
Cincinnati Reds	5
New York/San Francisco Giants	5
Pittsburgh Pirates	5
Detroit Tigers	4

Number of wins

SOURCE: Based on information from Major League Baseball

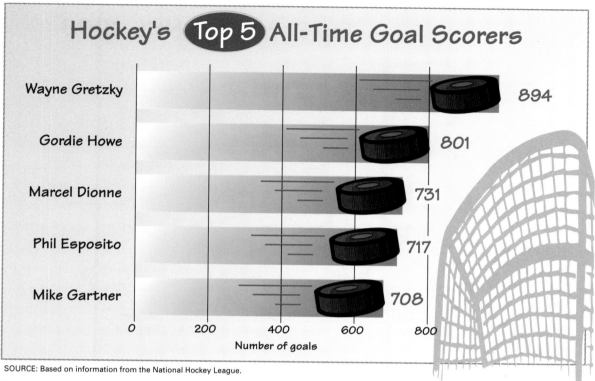

Hockey's Top 5 All-Time Goal Scorers

Player	Goals
Wayne Gretzky	894
Gordie Howe	801
Marcel Dionne	731
Phil Esposito	717
Mike Gartner	708

Number of goals

SOURCE: Based on information from the National Hockey League.

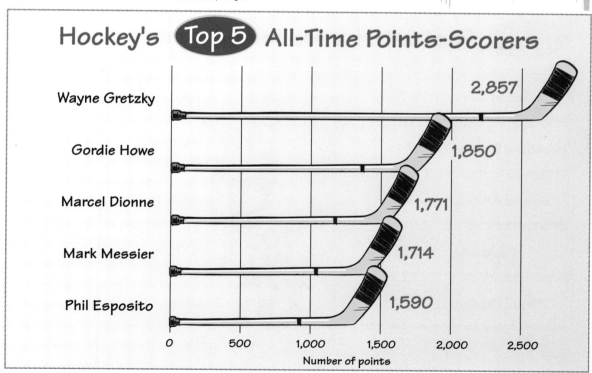

Hockey's Top 5 All-Time Points-Scorers

Player	Points
Wayne Gretzky	2,857
Gordie Howe	1,850
Marcel Dionne	1,771
Mark Messier	1,714
Phil Esposito	1,590

Number of points

SOURCE: Based on information from the National Hockey League

Pro Sports

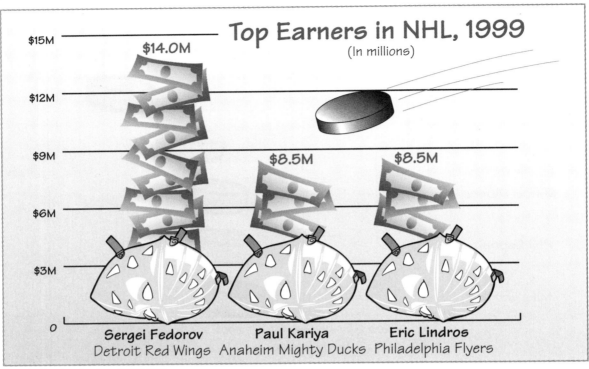

Top Earners in NHL, 1999
(In millions)

$15M — $14.0M

Sergei Fedorov — Detroit Red Wings

Paul Kariya — Anaheim Mighty Ducks — $8.5M

Eric Lindros — Philadelphia Flyers — $8.5M

SOURCE: Based on data from *USA TODAY*

Pro Sports

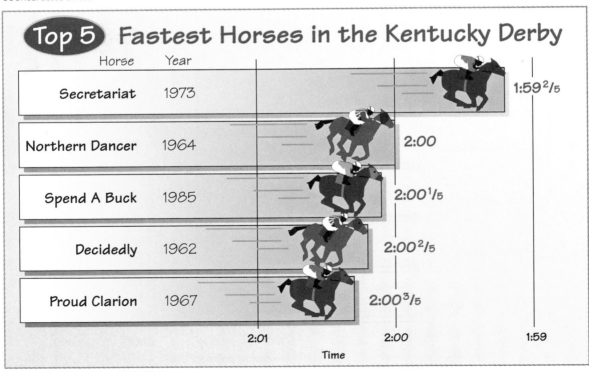

Top 5 Fastest Horses in the Kentucky Derby

Horse	Year	Time
Secretariat	1973	$1:59^2/_5$
Northern Dancer	1964	$2:00$
Spend A Buck	1985	$2:00^1/_5$
Decidedly	1962	$2:00^2/_5$
Proud Clarion	1967	$2:00^3/_5$

2:01   2:00   1:59

Time

SOURCE: Based on data from *USA TODAY*

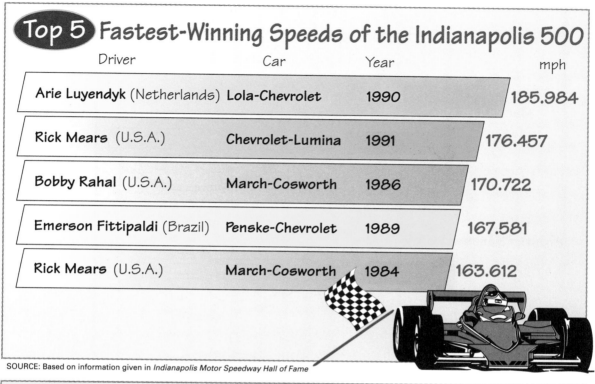

Top 5 Fastest-Winning Speeds of the Indianapolis 500

Driver	Car	Year	mph
Arie Luyendyk (Netherlands)	Lola-Chevrolet	1990	185.984
Rick Mears (U.S.A.)	Chevrolet-Lumina	1991	176.457
Bobby Rahal (U.S.A.)	March-Cosworth	1986	170.722
Emerson Fittipaldi (Brazil)	Penske-Chevrolet	1989	167.581
Rick Mears (U.S.A.)	March-Cosworth	1984	163.612

SOURCE: Based on information given in *Indianapolis Motor Speedway Hall of Fame*

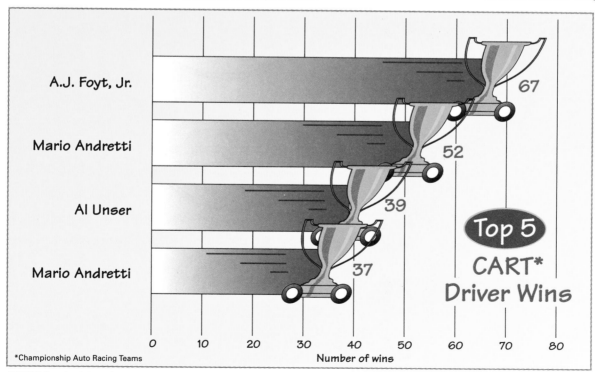

Top 5 CART* Driver Wins

Driver	Number of wins
A.J. Foyt, Jr.	67
Mario Andretti	52
Al Unser	39
Mario Andretti	37

*Championship Auto Racing Teams

SOURCE: Based on information given in *The Top 10 of Everything 2000*

Pro Sports

Pro Sports

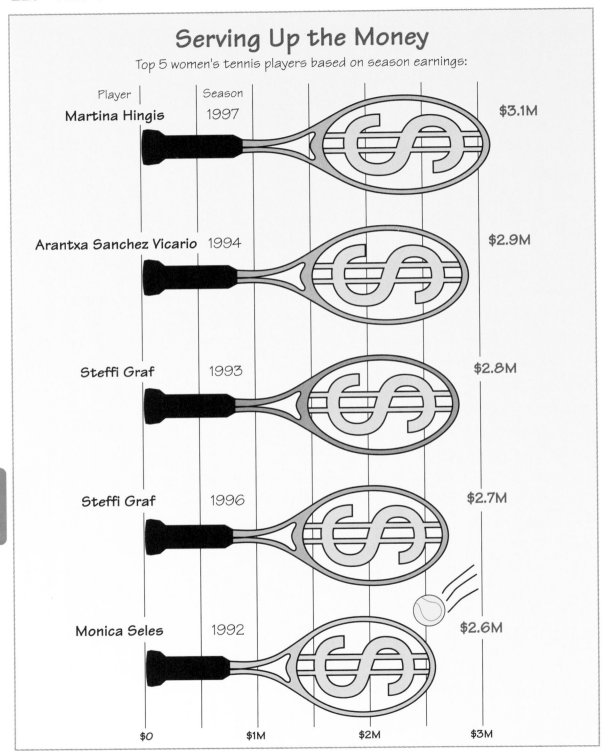

Serving Up the Money

Top 5 women's tennis players based on season earnings:

Player	Season		Earnings
Martina Hingis	1997		$3.1M
Arantxa Sanchez Vicario	1994		$2.9M
Steffi Graf	1993		$2.8M
Steffi Graf	1996		$2.7M
Monica Seles	1992		$2.6M

$0 $1M $2M $3M

SOURCE: Based on data from WTA Tour

Top Wimbledon Champions—Men

Player	# of titles	Years earned
William Renshaw	7	1880-89
Bjorn Borg	5	1975-81
H. Laurie Doherty	5	1897-1906
Reginald F. Doherty	4	1897-1905
Rod Laver	4	1959-71
Pete Sampras	4	1990-97
Tony Wilding	4	1906-14

SOURCE: Based on data from United States Tennis Association

Top Wimbledon Champions—Women

Player	# of titles	Years earned
Martina Navratilova	9	1974-95
Helen Wills Moody	8	1923-38
Steffi Graf	7	1987-96
Billie Jean King	6	1961-81
Suzanne Lenglen	6	1919-26

Pro Sports

SOURCE: Based on data from United States Tennis Association

Top U.S. Open Champions—Men

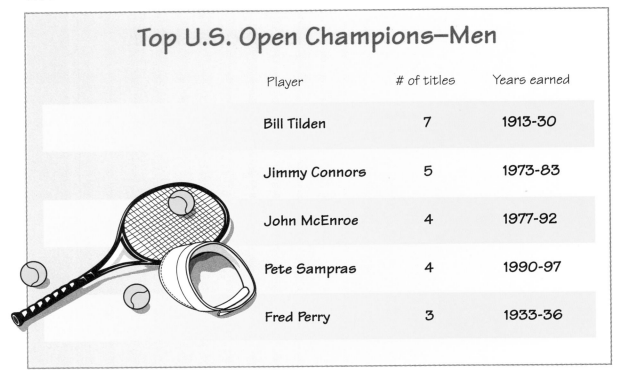

Player	# of titles	Years earned
Bill Tilden	7	1913-30
Jimmy Connors	5	1973-83
John McEnroe	4	1977-92
Pete Sampras	4	1990-97
Fred Perry	3	1933-36

SOURCE: Based on data from United States Tennis Association

Top U.S. Open Champions—Women

Player	# of titles	Years earned
Molla Mallory	8	1915-26
Helen Wills Moody	7	1923-38
Chris Evert	6	1974-86
Margaret Court	5	1960-75
Steffi Graf	5	1987-96

SOURCE: Based on data from United States Tennis Association

Top Grand Slam Champions—Men

Through 2000, only five men have won over ten total grand slam, or major, tournaments. The majors are the Australian Open, the French Open, Wimbledon, and the U.S. Open.

Player	# of titles	Years earned
Pete Sampras	13	1990-00
Roy Emerson	12	1959-71
Bjorn Borg	11	1975-81
Rod Laver	11	1959-71
Bill Tilden	10	1913-30

SOURCE: Based on data from United States Tennis Association

Top Grand Slam Champions—Women

Through 2000, only six women have won over ten total grand slam, or major, tournaments. The majors are the Australian Open, the French Open, Wimbledon, and the U.S. Open.

Player	# of titles	Years earned
Margaret Court	24	1960-75
Steffi Graf	22	1987-99
Chris Evert	18	1974-86
Martina Navratilova	18	1974-95
Billie Jean King	12	1961-81
Suzanne Lenglen	12	1919-26

SOURCE: Based on data from United States Tennis Association

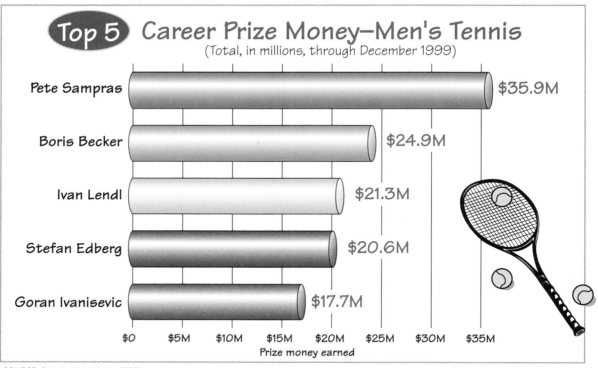

Top 5 Career Prize Money—Men's Tennis
(Total, in millions, through December 1999)

Player	Prize money earned
Pete Sampras	$35.9M
Boris Becker	$24.9M
Ivan Lendl	$21.3M
Stefan Edberg	$20.6M
Goran Ivanisevic	$17.7M

Prize money earned: $0 $5M $10M $15M $20M $25M $30M $35M

SOURCE: Based on data from ATP Tour

Top 5 Career Prize Money—Women's Tennis
(Total, in millions, through October 30, 2000)

Player	Prize money earned
Steffi Graf	$21.8M
Martina Navratilova	$20.3M
Arantxa Sanchez Vicario	$15.6M
Martina Hingis	$14.0M
Monica Seles	$12.6M

Prize money earned: $0 $5M $10M $15M $20M $25M

SOURCE: Based on data from CNN

Which Pros Do Kids Like Best?
Top 10 Most Popular Pro Athletes

(Ranked by TRU*SCORES of Teenage Research Unlimited)

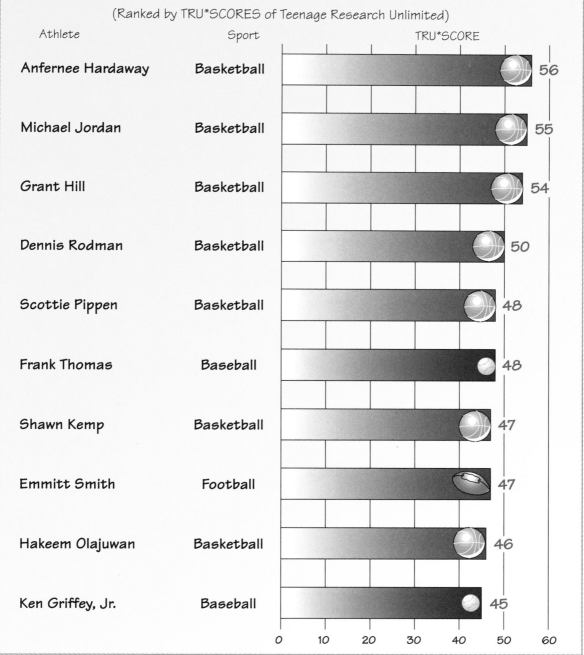

Athlete	Sport	TRU*SCORE
Anfernee Hardaway	Basketball	56
Michael Jordan	Basketball	55
Grant Hill	Basketball	54
Dennis Rodman	Basketball	50
Scottie Pippen	Basketball	48
Frank Thomas	Baseball	48
Shawn Kemp	Basketball	47
Emmitt Smith	Football	47
Hakeem Olajuwan	Basketball	46
Ken Griffey, Jr.	Baseball	45

Pro Sports

SOURCE: Based on data from Teenage Research Unlimited, Inc.

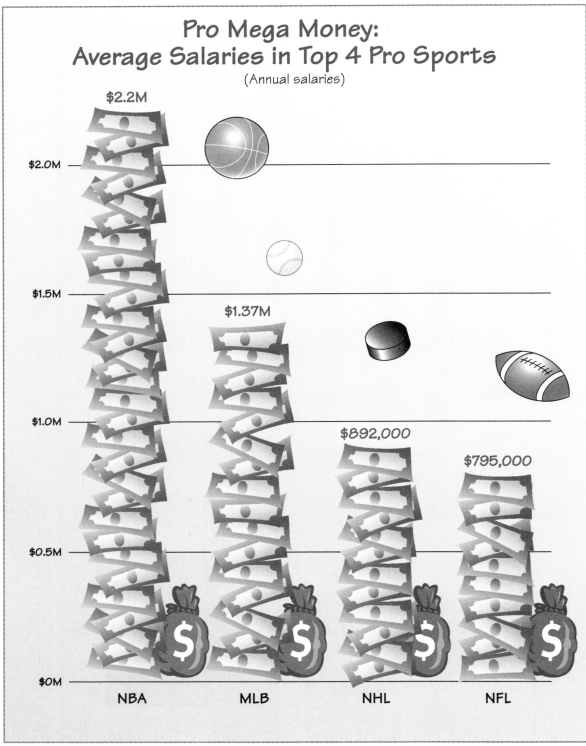

Pro Mega Money:
Average Salaries in Top 4 Pro Sports
(Annual salaries)

$2.2M

$2.0M

$1.5M

$1.37M

$1.0M

$892,000

$795,000

$0.5M

$0M

NBA   MLB   NHL   NFL

Pro Sports

SOURCE: Based on data from *USA TODAY*

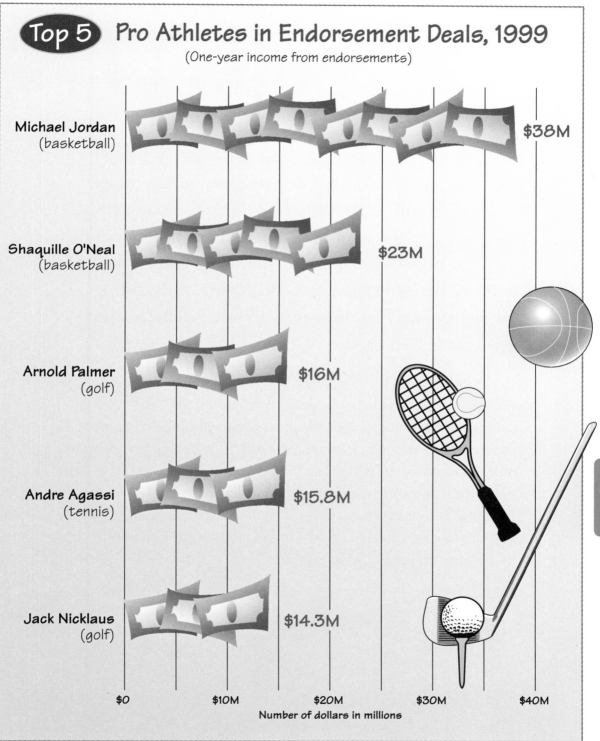

Top 5 Pro Athletes in Endorsement Deals, 1999

(One-year income from endorsements)

Michael Jordan (basketball) — $38M

Shaquille O'Neal (basketball) — $23M

Arnold Palmer (golf) — $16M

Andre Agassi (tennis) — $15.8M

Jack Nicklaus (golf) — $14.3M

$0 $10M $20M $30M $40M

Number of dollars in millions

Pro Sports

SOURCE: Based on data from The Sports Marketing Letter estimates

Pets

Look in an American home and you're likely to see a cat snoozing on a couch or a dog sleeping on the carpet. More than half of all households in America include at least one pet. Most of these homes have either dogs or cats—or both dogs and cats. But many other kinds of animals are also kept as pets, including birds, fish, rabbits, guinea pigs, hamsters, gerbils, ferrets, horses— even pot-bellied pigs!

More homes have dogs than cats. But there are more pet cats than any other kind of pet—more than 66 million felines were counted at the end of 2000. Most cat-owning homes—52 percent— have more than one cat, while less than 38% of dog owners have more than one dog. If you live in the midwest, chances are good you own a dog; on average that region has 37% to 47.9% of all households owning dogs. If you live in the northwest, chances are you own a cat. Between 30.6% and 42.7% of all households in that region contain at least one cat.

Kidbits Tidbits

- More than 58 million homes in the U.S. have at least one pet.
- About 13% of U.S. homes include both dogs and cats.
- Dogs have been the #1 pet in the White House; 23 presidents have had dogs.
- "First Pet" Millie, an English springer spaniel that lived with President and Mrs. Bush, made almost $1 million for charity by "authoring" *Millie's Book* with Mrs. Bush in 1990.
- The last president to have a pet reptile was John Quincy Adams, who owned an alligator.

Though it's often the children in a home who eagerly want a pet, it's most often the mother who has the main responsibility for caring for the animals, including taking them to veterinarians for vaccinations and other health care. The average cost for veterinary care depends on the type of pet. In 2000, the average yearly veterinary medical expenditure for a dog was $147, compared with $98 for a cat and under $9 for a bird.

Veterinary bills are only part of the cost of owning a pet. Other costs include food, grooming, toys, housing, and so on. For example, Americans spend about $4 billion on dog food each year, and $2.5 billion on cat food.

Many people obtain their pets for little or no cost, often from neighbors or animal shelters. Other people pay hundreds or even thousands of dollars for pedigreed animals—that is, animals that have been carefully bred and for whom there is a written record of parents, grandparents, etc. These animals are often shown professionally— they compete in judged events, such as dog shows and cat shows.

Ask a pet owner if the costs of owning an animal are worth it, and the answer is most likely to be a loud "yes!" Pets add fun, companionship, and love to people's lives. They are even beneficial to people's health. For example, research shows that owning a pet can lower a person's blood pressure and decrease chances of having a heart attack.

Kidbits Tidbits

- The great majority of Americans believe that pets play a positive role in people's lives.
- About 90% of cat and dog owners consider the animals to be members of the family.
- Labrador retrievers rank #1 in registrations with the American Kennel Club, followed by golden retrievers and German shepherds.
- The Cat Fanciers Association recognizes 36 breeds, of which Persians are #1 in number of registrations.

Pets

Pets

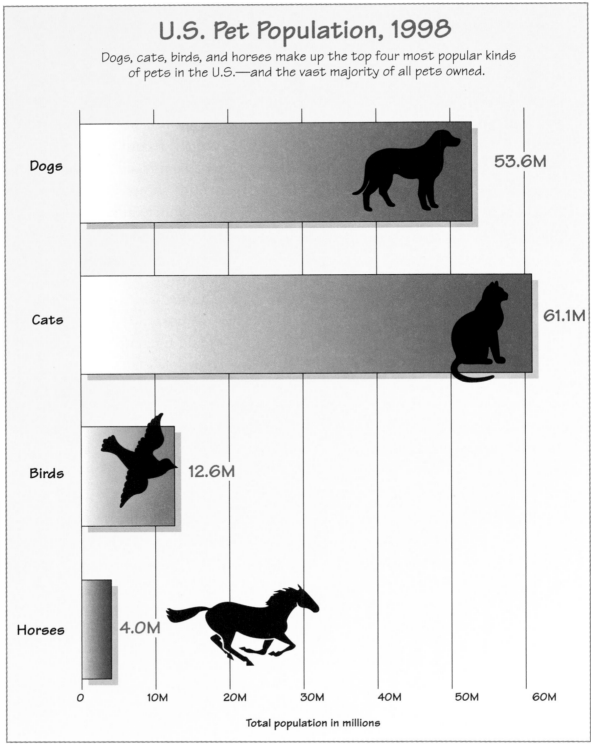

U.S. Pet Population, 1998

Dogs, cats, birds, and horses make up the top four most popular kinds
of pets in the U.S.—and the vast majority of all pets owned.

Dogs — 53.6M

Cats — 61.1M

Birds — 12.6M

Horses — 4.0M

0   10M   20M   30M   40M   50M   60M

Total population in millions

SOURCE: Based on data from American Veterinary Medical Association - Center for Information Management, 1997

U.S. Pet Ownership

Between 1987 and 1998 U.S. dog, cat, and horse ownership
declined while bird ownership rose.
Percentage of all U.S. households with selected pets, 1987 vs. 1998:

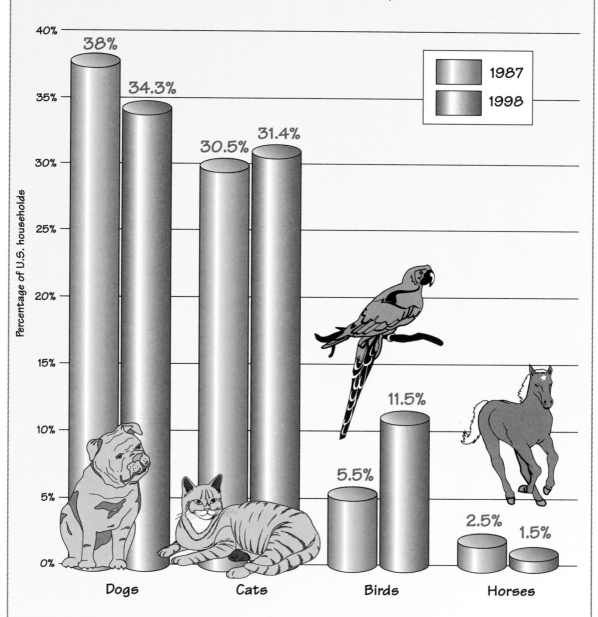

SOURCE: Based on data from American Veterinary Medical Association

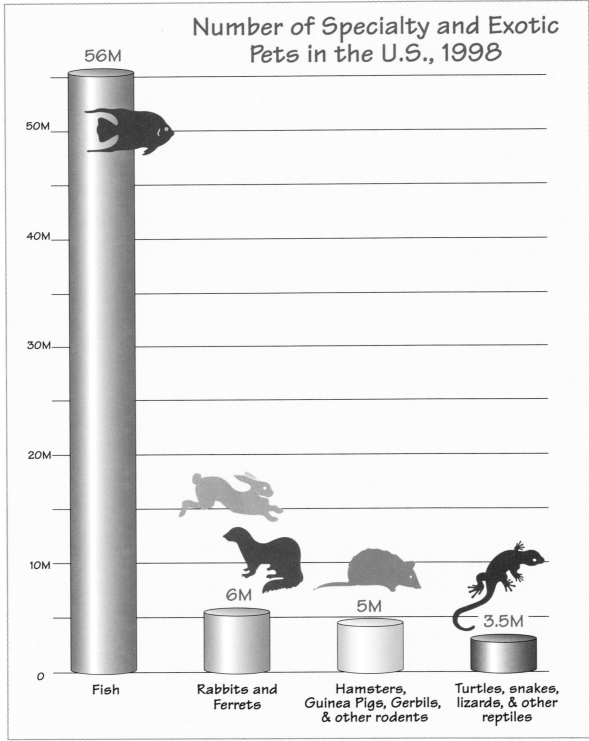

Number of Specialty and Exotic Pets in the U.S., 1998

56M — Fish
6M — Rabbits and Ferrets
5M — Hamsters, Guinea Pigs, Gerbils, & other rodents
3.5M — Turtles, snakes, lizards, & other reptiles

Pets

SOURCE: Based on data from American Veterinary Medical Association - Center for Information Management

U.S. Households with Pets, 1999

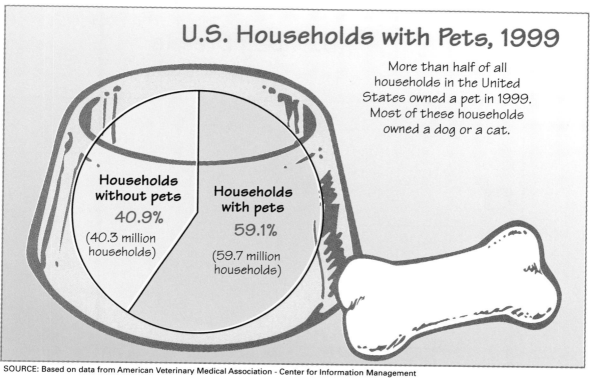

More than half of all households in the United States owned a pet in 1999. Most of these households owned a dog or a cat.

Households without pets
40.9%
(40.3 million households)

Households with pets
59.1%
(59.7 million households)

SOURCE: Based on data from American Veterinary Medical Association - Center for Information Management

Presidential Pets

Number of U.S. presidents who had at least one of these animals in the White House:

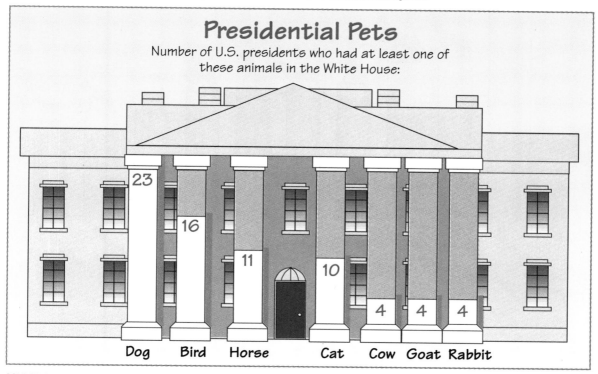

Dog	Bird	Horse	Cat	Cow	Goat	Rabbit
23	16	11	10	4	4	4

SOURCE: Based on data from *Presidential Pets* by Niall Kelly

Pets

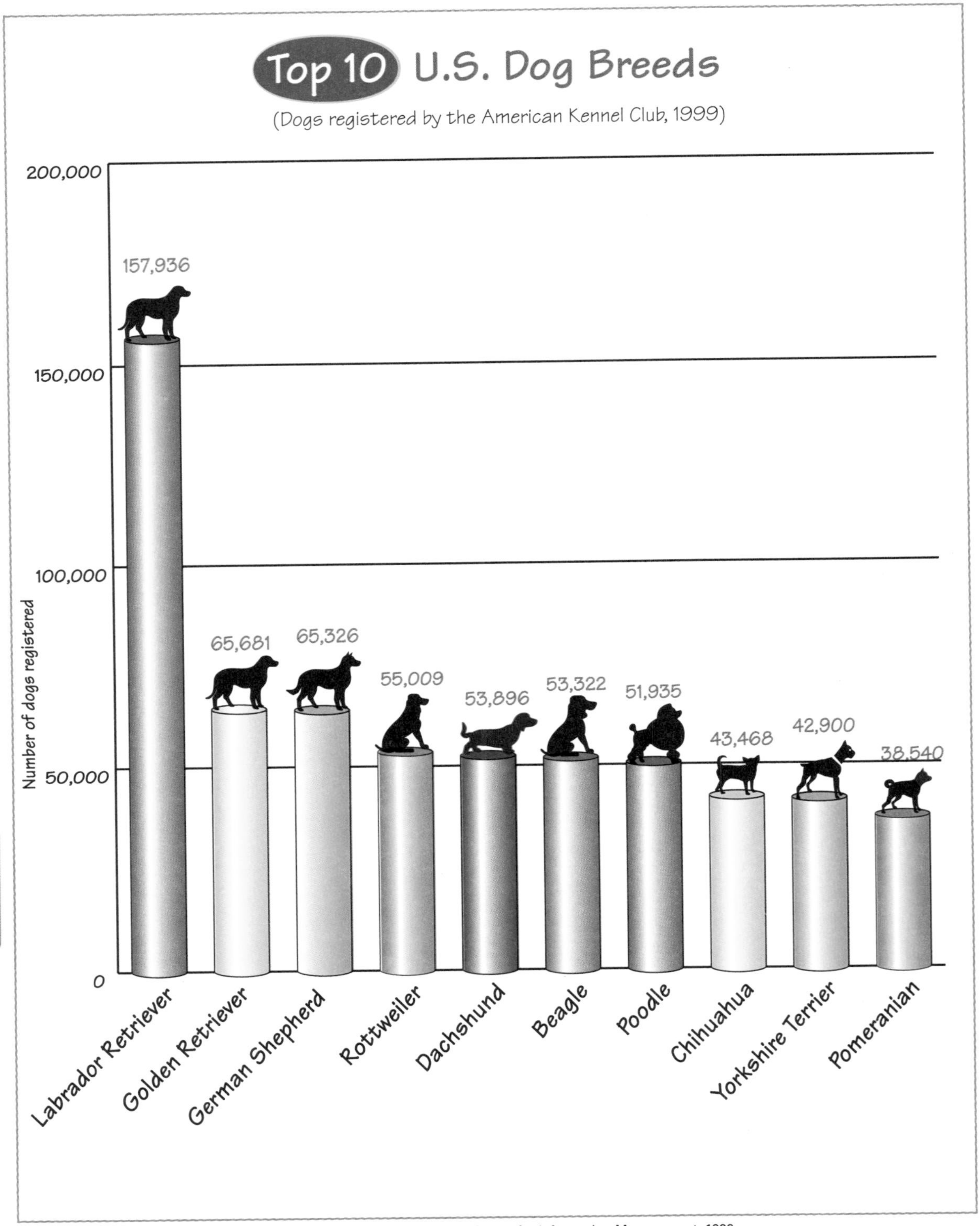

Top 10 U.S. Dog Breeds

(Dogs registered by the American Kennel Club, 1999)

Number of dogs registered

Breed	Number
Labrador Retriever	157,936
Golden Retriever	65,681
German Shepherd	65,326
Rottweiler	55,009
Dachshund	53,896
Beagle	53,322
Poodle	51,935
Chihuahua	43,468
Yorkshire Terrier	42,900
Pomeranian	38,540

Pets

SOURCE: Based on data from American Veterinary Medical Association - Center for Information Management, 1999

Top Dog-Loving States

(States where percentage of all households with dogs is between 37% and 47.9%)

SOURCE: Based on data from American Veterinary Medical Association - Center for Information Management, 1997

Number of Dogs Owned per U.S. Dog-Owning Household, 2000

The vast majority of U.S. dog owners own only one dog.

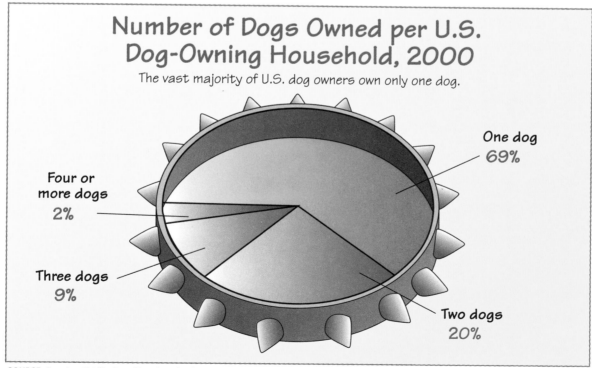

One dog
69%

Four or more dogs
2%

Three dogs
9%

Two dogs
20%

SOURCE: American Pet Products Manufacturing Association

Pets

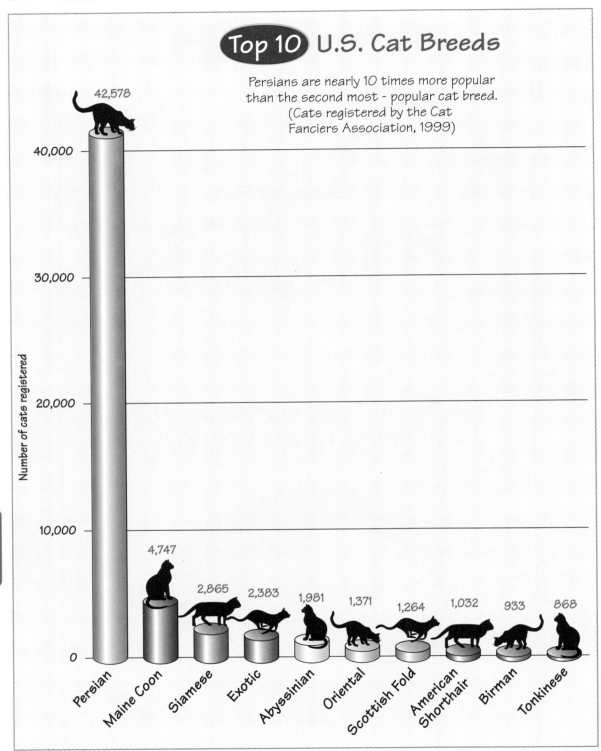

Top 10 U.S. Cat Breeds

Persians are nearly 10 times more popular than the second most - popular cat breed. (Cats registered by the Cat Fanciers Association, 1999)

Number of cats registered

- Persian — 42,578
- Maine Coon — 4,747
- Siamese — 2,865
- Exotic — 2,383
- Abyssinian — 1,981
- Oriental — 1,371
- Scottish Fold — 1,264
- American Shorthair — 1,032
- Birman — 933
- Tonkinese — 868

SOURCE: Based on data from American Veterinary Medical Association - Center for Information Management, 1997

Pets

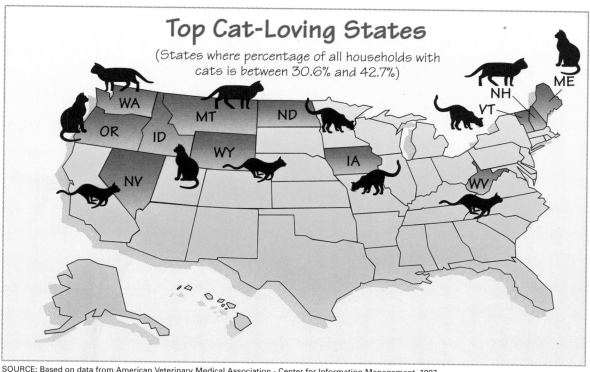

Top Cat-Loving States

(States where percentage of all households with cats is between 30.6% and 42.7%)

SOURCE: Based on data from American Veterinary Medical Association - Center for Information Management, 1997

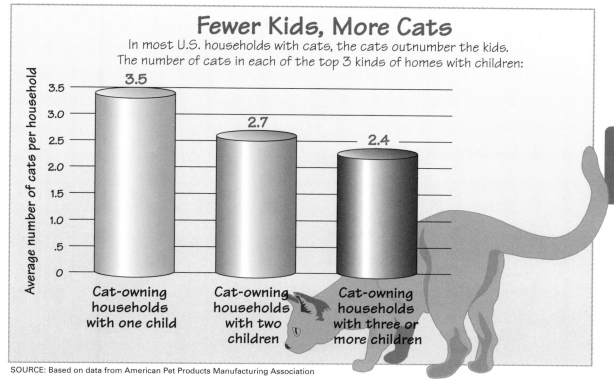

Fewer Kids, More Cats

In most U.S. households with cats, the cats outnumber the kids.
The number of cats in each of the top 3 kinds of homes with children:

Average number of cats per household

3.5 — Cat-owning households with one child
2.7 — Cat-owning households with two children
2.4 — Cat-owning households with three or more children

SOURCE: Based on data from American Pet Products Manufacturing Association

Pets

Number of Birds Owned per U.S. Bird-Owning Household

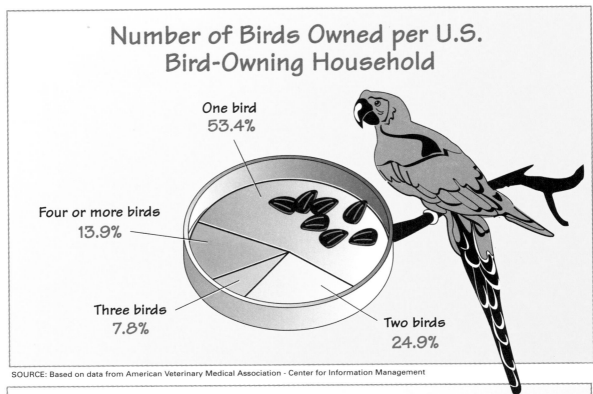

One bird
53.4%

Four or more birds
13.9%

Three birds
7.8%

Two birds
24.9%

SOURCE: Based on data from American Veterinary Medical Association - Center for Information Management

How Do Owners Celebrate Their Dogs' Birthdays?

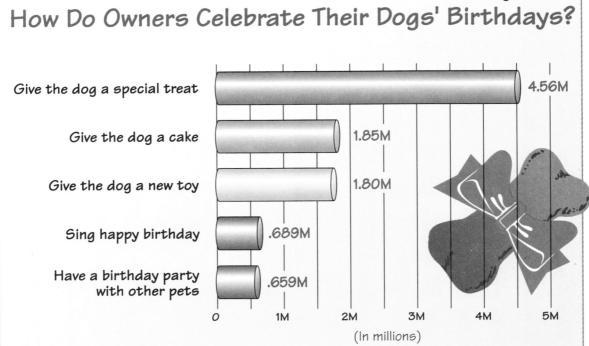

Give the dog a special treat — 4.56M

Give the dog a cake — 1.85M

Give the dog a new toy — 1.80M

Sing happy birthday — .689M

Have a birthday party with other pets — .659M

0   1M   2M   3M   4M   5M

(In millions)

SOURCE: American Pet Association

How Are Pets Combined?

U.S. horse owners are the most likely to also own dogs and cats.
Percentage of U.S. pet-owning households with pet combinations, 1996:

Dog-owning households that also own:	Cat-owning households that also own:	Bird-owning households that also own:	Horse-owning households that also own:
Cats 42.0%	Dogs 48.5%	Dogs 63.0%	Dogs 81.3%

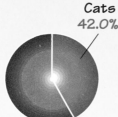   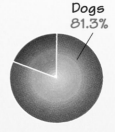

| Birds 9.2% | Birds 8.0% | Cats 47.5% | Cats 69.1% |

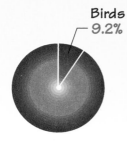 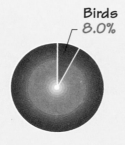 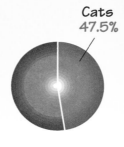 

| Horses 3.9% | Horses 3.9% | Horses 4.8% | Birds 14.6% |

  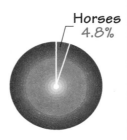 

Pets

SOURCE: Based on data from American Veterinary Medical Association - Center for Information Management, 1997

Percentage of All U.S. Households with Dogs and Cats or Both

Combination of dogs and cats owned:

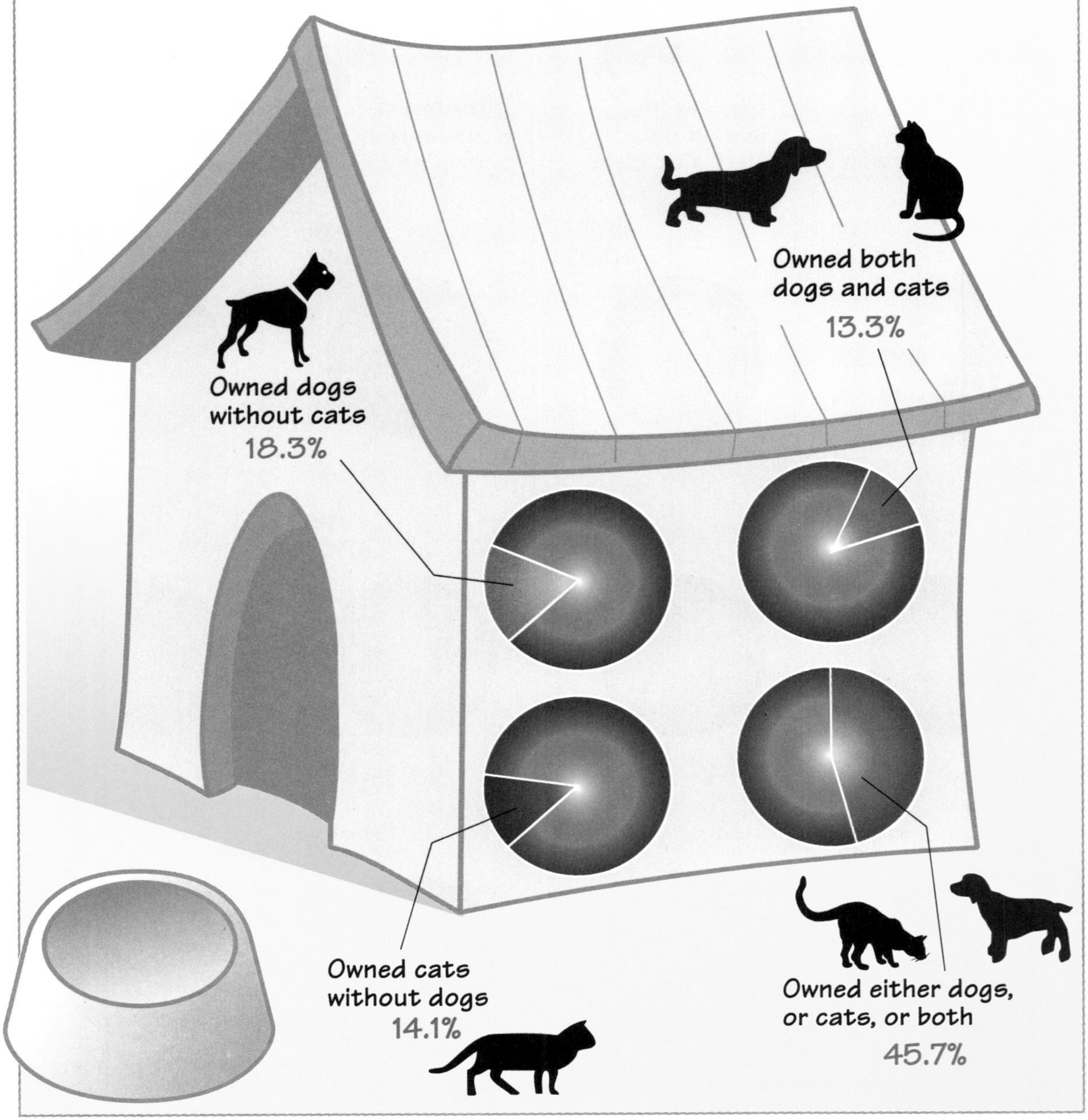

Owned dogs
without cats
18.3%

Owned both
dogs and cats
13.3%

Owned cats
without dogs
14.1%

Owned either dogs,
or cats, or both
45.7%

SOURCE: Based on data from American Veterinary Medical Association - Center for Information Management

Who Takes Care of Our Pets?

When it comes to caring for a pet in the U.S., nearly three-quarters of caregivers are women. More than half of caregivers are between 30- to 49-years-old.

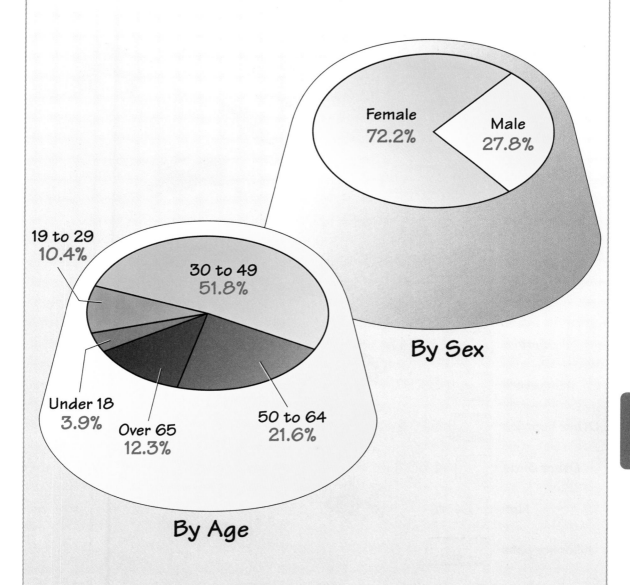

Female
72.2%

Male
27.8%

By Sex

30 to 49
51.8%

19 to 29
10.4%

Under 18
3.9%

Over 65
12.3%

50 to 64
21.6%

By Age

Pets

SOURCE: Based on data from American Veterinary Medical Association - Center for Information Management, 1997

Pets

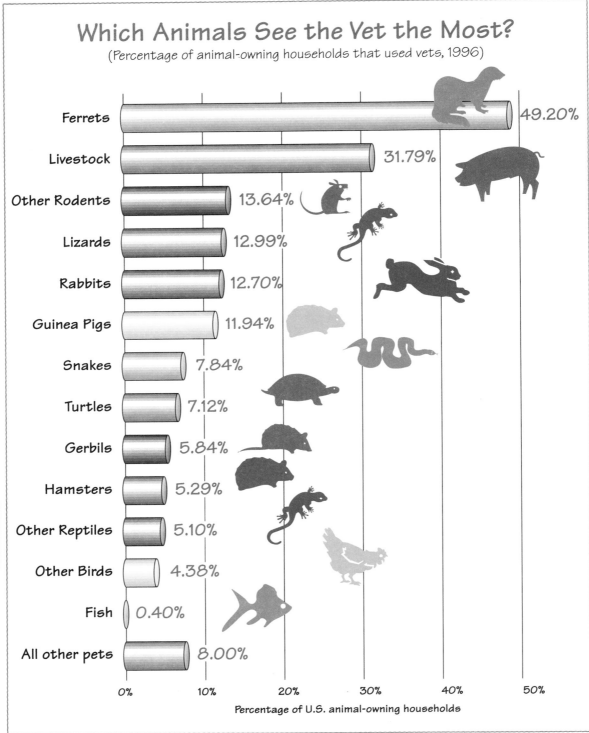

Which Animals See the Vet the Most?

(Percentage of animal-owning households that used vets, 1996)

Animal	Percentage
Ferrets	49.20%
Livestock	31.79%
Other Rodents	13.64%
Lizards	12.99%
Rabbits	12.70%
Guinea Pigs	11.94%
Snakes	7.84%
Turtles	7.12%
Gerbils	5.84%
Hamsters	5.29%
Other Reptiles	5.10%
Other Birds	4.38%
Fish	0.40%
All other pets	8.00%

Percentage of U.S. animal-owning households

SOURCE: Based on data from American Veterinary Medical Association - Center for Information Management, 1997

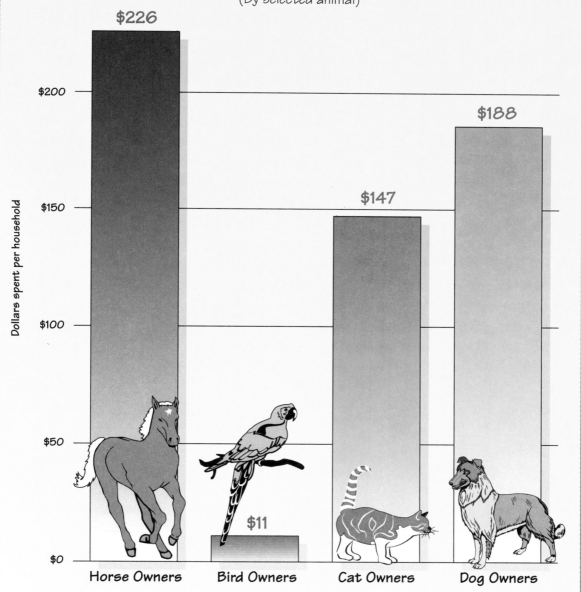

Average Yearly Cost for Veterinary Care, per Animal-Owning Household

U.S. horse owners spend the most on vets each year,
but dog owners spend only 16.8% less.
(By selected animal)

Dollars spent per household

$226

$200

$188

$150

$147

$100

$50

$11

$0

Horse Owners   Bird Owners   Cat Owners   Dog Owners

Pets

SOURCE: Based on data from American Veterinary Medical Association, *U.S. Pet Ownership and Demographics Sourcebook*, 1997

Pets

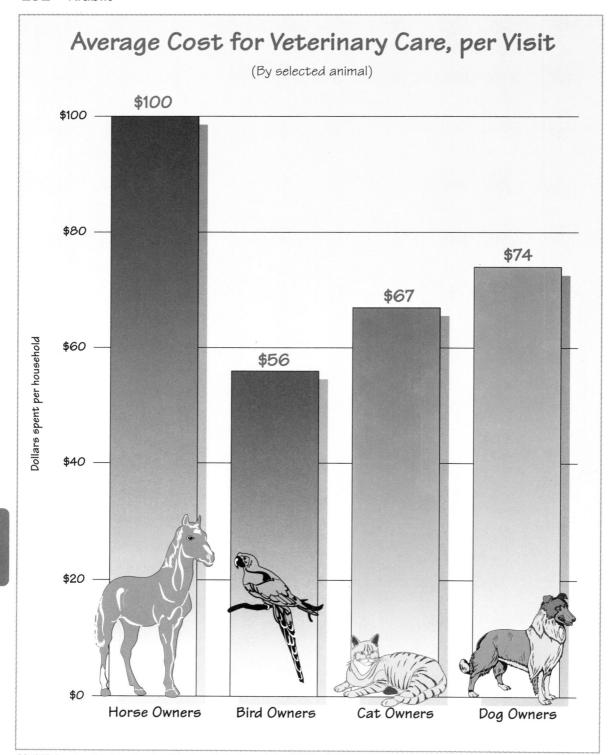

Average Cost for Veterinary Care, per Visit

(By selected animal)

Dollars spent per household

$100 — Horse Owners

$56 — Bird Owners

$67 — Cat Owners

$74 — Dog Owners

SOURCE: Based on data from American Veterinary Medical Association, *U.S. Pet Ownership and Demographics Sourcebook*, 1997

Average Yearly Cost for Veterinary Care, per Animal

On an animal-by-animal basis, dogs cost the most in medical care—
nearly 25% more than horses and about 37% more than cats.
(By selected animal)

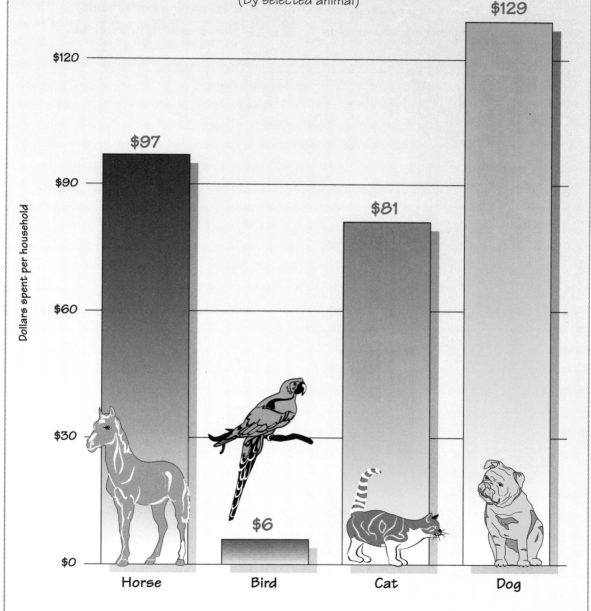

SOURCE: Based on data from American Veterinary Medical Association, *U.S. Pet Ownership and Demographics Sourcebook*, 1997

Pet-Owning Households: What Kind of Home?

Americans living in houses are the vast majority of pet owners.
(Percentage of U.S. households, 1996)

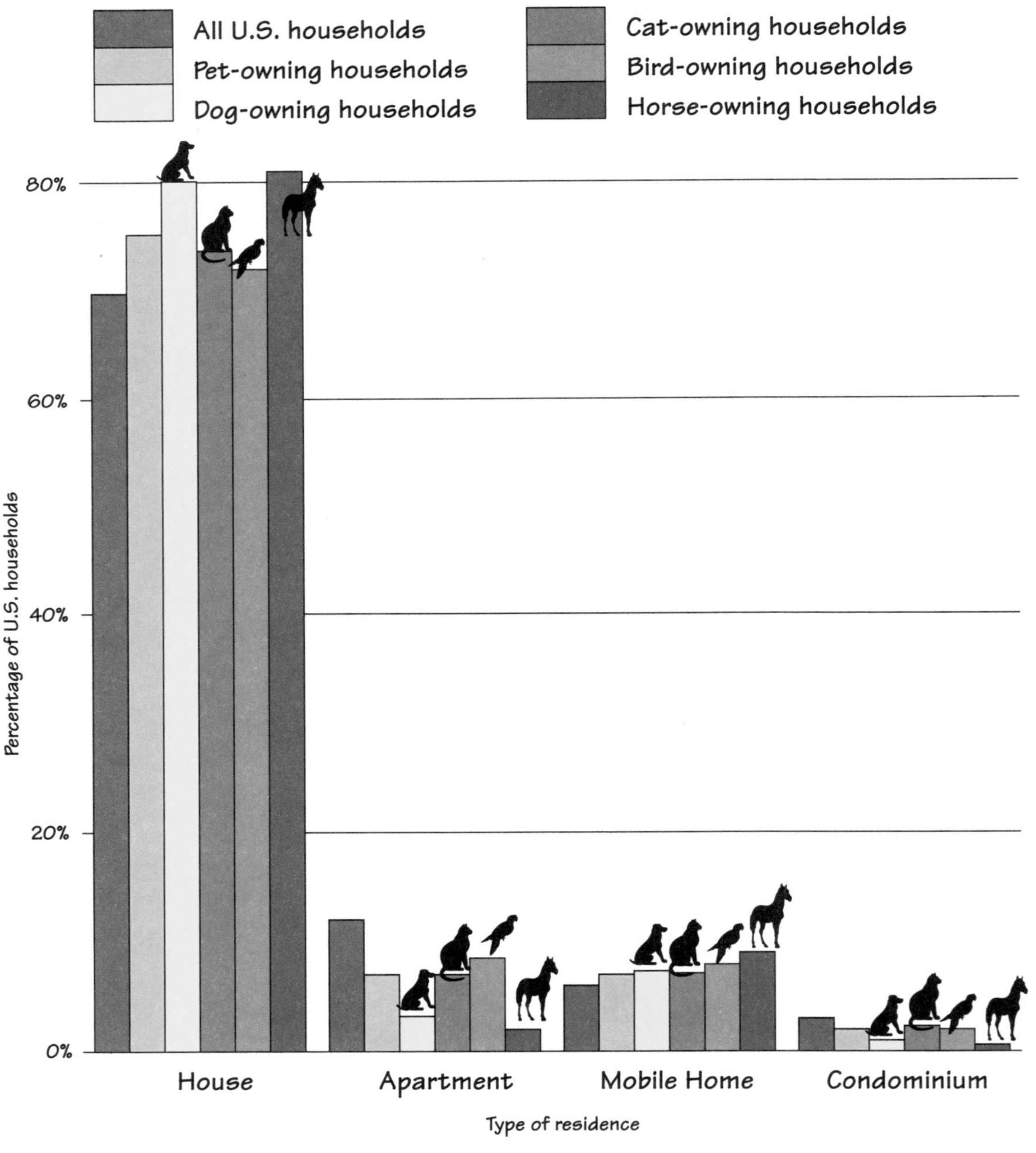

Legend:
- All U.S. households
- Pet-owning households
- Dog-owning households
- Cat-owning households
- Bird-owning households
- Horse-owning households

Percentage of U.S. households (y-axis: 0%, 20%, 40%, 60%, 80%)

Type of residence (x-axis: House, Apartment, Mobile Home, Condominium)

Pets

SOURCE: Based on data from American Veterinary Medical Association - Center for Information Management, 1997

Pet-Owning Households: Average Yearly Household Income

U.S. households with incomes greater than $25,000 own the most pets.
(Percentage of U.S. households, 1996)

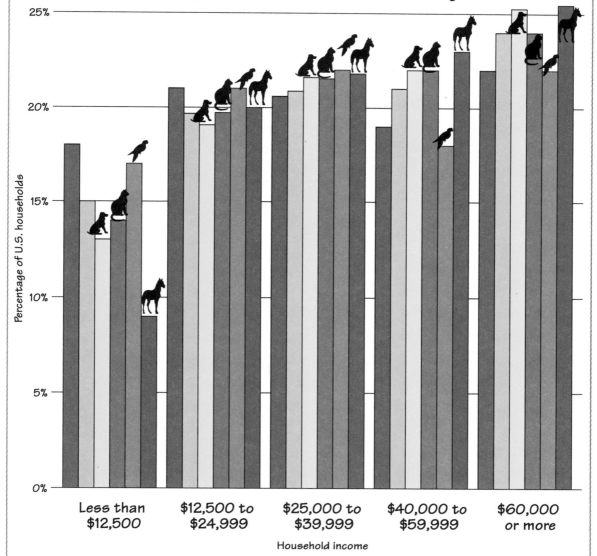

SOURCE: Based on data from American Veterinary Medical Association - Center for Information Management, 1997

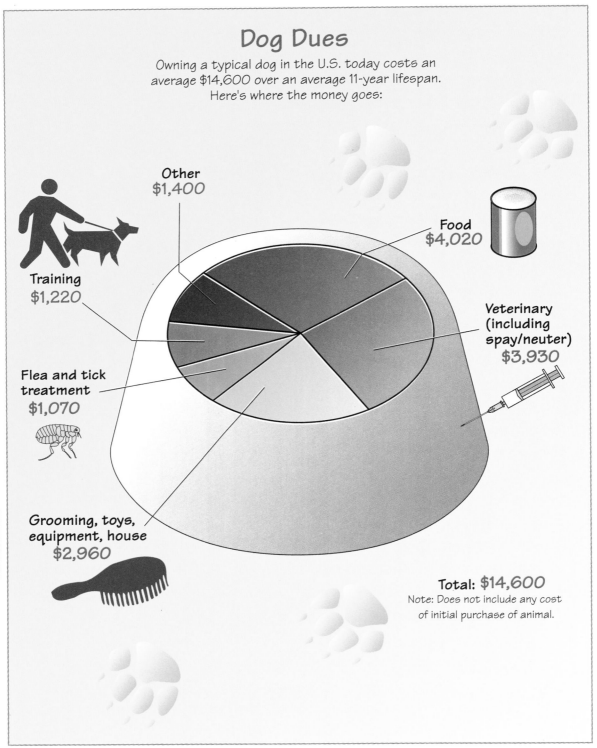

Dog Dues

Owning a typical dog in the U.S. today costs an average $14,600 over an average 11-year lifespan. Here's where the money goes:

Other
$1,400

Food
$4,020

Training
$1,220

Veterinary
(including
spay/neuter)
$3,930

Flea and tick
treatment
$1,070

Grooming, toys,
equipment, house
$2,960

Total: **$14,600**
Note: Does not include any cost
of initial purchase of animal.

Pets

Average Lifespan of Selected Pets

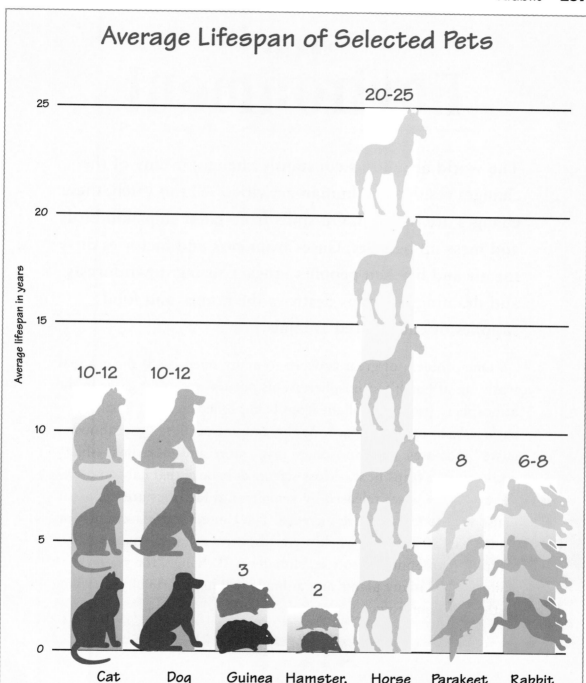

The Environment

The world around us constantly changes. Many of the changes result from human activities. All too often, these changes are harmful. Oil spills from giant ships kill birds and mess up beaches. Gases from cars and factories dirty the air and blacken people's lungs. Cutting down forests and draining wetlands destroys the homes and food supplies of endangered animals.

One problem of great concern to many scientists is the gradual warming of Earth's atmosphere. This occurs as certain gases in the atmosphere prevent sunlight from being reflected from Earth's surface back out into space. As the amount of these "greenhouse gases" increases, the atmosphere traps more and more heat—like a greenhouse traps heat. Most scientists believe that carbon dioxide and other gases released by vehicles and factories are the main cause for the temperature increase. The United States accounts for more than 20% of the world's greenhouse gas emissions. As temperatures continue to rise, climates will change, the sea level will rise, and many plants and animals will have difficulty surviving in their current homes.

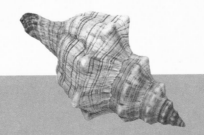

Another serious problem is the effect of air pollution on people's health. People with lung and heart disease are very sensitive to air pollution. So, too, are children and elderly people. The U.S. government measures air quality in approximately 3,000 places. In 1998, Riverside, California, had 106 days when there was so much pollution that the air was classified as unhealthy. (California cities consistently rate the worst in this regard.) Los Angeles, California, had 63 unhealthy days and Bakersfield, California, had 55 unhealthy days.

Some people are taking action to solve environmental problems. Engineers have designed cars and home appliances that use less energy. Homes are better insulated, so that less energy is needed for heating and cooling. Parks around the world have been established, where wild animals and their homes are protected. Communities have recycling programs that enable us to reuse paper, plastic, glass, and other materials. This all saves energy and other valuable natural resources. It also limits pollution.

Many kids take part in projects that improve the environment. They clean up local parks and start school recycling programs. Most importantly, they spread the word about the environment's three R's: reduce, reuse, and recycle.

Top 5 Most-Polluted U.S. Cities, by Air Quality

(Number of unhealthy days in 1998)

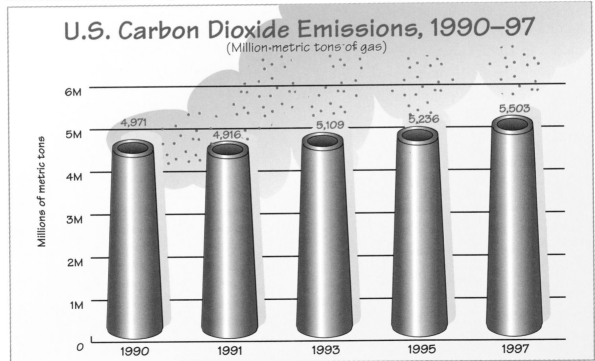

3.
Bakersfield, CA
55

4.
Fresno, CA
50

1.
Riverside–
San Bernardino, CA
106

2.
Los Angeles, CA
63

5.
Houston, TX
47

SOURCE: Environmental Protection Agency, *National Air Quality and Emissions Trends Report*

U.S. Carbon Dioxide Emissions, 1990–97

(Million-metric tons of gas)

Millions of metric tons

Year	Emissions
1990	4,971
1991	4,916
1993	5,109
1995	5,236
1997	5,503

SOURCE: U.S. Environmental Protection Agency

Where Carbon Monoxide & Lead Pollution Come From

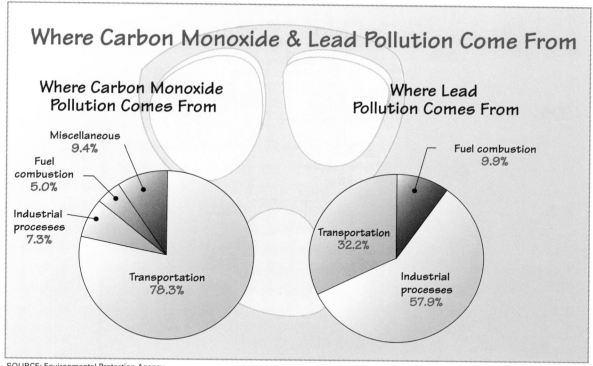

Where Carbon Monoxide Pollution Comes From

Miscellaneous 9.4%

Fuel combustion 5.0%

Industrial processes 7.3%

Transportation 78.3%

Where Lead Pollution Comes From

Fuel combustion 9.9%

Transportation 32.2%

Industrial processes 57.9%

SOURCE: Environmental Protection Agency

Emissions of Greenhouse Gases, by Type

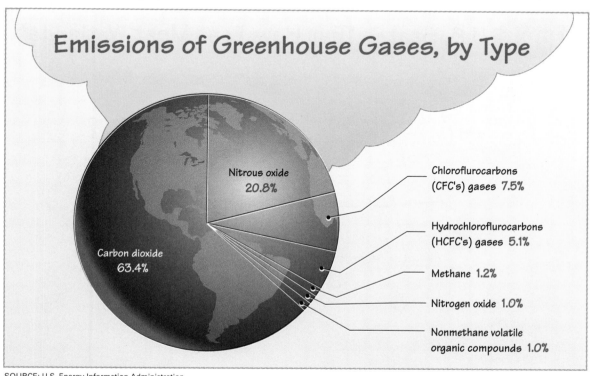

Nitrous oxide 20.8%

Carbon dioxide 63.4%

Chloroflurocarbons (CFC's) gases 7.5%

Hydrochloroflurocarbons (HCFC's) gases 5.1%

Methane 1.2%

Nitrogen oxide 1.0%

Nonmethane volatile organic compounds 1.0%

SOURCE: U.S. Energy Information Administration

The Environment

America's Ten Most Endangered Rivers

1. Lower Snake River
2. Missouri River
7. Fox River
6. Cedar River
9. Coal River
5. Yellowstone River
10. Bear River
8. Carmel River
4. Upper San Pedro River
3. Alabama-Coosa-Tallapoosa River

SOURCE: American Rivers, *America's Most Endangered Rivers of 1999*

Top 5 U.S. States That Have Lost Most Wetlands*
(In percent of total area)

1. California -91%
3. Iowa -89%
2. Ohio -90%
4. Missouri -87%
5. Illinois -87%

*From 1780 to the late 1990s

SOURCE: Environmental Protection Agency

The Environment

Top 5 Superfund Hazardous Waste Sites

About 70 million Americans live within 4 miles of a toxic waste site.

Number of sites

- Oct. 23 1981 — 115*
- June 10 1986 — 703
- Feb. 11 1991 — 1,891
- June 17 1996 — 1,227
- July 22 1999 — 1,226

*proposed sites

SOURCE: Environmental Protection Agency

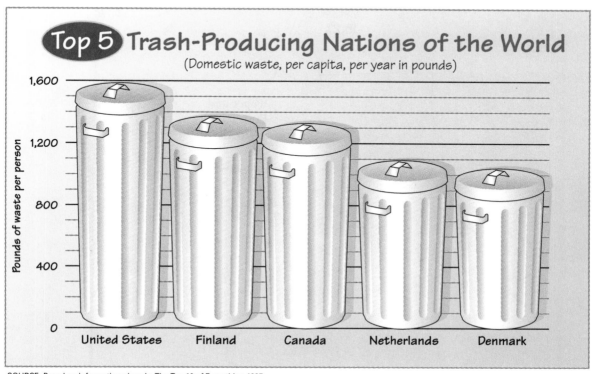

Top 5 Trash-Producing Nations of the World

(Domestic waste, per capita, per year in pounds)

Pounds of waste per person

United States · Finland · Canada · Netherlands · Denmark

SOURCE: Based on information given in *The Top 10 of Everything 1997*

The Environment

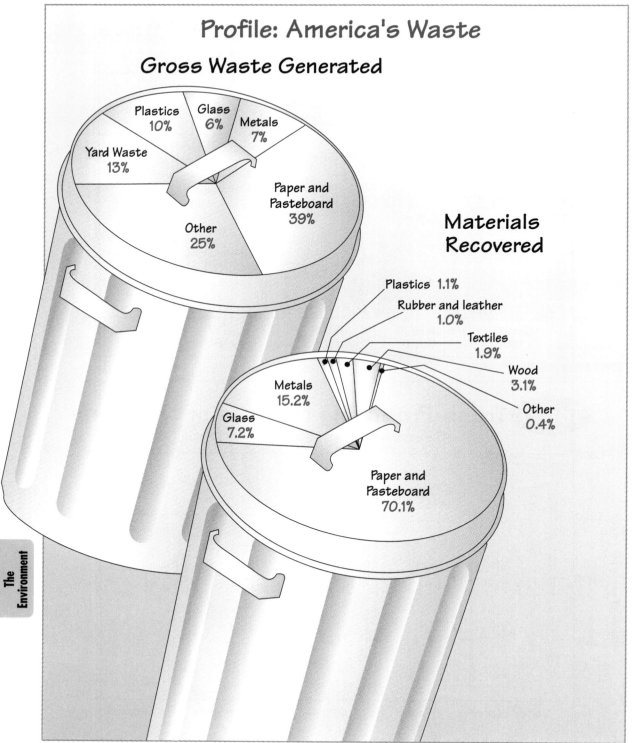

Profile: America's Waste

Gross Waste Generated

Plastics 10%
Glass 6%
Metals 7%
Yard Waste 13%
Paper and Pasteboard 39%
Other 25%

Materials Recovered

Plastics 1.1%
Rubber and leather 1.0%
Textiles 1.9%
Wood 3.1%
Other 0.4%
Metals 15.2%
Glass 7.2%
Paper and Pasteboard 70.1%

The Environment

How Much Trash Gets Recycled?

On average, Americans create about 208 million tons of trash each year. That averages out to about 4.3 pounds of garbage created per person, per day. (Percentage of total trash, by type)

 Percent of total that is recycled

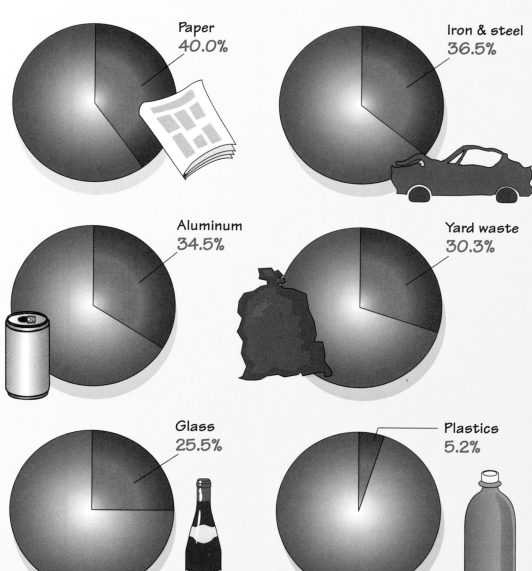

Paper
40.0%

Iron & steel
36.5%

Aluminum
34.5%

Yard waste
30.3%

Glass
25.5%

Plastics
5.2%

SOURCE: Environmental Protection Agency

Top 5 U.S. States with Most Hazardous Waste Sites, 1999

3. California 91 Sites

2. Pennsylvania 97 Sites

4. New York 79 Sites

5. Michigan 72 Sites

1. New Jersey 108 Sites

SOURCE: Environmental Protection Agency

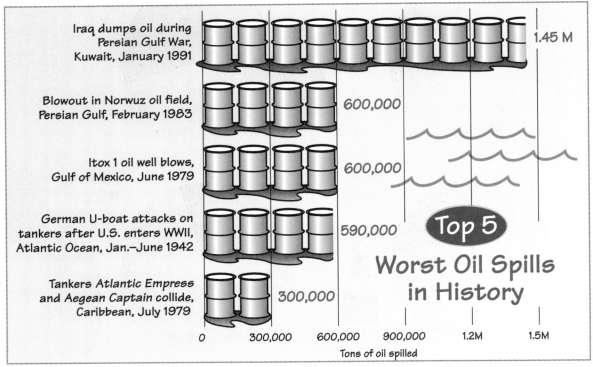

Top 5 Worst Oil Spills in History

Iraq dumps oil during Persian Gulf War, Kuwait, January 1991 — 1.45 M

Blowout in Norwuz oil field, Persian Gulf, February 1983 — 600,000

Itox 1 oil well blows, Gulf of Mexico, June 1979 — 600,000

German U-boat attacks on tankers after U.S. enters WWII, Atlantic Ocean, Jan.–June 1942 — 590,000

Tankers Atlantic Empress and Aegean Captain collide, Caribbean, July 1979 — 300,000

0   300,000   600,000   900,000   1.2M   1.5M

Tons of oil spilled

SOURCE: United Nations

Top 10 U.S. Producers of Toxic Wastes, by Industry

(In millions and billions)

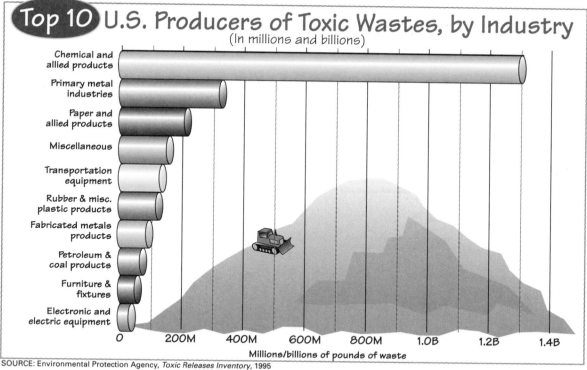

Chemical and allied products
Primary metal industries
Paper and allied products
Miscellaneous
Transportation equipment
Rubber & misc. plastic products
Fabricated metals products
Petroleum & coal products
Furniture & fixtures
Electronic and electric equipment

0   200M   400M   600M   800M   1.0B   1.2B   1.4B

Millions/billions of pounds of waste

SOURCE: Environmental Protection Agency, *Toxic Releases Inventory*, 1995

Nations with the Most Species of Threatened Mammals and Birds

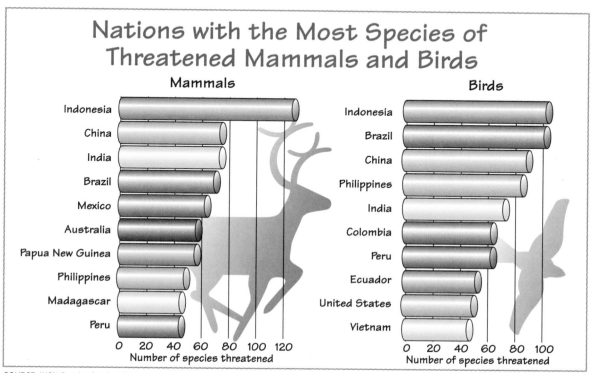

Mammals

Indonesia
China
India
Brazil
Mexico
Australia
Papua New Guinea
Philippines
Madagascar
Peru

0   20   40   60   80   100   120
Number of species threatened

Birds

Indonesia
Brazil
China
Philippines
India
Colombia
Peru
Ecuador
United States
Vietnam

0   20   40   60   80   100
Number of species threatened

SOURCE: IUCN Species Survival Commission

The Environment

Animal Species in Trouble, 1999
Endangered Species

Animal	U.S.	Foreign
Mammals	60	251
Birds	75	178
Reptiles	14	65
Amphibians	9	8
Fish	70	11
Snails	18	1
Clams	61	2
Crustaceans	17	0
Insects	28	4
Arachnids	5	0

Legend: U.S. / Foreign

Total animals in the U.S.: 357

Number of species endangered (0, 50, 100, 150, 200, 250)

Threatened Species

Animal	U.S.	Foreign
Mammals	8	16
Birds	6	15
Reptiles	21	14
Amphibians	7	1
Fish	40	0
Snails	10	0
Clams	8	0
Crustaceans	3	0
Insects	9	0
Arachnids	0	0

Legend: U.S. / Foreign

Total animals in the U.S.: 121

Number of species threatened (0, 5, 10, 15, 20, 25, 30, 35, 40)

SOURCE: U.S. Fish and Wildlife Service, *List of Endangered and Threatened Species,* March 31, 1999

The Environment

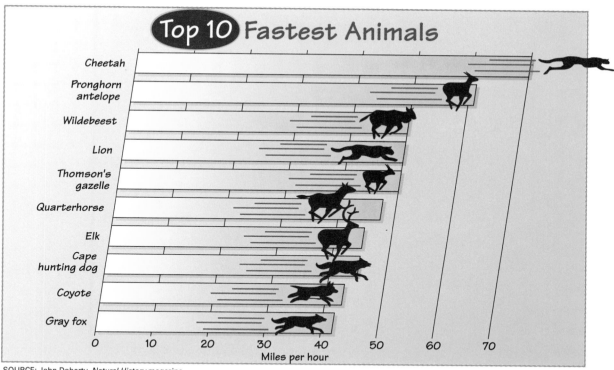

Top 10 Fastest Animals

Cheetah
Pronghorn antelope
Wildebeest
Lion
Thomson's gazelle
Quarterhorse
Elk
Cape hunting dog
Coyote
Gray fox

0   10   20   30   40   50   60   70
Miles per hour

SOURCE: John Doherty, *Natural History* magazine

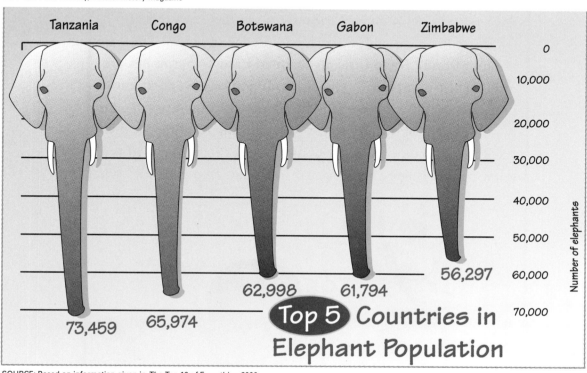

Tanzania   Congo   Botswana   Gabon   Zimbabwe

0
10,000
20,000
30,000
40,000
50,000
60,000
70,000

Number of elephants

56,297
62,998   61,794

Top 5 Countries in Elephant Population

73,459   65,974

SOURCE: Based on information given in *The Top 10 of Everything 2000*

Attitudes

So what do you think about fashion, politics, religion, dating, music, drinking, and a zillion other things? What's your favorite cereal, hobby, TV show? What are your attitudes toward people who cheat, people of different races, elderly people?

Who—and what—influences your opinions? Your parents, teachers, or friends? What you see on television or read in books?

How quickly do you form opinions? What does it take to make you change your attitude toward something, or someone? Are you willing to consider the facts and listen to reason?

Everyone has opinions on a wide range of issues. These opinions are important. Town officials want to know what issues are important to taxpayers. Jacket manufacturers want to know what brands are "in" with teenage buyers. Politicians want to know for whom people of different ages are planning to vote—and why.

Research companies are constantly taking surveys to find out what people think about everything, what they like, and what they

plan to do in the future. For instance, one survey of teenagers ages 15 through 18 found that their main concern was getting a good job. A survey of pre-teens found that more 7 to 12 year olds preferred to play outside than to go to a sports event. Another survey found that kids think playing sports is more fun that going to the movies—and much, much more fun than watching TV!

Opinions can differ widely depending on age, sex, education, economic status, and other factors. For example, romance books are more popular with girls than with boys, but science fiction tales are favorites of more boys than girls. Men say a person's eyes are the first thing they notice when they meet someone; women are most likely to notice a person's smile and teeth when they're first introduced. College graduates are more likely than high school dropouts to support women's right to have abortions.

Many surveys suggest that young people are more tolerant than older people. For example, there are indications that teenagers are more tolerant than adults of racial diversity. Young adults also seem to be more accepting than older adults of single parenthood.

Attitudes

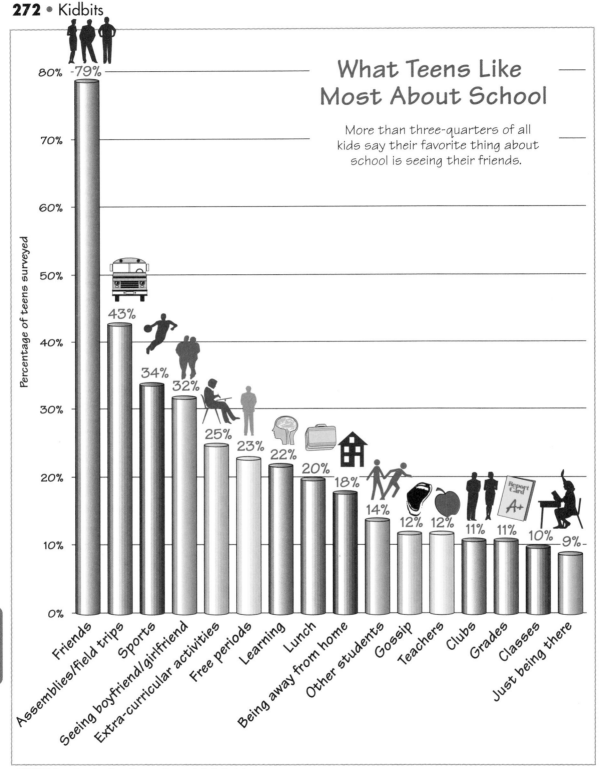

What Teens Like Most About School

More than three-quarters of all kids say their favorite thing about school is seeing their friends.

Percentage of teens surveyed

- Friends — 79%
- Assemblies/field trips — 43%
- Sports — 34%
- Seeing boyfriend/girlfriend — 32%
- Extra-curricular activities — 25%
- Free periods — 23%
- Learning — 22%
- Lunch — 20%
- Being away from home — 18%
- Other students — 14%
- Gossip — 12%
- Teachers — 12%
- Clubs — 11%
- Grades — 11%
- Classes — 10%
- Just being there — 9%

Attitudes

SOURCE: Based on data from Teenage Research Unlimited, Inc.

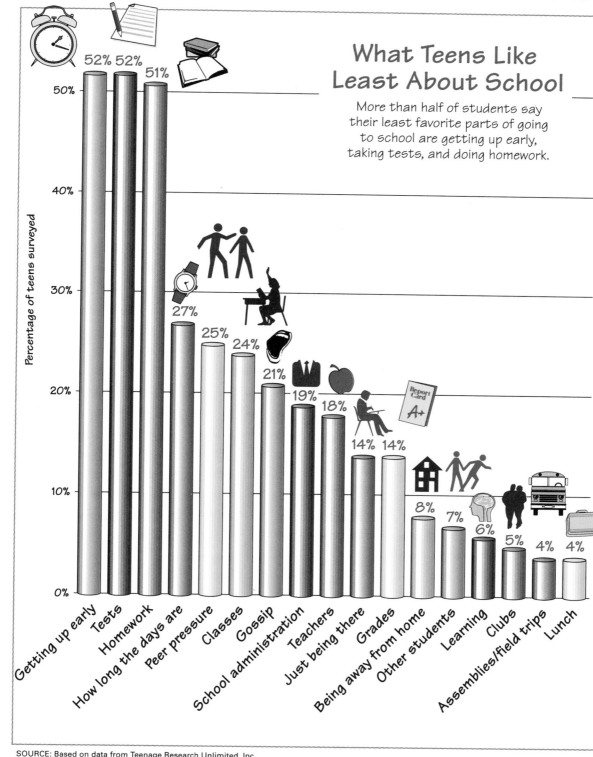

What Teens Like Least About School

More than half of students say their least favorite parts of going to school are getting up early, taking tests, and doing homework.

Percentage of teens surveyed

52% Getting up early
52% Tests
51% Homework
27% How long the days are
25% Peer pressure
24% Classes
21% Gossip
19% School administration
18% Teachers
14% Just being there
14% Grades
8% Being away from home
7% Other students
6% Learning
5% Clubs
4% Assemblies/field trips
4% Lunch

Attitudes

SOURCE: Based on data from Teenage Research Unlimited, Inc.

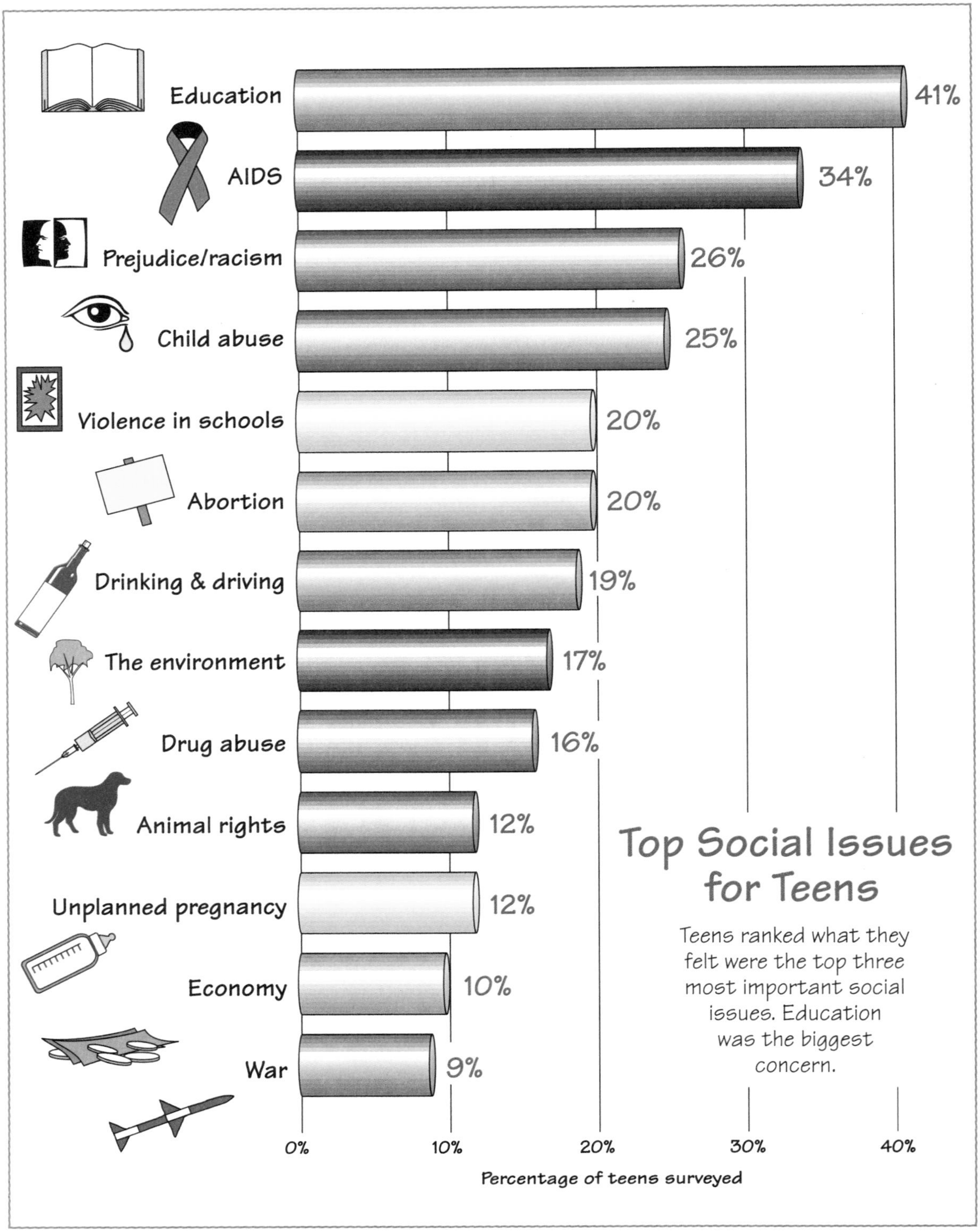

Attitudes

Top Social Issues for Teens

Education — 41%

AIDS — 34%

Prejudice/racism — 26%

Child abuse — 25%

Violence in schools — 20%

Abortion — 20%

Drinking & driving — 19%

The environment — 17%

Drug abuse — 16%

Animal rights — 12%

Unplanned pregnancy — 12%

Economy — 10%

War — 9%

0%   10%   20%   30%   40%

Percentage of teens surveyed

Teens ranked what they felt were the top three most important social issues. Education was the biggest concern.

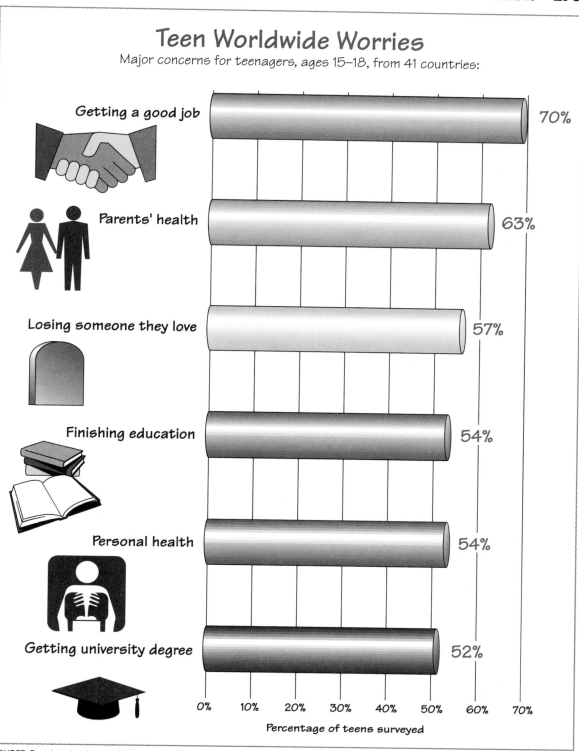

Teen Worldwide Worries

Major concerns for teenagers, ages 15–18, from 41 countries:

- Getting a good job — 70%
- Parents' health — 63%
- Losing someone they love — 57%
- Finishing education — 54%
- Personal health — 54%
- Getting university degree — 52%

Percentage of teens surveyed

Attitudes

SOURCE: Based on data from BrainWaves Group's New World Teen Study

Teachers Think Less of Students

Percentage of teachers who think their students have
declined over the years because students today are:

Less respectful
of authority — 81%

Less
ethical/moral — 73%

Less
responsible — 65%

More
self-centered — 60%

Less
studious — 57%

0%   20%   40%   60%   80%

Percentage of teachers

Attitudes

SOURCE: Based on data from Educational Communications for *Who's Who Among America's Teachers*

Adults Know Kids Are Internet Experts

Who did adults say knew the
most about the Internet?

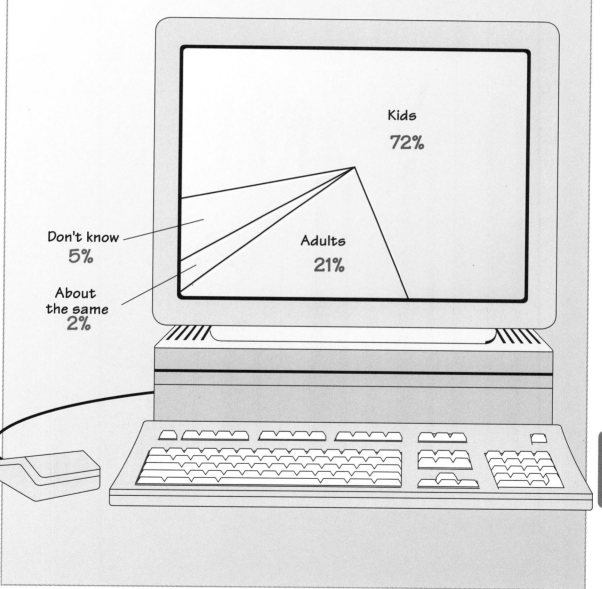

Kids
72%

Don't know
5%

Adults
21%

About
the same
2%

Attitudes

SOURCE: Based on data from The Direct Marketing Association

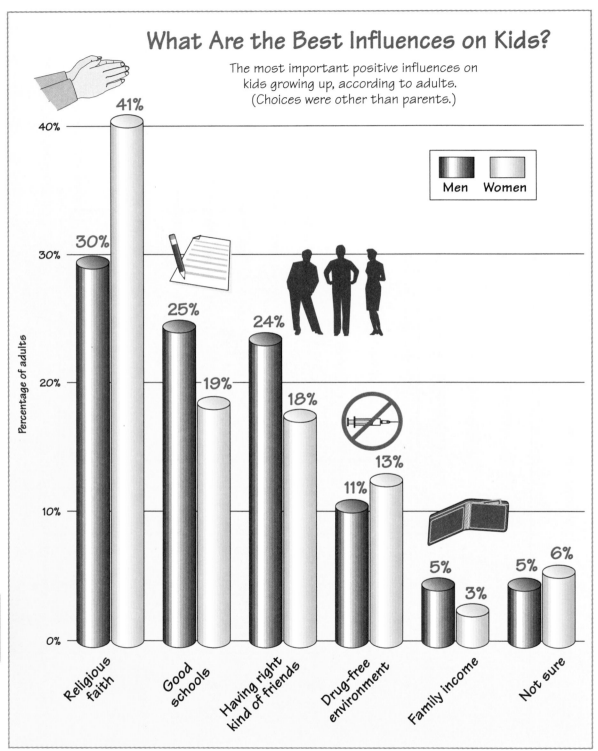

What Are the Best Influences on Kids?

The most important positive influences on kids growing up, according to adults. (Choices were other than parents.)

Men   Women

Percentage of adults

- Religious faith: 30% (Men), 41% (Women)
- Good schools: 25% (Men), 19% (Women)
- Having right kind of friends: 24% (Men), 18% (Women)
- Drug-free environment: 11% (Men), 13% (Women)
- Family income: 5% (Men), 3% (Women)
- Not sure: 5% (Men), 6% (Women)

SOURCE: Based on data from Lutheran Brotherhood

Attitudes

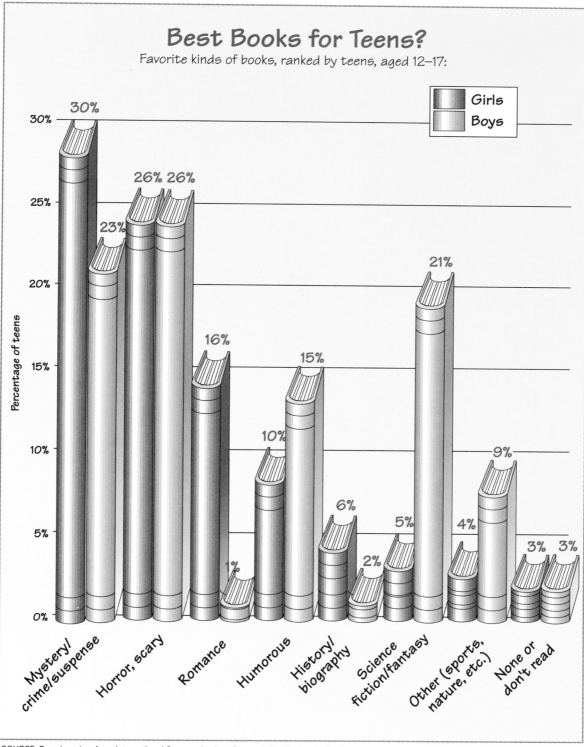

Best Books for Teens?

Favorite kinds of books, ranked by teens, aged 12–17:

Girls
Boys

Percentage of teens

- Mystery/crime/suspense — 30%, 23%
- Horror, scary — 26%, 26%
- Romance — 16%, 1%
- Humorous — 10%, 15%
- History/biography — 6%, 2%
- Science fiction/fantasy — 5%, 21%
- Other (sports, nature, etc.) — 4%, 9%
- None or don't read — 3%, 3%

Attitudes

SOURCE: Based on data from International Communications Research for Hewlett-Packard

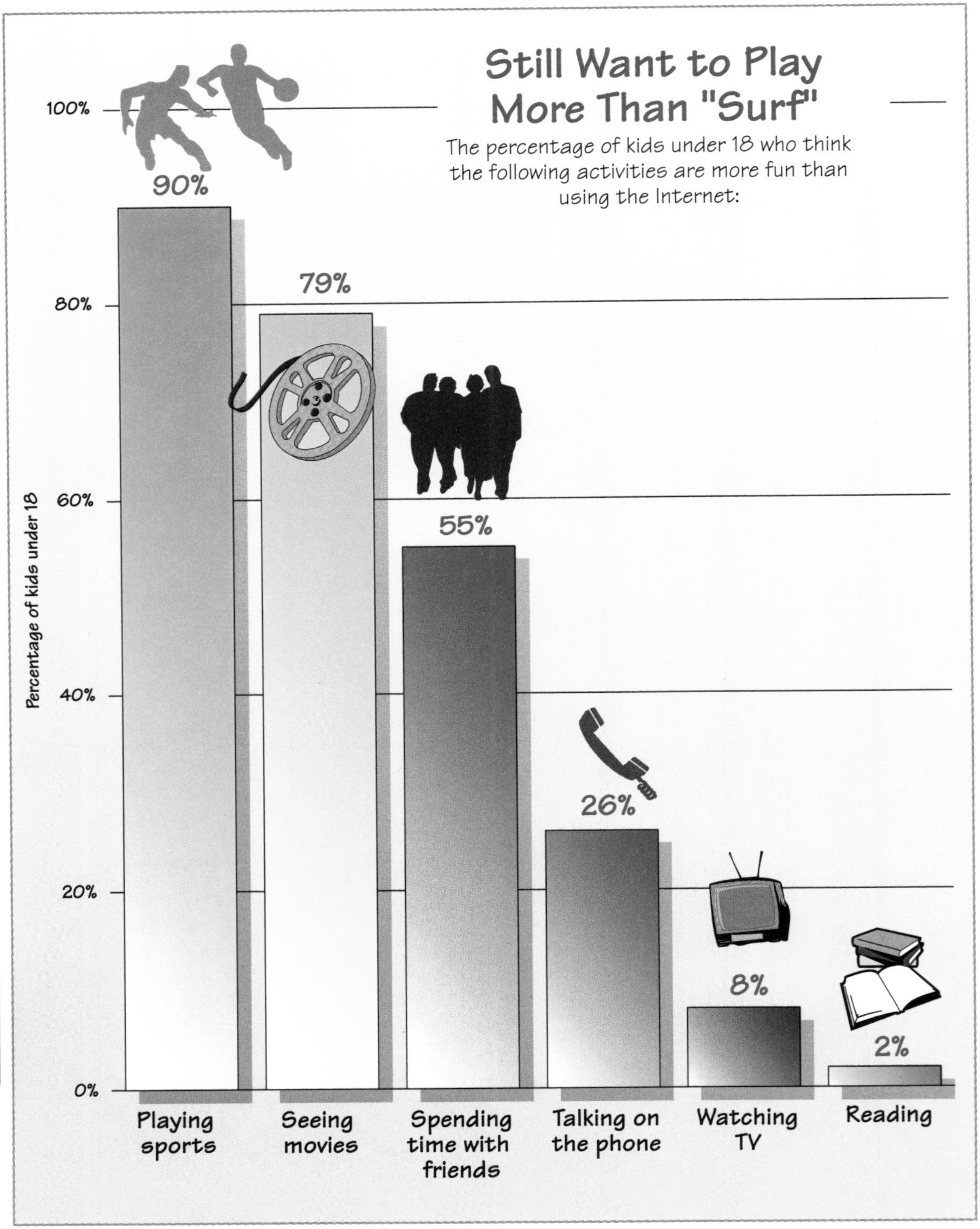

Still Want to Play More Than "Surf"

The percentage of kids under 18 who think the following activities are more fun than using the Internet:

Percentage of kids under 18

Activity	Percentage
Playing sports	90%
Seeing movies	79%
Spending time with friends	55%
Talking on the phone	26%
Watching TV	8%
Reading	2%

Attitudes

SOURCE: Based on data from Jupiter Communications' *1997 Online Kids Report*

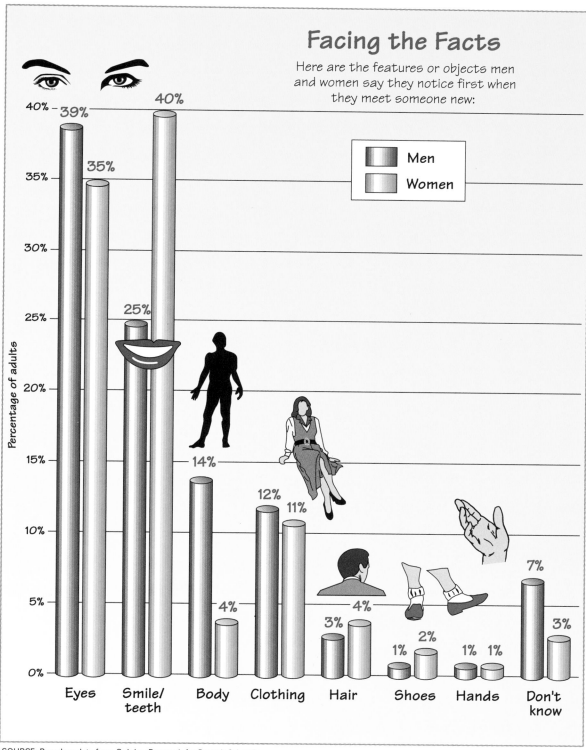

Facing the Facts

Here are the features or objects men and women say they notice first when they meet someone new:

Men
Women

Percentage of adults

Feature	Men	Women
Eyes	39%	35%
Smile/teeth	25%	40%
Body	14%	4%
Clothing	12%	11%
Hair	3%	4%
Shoes	1%	2%
Hands	1%	1%
Don't know	7%	3%

SOURCE: Based on data from Opinion Research for Bausch & Lomb

Attitudes

Food

Food gives you energy, helps you grow, and keeps you healthy. It can also give you lots of pleasure. A meal of your favorite foods is always a treat. So, too, are those after-school snacks!

It's important to eat lots of fruit, veggies, and whole-grain starchy foods, such as bread and pasta. You should eat meat only in moderation. And, by proportion, you should eat very little fat. Many Americans do not follow this advice. They eat more cheese than lettuce, more fatty beef than lean chicken, more pepperoni pizzas than pizzas topped with vegetables. A diagram called a food pyramid shows which foods make up a healthy diet (look on page 297—or you can usually find one on your favorite cereal box or loaf of bread). But a recent study found that only 1% of American children met the food pyramid's guidelines.

Many factors influence what we eat. These include where we live, our religious beliefs, the amount of money we have, and how much time we have to prepare and eat meals.

People in different places have different food favorites. People in Philadelphia, for example, like pepper pot soup. In New

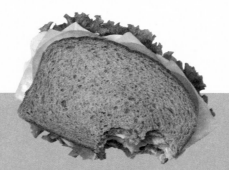

stock—beef is the main source of protein.

Cow milk is drunk in Canada, sheep and goat milk in Turkey, and reindeer milk is a staple in Finland.

Advertising plays a role in food preferences, too. A large supermarket may carry 20,000 different items, including dozens of brands of bread, breakfast cereal, cookies, and frozen desserts. Advertising helps persuade buyers to select a certain brand or item. General Mills spent $430 million advertising its products in 1998; Kellogg was close behind with $324 million; Coca-Cola spent $315 million, but McDonald's was the top spender at $571 million.

Orleans, French onion soup is the favorite. In New York and New England people prefer white cheddar cheese. Elsewhere in the U.S., yellow cheddar is the hands-down favorite. The popularity of brands also varies from region to region. For example, people who live in the South prefer one brand of peanut butter. On the West Coast, another brand is much more popular.

People in different countries also have different eating habits. Rice is the basic starchy food in Asia, while potatoes fill this role in northern Europe. Fish is the main source of protein in Japan, but in Argentina—which has broad plains for raising live-

Food

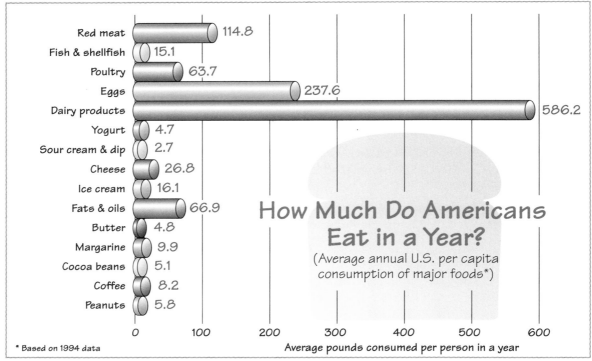

How Much Do Americans Eat in a Year?
(Average annual U.S. per capita consumption of major foods*)

Food	Average pounds consumed per person in a year
Red meat	114.8
Fish & shellfish	15.1
Poultry	63.7
Eggs	237.6
Dairy products	586.2
Yogurt	4.7
Sour cream & dip	2.7
Cheese	26.8
Ice cream	16.1
Fats & oils	66.9
Butter	4.8
Margarine	9.9
Cocoa beans	5.1
Coffee	8.2
Peanuts	5.8

* Based on 1994 data

SOURCE: U.S. Dept. of Agriculture

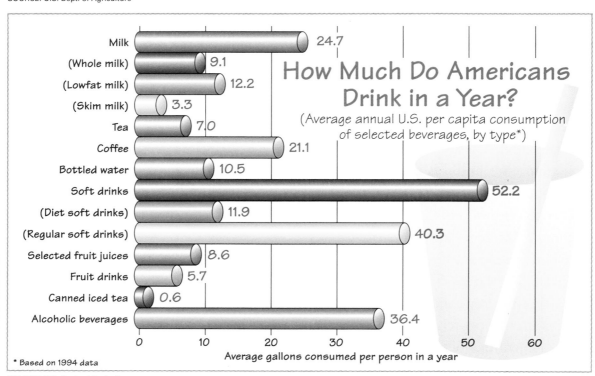

How Much Do Americans Drink in a Year?
(Average annual U.S. per capita consumption of selected beverages, by type*)

Beverage	Average gallons consumed per person in a year
Milk	24.7
(Whole milk)	9.1
(Lowfat milk)	12.2
(Skim milk)	3.3
Tea	7.0
Coffee	21.1
Bottled water	10.5
Soft drinks	52.2
(Diet soft drinks)	11.9
(Regular soft drinks)	40.3
Selected fruit juices	8.6
Fruit drinks	5.7
Canned iced tea	0.6
Alcoholic beverages	36.4

* Based on 1994 data

SOURCE: U.S. Dept. of Agriculture

Food